BRETHREN

DRAWING-ROOM MEETING.

From an old Picture.

Among the figures depicted by the artist may be observed:
J. N. Darby, Lady Powerscourt, J. G. Bellett, C. H. Mackintosh, and Sir Edward Denny.

BRETHREN
THE STORY OF A GREAT RECOVERY

DAVID J. BEATTIE

40 Beansburn, Kilmarnock, Scotland

ISBN-13: 978 1 904064 80 0
ISBN-10: 1 904064 80 9

Copyright © 2009 by John Ritchie Ltd.
40 Beansburn, Kilmarnock, Scotland

www.ritchiechristianmedia.co.uk

The *Classic Reprint Series* is derived from facsimile copies of the originally published material.

At times the quality of print and typeface may have been compromised as a result of either inferior original copy or the facsimile process itself.

We are confident, however, that the vast majority of the printed content is of reasonable quality and most importantly is legible.

All rights reserved. No part of this publication may be reproduced, stored in a retrievable system, or transmitted in any form or by any other means – electronic, mechanical, photocopy, recording or otherwise – without prior permission of the copyright owner.

Typeset by John Ritchie Ltd., Kilmarnock
Printed by Bell & Bain Ltd., Glasgow

FOREWORD

The sub-title of this book is excellently chosen, for the remarkable movement that it relates was no new thing, no novelty, but the recovery of truth that had become obscured by the encroachments of tradition and clericalism.

Our Lord rebuked the religionists of His day for making the Word of God of none effect by their traditions; He told them that in vain did they attempt to worship the Father teaching for doctrines the commandments of men. This has happened again. A monopoly unauthorised by the Scriptures has been given to a caste of priests or clerics who have so obscured the truth that in the Establishment itself there are such differences that no one can be sure of what is the way of Salvation. The Sacerdotalist says one thing, the Modernist says another, and the "low" Church seeks to explain away the doctrine of infant baptism and regeneration taught in the Prayer Book, and attempts in face of its plain words to teach the necessity of a new birth and salvation through faith alone. Was it any wonder that believers began to question the traditions in which they had been brought up and to search the Scriptures daily to see if those things were so?

They quickly discovered that they had no warrant in Scripture—nowhere is a Christian teacher called a priest in the New Testament in any other sense than that in which all believers are priests. No such monopoly as is claimed is to be found in the Word of God; no restriction is put upon the Liberty of the Spirit or the exercise of God-given gifts.

That the movement is no novelty can be learned from Mr. E. Hamer Broadbent's illuminating book, *The Pilgrim Church*. All down the ages there have been faithful souls who have met and worshipped in the simple way laid down in the word of the Lord. They have been hunted down as heretics by those who say they are apostles but are not, but have never been stamped out.

The movement seeks to avoid sectarianism. In the words of Mr. Lincoln, quoted on p. 88, the attitude of the brethren is, "*May I be kept by God's grace from joining anything.*" Their only creed is the Bible, from which they are seeking to receive all the truth as it is revealed to them by the Holy Spirit.

In an issue of *The Evening Standard* (19th April 1937) there appeared an article by Patrick Monkhouse, a journalist, on "The Brethren." It is so well informed and aptly expressed that I take the liberty of quoting from it. He says:

"This is the century of over-organisation. Every trade, every art, almost every Church, is organised, associated, federated; councils and committees multiply; annual conferences meet incessantly to pass resolutions on every subject under the sun.

"In the midst of these imposing structures there is one body which has found the secret of vitality in a completely contrary policy. . . .

"From the very first, it has been the endeavour of the Brethren to eliminate from their Church every trace of clerical procedure for which they could not find warrant in the New Testament.

"They have no clergy. They have no fixed order of service. They have no central organisation or officers with authority over the various assemblies.

"A minority, known as the Exclusive Assemblies, did indeed break away in the middle of the nineteenth century and establish an authoritative Central Meeting with power to censure or exclude adherents or assemblies. But the main body of the movement, known as the Open Assemblies, has continued its traditional freedom from organisation or authority. . . .

"So far, indeed, does this refusal to organise go that the Brethren have no sure idea what their own numbers are. It has been estimated roughly that they come to 80,000 in England alone. But the movement is strong as well not only in Scotland, Wales and Ireland—it sprang from Dublin, which has still one of the largest assemblies—but also in many foreign countries.

"Their numbers are still increasing. A knowledgeable member gave me an estimate that they have gone up by 50 per cent. in the last twenty years. . . .

"At their principal service, the breaking of bread, corresponding to the Communion Service in the Church of England, no one person presides, or performs any priestly function. Nor is there any fixed order of service. One member will offer up a prayer, another suggest a hymn, as the Spirit moves him.

"There are some evangelists and teachers who serve the movement full time. But they have no official title or position, nor do they receive any fixed salary. They depend on gifts made to them by the Assemblies which they visit.

"The Open Assemblies do not bar from their service members of other denominations who profess themselves believers in Jesus Christ. . . .

"At all events, the Brethren have not found their high standards of personal conduct any more a bar to their vigorous progress than is the deliberate lack of hierarchical organisation which is what makes their churches so distinctive and so interesting."

It is interesting to see ourselves as others see us. Mr. Beattie is eminently fitted to tell the story of the movement. He has a gifted and facile pen, and has given a charm to the history he records that cannot fail to reach the hearts of sincere believers, even though they may yet be satisfied to remain in the traditional churches.

I wish the book every success.

GEO. GOODMAN.

September '39.

AUTHOR'S NOTE

THE title given to this book is the name common to all true Christians and is, therefore, unsectarian. In this sense only is the title used, and it has been chosen to convey this message.

In compiling this record of the work of the Holy Spirit, covering the last hundred years, since the inception of what became known as the Brethren Movement, it would be superfluous to state that no attempt has been made to follow every bypath leading from the main arteries of that spiritual movement. To have set out upon such an expedition would have entailed research work which could hardly have warranted the labour expended, and must surely have been a task altogether too formidable to contemplate.

A faithful endeavour has been made to trace the path of the pioneers of faith, and record the founding of such assemblies which lay along that path in our sojourn through the British Isles.

Owing to the exigencies of space it has been impossible to include many assemblies worthy of permanent record. The omission of others equally deserving of a place has been the lack of reliable data or the absence of definite information.

The author has spared no effort in an endeavour to trace the history of assemblies, particularly those whose birth took place before the present century. In this task he has been ably assisted by those who so kindly furnished valuable material which otherwise would have been irretrievably lost. To all who have lent a helping hand he takes this opportunity of expressing his sincere thanks.

D. J. B.

CARLISLE.

CONTENTS

PART I

ENGLAND AND WALES

CHAPTER		PAGE
I.	Early Days	3
II.	First Public Meeting	12
III.	At Plymouth	16
IV.	Early Brethren	22
V.	Bristol Bethesda	27
VI.	Around Bristol	32
VII.	Early Days in Hereford	35
VIII.	Ross-on-Wye	42
IX.	Exeter	47
X.	Robert Chapman and Barnstaple	52
XI.	Weston-super-Mare	57
XII.	Early Days at Teignmouth	59
XIII.	The First Gathering at Torquay	63
XIV.	Bridford Mills Assembly	69
XV.	In Dorset: Early Ministry of Henry Dyer	72
XVI.	Early Days in London	77
XVII.	Beresford Chapel and William Lincoln	87
XVIII.	Leyton and East London	92
XIX.	The Old Clock Factory at Wimbledon	98
XX.	The Archway Assembly	102
XXI.	The Testimony at Woolwich	103
XXII.	Early History of Welbeck Assembly	110
XXIII.	The Story of the London Missionary Meetings	118
XXIV.	Suffolk and Henry Heath	122
XXV.	St. Albans	127
XXVI.	Eastbourne—1872	129
XXVII.	Shanklin, Isle of Wight	134

CONTENTS

CHAPTER		PAGE
XXVIII.	Kingston-on-Thames—1867	136
XXIX.	Cheltenham Assembly	141
XXX.	Leeds—and Harry Moorhouse	145
XXXI.	Cutsyke	151
XXXII.	Early Days at Bath	153
XXXIII.	Swindon	159
XXXIV.	In South Wales	162
XXXV.	Light at Tredegar	167
XXXVI.	Merseyside	173
XXXVII.	Isle of Man	175
XXXVIII.	Manchester	176
XXXIX.	Warrington	180
XL.	Barrow-in-Furness	181
XLI.	Walney	183
XLII.	Lancaster	184
XLIII.	In Westmorland	186
XLIV.	Carlisle and William Reid	192

PART II

SCOTLAND AND IRELAND

I.	Across the Scottish Border	201
II.	In Lanarkshire—Larkhall	206
III.	Early Days in Ayrshire	218
IV.	Early Days in Glasgow: The Marble Hall	238
V.	In the Scottish Capital	260
VI.	Chirnside	265
VII.	In the Highlands of Scotland	266
VIII.	Early Days in Ireland	279

PART III

EARLY DAYS IN THE FOREIGN FIELD

EARLY DAYS IN THE FOREIGN FIELD	313
INDEX OF NAMES	321
INDEX OF PLACES	331

LIST OF ILLUSTRATIONS

Bible Reading, 1838		*Frontispiece*
J. G. Bellett		*Facing page* 16
John Nelson Darby		,, ,, 16
Meeting Room, Aungier Street, Dublin		,, ,, 17
Dr. Edward Cronin		,, ,, 32
Francis Hutchinson's House, Dublin		,, ,, 32
Captain Percy Hall		,, ,, 33
George Viceimus Wigram		,, ,, 33
George Müller		,, ,, 48
Bethesda Chapel, Bristol		,, ,, 49
Henry Craik		,, ,, 49
Captain W. G. Rhind		,, ,, 64
Henry W. Soltau		,, ,, 64
Lord Congleton		,, ,, 65
Home of R. C. Chapman, Barnstaple		,, ,, 80
R. C. Chapman		,, ,, 80
Sir Edward Denny		,, ,, 81
C. H. Mackintosh		,, ,, 81
Henry Dyer		,, ,, 96
John Morley		,, ,, 96
Meeting Room, Paragon Road		,, ,, 97
James Wright		,, ,, 97
John Churchill		,, ,, 112
Captain Orde-Browne		,, ,, 112
James W. C. Fegan		,, ,, 113

LIST OF ILLUSTRATIONS

Leonard Strong	*Facing page*	113
Fred. Stanley Arnot	,, ,,	128
Missionary Pioneers	,, ,,	129
John Marsden Code	,, ,,	144
J. Denham Smith	,, ,,	144
Henry Groves	,, ,,	145
William Wilson	,, ,,	145
William Reid	,, ,,	160
John Wardrop	,, ,,	160
James Anderson	,, ,,	161
John Ritchie	,, ,,	161
John Dickie	,, ,,	176
Thomas McLaren	,, ,,	176
John Stewart	,, ,,	176
Gordon Forlong	,, ,,	176
Samuel Dodds	,, ,,	177
Peter Hynd	,, ,,	177
Alexander Bayne	,, ,,	192
Robert Fyfe	,, ,,	192
Alexander Marshall	,, ,,	192
J. R. Caldwell	,, ,,	193
Dr. James Wardrop	,, ,,	193
Donald Munro	,, ,,	224
Donald Ross	,, ,,	224
William Mackenzie	,, ,,	225
Alexander Stewart	,, ,,	225
W. H. McLaughlin	,, ,,	240
William McLean	,, ,,	240
Archibald Bell	,, ,,	241
Dr. John Singleton Darling	,, ,,	241
F. C. Bland	,, ,,	272

LIST OF ILLUSTRATIONS

DAVID REA	*Facing page*	272
WILLIAM TALBOT CROSBIE	,, ,,	273
RICHARD J. MAHONY	,, ,,	273
HENRY BEWLEY	,, ,,	288
WILLIAM FRY	,, ,,	288
J. G. MCVICKER	,, ,,	289

PART I

ENGLAND AND WALES

CHAPTER I

EARLY DAYS

LOOKING back over a hundred years, years pregnant with a multitude of events, which in their course were to become living milestones in the long march of Church history, one cannot but be sensibly impressed as, in panoramic sequence, the picture of a century's triumphs and failures slowly passes before our vision, leaving on the mind an indelible impression. We stand aside that one might view the historic picture in its true perspective, at the same time unconsciously eliminating the many recurring shadows which ever and anon would seek to darken an otherwise fascinating canvas.

There, in the forefront, are the stalwarts of the faith, Groves and Bellett; Darby and Parnell; Craik and Müller; Deck and Chapman. The scroll is unfolded and we catch a glimpse of a familiar location in these islands. Instinctively our eyes are focussed on a clearly defined spot beyond the Irish Sea, which was to become the virtual birthplace of a great and wonderful movement. And as we watch, we see the living line move—Dublin—Plymouth—Bristol—to encompass the world.

This graphic picture momentarily portrayed on the mind, looms up afresh as we seek to review God's wonderful ways in leading out His beloved people from the bewildering maze of ecclesiastical intricacies, doubtless inborn by generations of unquestioned usage, to the simple and unostentatious gathering of themselves together on lines untrammelled by man, and solely according to Scripture.

Before coming to more recent times and events in the history of the various assemblies throughout this land and the lands beyond the seas, it is necessary to give a brief survey of the early days of a remnant of God's people, who came to be known by the sobriquet of Plymouth Brethren.

Years before what is now regarded as the first public

meeting of Brethren, which, as we know, took place in Dublin in 1830, there were, in different parts of the country, many godly Christians, who, unknown to each other, had had their thoughts directed along similar lines to those eventually adopted, and pursued by men of God who were to form the nucleus of a world-wide movement. These faithful believers were known to have met together on the first day of the week for the purpose of promoting New Testament principles—which to them had long since been a dead letter—including the fellowship with all those who love the Lord, irrespective of sect or religious denomination, the celebration of the Lord's Supper, and the observance of believers' baptism, according to light received through a diligent study of the Scriptures. Very little is left on record of those early Christians, and it was only when development of a more pronounced character made itself evident in the region of the Irish Capital, that these isolated gatherings became known.

J. G. Bellett in his *Reminiscences* mentions an instance of the independent action of the Spirit of God in the case of J. Mahon, an honoured servant of the Lord living at Ennis, County Clare, who, with other Christians, prior to the first public meeting in Dublin, had been meeting together in his house, where the little party had "breaking of bread" each Lord's Day morning. Bellett further tells of a visit to Somerset in 1831 or 1832, to the residence of Sir Edward Denny—who afterwards wrote many beautiful hymns in use in our assemblies to-day—when Sir Edward asked Bellett to give him some idea of the "Brethren." "We were sitting round the fire," he writes, "and the daughter of a clergyman was present. As I stated our thoughts, she said they had been hers for the last twelve months, and that she had no idea that anyone had them but herself. So also being at ―― shortly afterwards, a dear brother, now with the Lord, told me that he, his wife, and his wife's mother were meeting in the simplicity of the 'Brethren's' way for some time before he ever heard of such people."

It is of interest to trace these circumstances, for they help to assure us that the Lord's hand was independently

EARLY DAYS

at work designing to revive a testimony here, and another there, in the midst of His own children. But there have been faithful followers of the Lord since the days of Paul, and though the vicissitudes of time and circumstance may have obscured all trace of their existence there were ever those faithful to Apostolic teaching who came together under the Holy Spirit's influence and guidance, in like manner as we assemble ourselves to-day. Indeed, God has maintained a simple testimony of the Church on Scriptural lines since Pentecost; and down through the ages many at the cost of martyrdom witnessed to the faith once for all delivered to the saints. Thus while we seek to review a spiritual movement of more recent times, which because of certain circumstances may have received undue emphasis, it should not be assumed that the gathering to the Lord is a new movement.

To regard such would be to set on one side the faithfulness and loyalty of those early saints who paid such a price for the Testimony, while the present gatherings, to whom the cost of witnessing for the truth was not so great, are given a unique position.

The period around the late 'twenties of the nineteenth century was to become a memorable landmark, when the smouldering fires of past centuries were to burst forth into a radiant flame, heralding a new era in the vicissitudinary history of the Church. Men chosen of God were to be raised up, a serious attempt was to be made to break down Church differences amongst the Lord's people, with an immediate return to the true teachings of Scripture, so long obscured and overruled by petty ecclesiastical prejudices.

Foremost amongst those who took a prominent part and exercised a powerful influence of the founding and the development of the newly formed company of Christians were: Anthony Norris Groves, John Gifford Bellett and John Nelson Darby. In addition to these, two others, John Vesey Parnell (afterwards Lord Congleton) and Dr. Edward Cronin, were also closely identified with those early proceedings.

So that the reader may be better able to follow the somewhat erratic course of events, it is necessary that a brief sketch be given of the men whose names are inseparably associated with those primitive beginnings which were to become historic.

Anthony Norris Groves was born at Newton, in Hampshire, in the year 1795. He received in London a professional training as a dentist, and after practising for a time in Plymouth, removed to Exeter, where he built up a successful business. Before he was thirty years of age his income was over £1500. Early in his career Groves decided to devote the whole of his property, including the greater part of his large income, to the Lord's work, freely distributing to the poor, of his bountiful store, and leaving only a small balance for his household and personal needs. A tract published by Groves, entitled *Christian Devotedness*, very clearly taught this line of doctrine as a distinct evangelical duty.

Mr. Groves was married at twenty-one, and it was about this time that the desire was laid on his heart to go abroad as a missionary, but the opposition of his wife, who could not yet see the way clear, kept him from taking the step till some years later.

It was with a view to preparing himself for missionary work that Anthony Groves, in 1825, after giving up his professional business, journeyed to Dublin for the purpose of entering Trinity College, that he might study for ordination in the Church of England, a circumstance which had such far-reaching results, as we shall see. Groves was a non-resident student, and during his frequent visits to the Irish metropolis he made the acquaintance of J. G. Bellett, a fellow churchman who, with other Christians, came together for prayer and study of the Scriptures. Those evening meetings were productive of bringing together a number of believers of deep spirituality who began to discern altogether new truths never before revealed to them, and it would appear that Groves was mainly instrumental in directing the company of believers in taking a very significant step towards the realisation of what he considered to be the true interpretation of Scripture regarding the union of the Lord's people, and their practical observation of apostolic teaching. We learn from Groves' Memoir that at one of these meetings J. G. Bellett made this significant statement —"Groves has just been telling me that it appeared to him from Scripture, that believers meeting together as disciples of Christ, were free to break bread together, as their Lord had admonished them; and that, in as far as the practice of the apostles could be a guide, every Lord's Day should be set apart for thus remembering the Lord's death, and obeying His parting command." "This suggestion of Mr. Groves," continues his biographer, "was immediately carried out by himself and his friends in Dublin."

Such thoughts and convictions simply expressed by Groves may to the casual reader seem commonplace, and may give no occasion for surprise. It is well to remember, however, that both Groves and Bellett were ardent churchmen, as were possibly the greater number of those who attended these meetings; but it was unmistakably evident that many of their deep-rooted prejudices were now breaking down under the penetrating influence of the Holy Spirit's teaching, in the light of the new truths discovered.

Having seen from the Scriptures of the liberty and power through the Holy Spirit in the ministry of the Word, Groves now began to wonder whether he should further pursue his studies towards ordination. With these thoughts in his mind he made application in London to the Church Missionary Society to arrange for his going out to the foreign field as a layman. Their refusal to allow him to celebrate the Lord's Supper when no minister was near came as a rude shock. Soon afterwards he was forcibly impressed with the conviction "that ordination of any kind to preach the Gospel is no requirement of Scripture. To me," he continues, "it was the removal of a mountain." This revelation he communicated to his friend Bellett, to whom it came with startling force.

This absorbing matter still occupied the attention of the latter when Groves returned to Dublin just previous to his departure for Baghdad, where he felt called of the Lord to carry the Gospel, relying solely upon Him to meet his needs. This was towards the close of 1828. The two friends were passing along Lower Pembroke Street when Groves remarked: "This I doubt not is the mind of God concerning us—we should come together in all simplicity as disciples, not waiting on any pulpit or ministry, but trusting that the Lord would edify us together by ministering as He pleased and saw good from the midst of ourselves." In giving an account of the incident Bellett relates: "At the moment he spoke the words, I was assured my soul had got the right idea; and that moment I remember as if it were yesterday, and could point out the place. It was the birthday of my mind, may I so speak, as a brother."

In 1829 Groves with his wife and two boys, and accompanied by three Christian friends—including a poor deaf and dumb lad, who afterwards became the famous Dr. Kitto, the author of *The Pictorial Bible*—set out for Baghdad. They sailed up the Baltic Sea to St. Petersburg, and travelled overland by way of Tiflis, their heavy lumbering wagons traversing the rough mountainous roads and passes where, during the wearisome journey, the travellers were exposed to great hardship and encountered many perils on the way. The journey took six months to accomplish. The story of his life at Baghdad, where the little household was established, is one which will always take an honoured place in the annals of pioneer missionary work. The ravages of plague, followed by flood, famine and war, almost wiped out the densely crowded city, sixty thousand dying out of a total population of eighty-five thousand, and Mrs. Groves was one of the victims. Yet, amidst the horrors of it all the faith of Anthony Groves was still in his God, and he was able to write home at this time: "The Lord has allowed us great peace, and assured confidence in His loving care, and in the truth of His promise that our bread and our water shall be sure; but certainly nothing but the service of such a Lord as He is would keep me in the scenes which these countries do exhibit, and I feel assured will, till the Lord has finished His judgments on them for the contempt of the name, nature and offices of the Son of God; yet I linger in the hope that He has a remnant even among them, for whose return these convulsions are preparing the way."

The little missionary party were greatly cheered by the arrival in the summer of 1832 of Dr. Cronin, John Parnell and Francis W. Newman (whose brother later became the Cardinal, the well-known author of "Lead, kindly Light"). Soon after this, Groves made a journey to India, having as his travelling companion Colonel Cotton, the noted engineer whose skill and Christian care for the people of India abolished the dreadful famines of the Godaveri Delta, and brought prosperity to the people of that region. Groves tells us that one object in going to India was "to become united more truly in heart with all the missionary band there, and show that, notwithstanding all differences, we are one in Christ; sympathising in their sorrows and rejoicing in their prosperity."

After a sojourn in India, Groves visited Britain, and following a stay of fifteen months, when he freely associated with the brethren at Plymouth and Bristol (which will be referred to later), he returned to India, taking with him a missionary party including the brethren Beer and Bowden and their wives from Barnstaple. It is interesting to note that the children and grandchildren of those pioneer missionaries are still carrying on the work. Groves himself proceeded to Madras where he was soon afterwards rejoined by the brethren he had left behind at Baghdad. "Having long depended for his supplies on such gifts as the Lord sent through His servants, he felt that now, in Madras, the circumstances were such that it would be better for the testimony that he should follow the example of Paul, who was ready, according to circumstances, either to live from the gifts of the churches, or from his own labour and earn his own living. He therefore took up practice again as a dentist and was successful in this."

We have gone to some length in sketching the missionary enterprise of A. N. Groves, but so many circumstances converge upon this initial undertaking and all that transpired thereto, that one has found it imperative to include such matter that the reader might more fitly be able to follow the trend of things, at the same time observing the working of the minds of these early brethren, thus using in some measure what has been set down as a background to the momentous events which were taking place at home.

While Groves was pursuing his labours in other lands, the feeble light that had been kindled ere he left these shores had not been permitted to die out. On the contrary, its influence was beginning to make itself felt in a very marked way. The friends he had left behind in Ireland were steadily moving along lines propounded by Groves, and had by the close of 1829 made notable progress towards the fruition of the ideal he longed might some day take tangible shape.

The remarkable development was due in no small measure to John Gifford Bellett. Born in Dublin on the 19th of July 1795, he was thus about the same age as his friend A. N. Groves. Bellett was educated at the Grammar School, Exeter, where he gave high promise as a classical scholar, and with a view to studying for the Bar he proceeded to Trinity College, Dublin. Here he first met J. N. Darby. Both were decided Christians, and an intimacy soon sprang up between the two young students which ripened into a life-long friendship.

Bellett was called to the Bar in Dublin but practised little if any at all, his interests evidently running along an altogether different groove. He came of a family having strong religious connections, both his brothers being clergymen and his only sister was married to a clergyman. Breaking away from the restraining conventionalities of the Established Church, Bellett lost no opportunity in devoting himself as a layman in whatever religious service exalted his Lord.

As we have seen, the coming of Groves to Dublin not only accentuated the beliefs which were gradually maturing in the mind of his friend, but opened up an entirely new field of religious thought which had its consummation in the hallowed atmosphere of those informal Bible Readings.

While the Movement in Dublin was yet in its embryonic state, J. G. Bellett brought into the circle of those devoted

Christians one who for some time to come was destined to wield a powerful influence.

John Nelson Darby—for he it was—was born at Westminster in 1800 of Irish parents. He received his early education at Westminster School, and as we have already seen, he afterwards prosecuted his studies at Trinity College, Dublin, where he graduated as Classical Gold Medallist, before he was nineteen. Though called to the Irish Bar about the same time as Bellett, he soon afterwards gave up the profession for the Church. In 1825 Darby was ordained by Bishop Magee, and accepted the curacy of the Wicklow parish of Calary. Bellett never lost contact with his old college friend, and in course of events as Darby's High Church ideas began to wane, because of internal ecclesiastical differences brought about by the controversy over the union of Church and State, which Darby in a pamphlet vehemently declared to be Babylonish, his visits to Dublin and his intercourse with those Christians who had a sincere love for the divine teaching of the Scriptures became more frequent.

CHAPTER II

FIRST PUBLIC MEETING

We are now approaching a decisive epoch in the history of those early beginnings, but ere we proceed further along the road which was to become fraught with countless difficulties, it is necessary to retrace our steps to the summer of 1826, when a young medical student in search of health came up from the south of Ireland to Dublin. He was a member of an Independent Church. His father was a Romanist, in which faith the son had been nurtured. The high spiritual character of his Protestant mother, however, appears to have had an impelling influence over the thoughtful boy, and before he had entered manhood, not only had he renounced the Roman Catholic hierarchy, but had taken a definite stand as a true believer in the Lord Jesus Christ. His name was Edward Cronin.

On his arrival in Dublin he visited the different Dissenting chapels, where he enjoyed communion. When it was learned that Cronin's stay in the city was to be permanent, he was informed that he could no longer be allowed to take his place at the Lord's Table as a communicant without *special membership* with one particular congregation. This to his mind appeared contrary to what the Scriptures taught. Reasoning within himself that all true believers are members of the body of Christ, he refused to submit to their Church order and was soon afterwards publicly excommunicated. Thus cut off from fellowship and feeling the separation very keenly, Cronin spent the following Lord's Day mornings in quiet meditation under a tree or a haystack during the hour for service. Soon afterwards one of the Deacons of the Dissenting Chapel, Edward Wilson (assistant secretary to the Bible Society), protesting against the action of the minister, also left. Thus cut off, the two began to study the Word with a fresh earnestness of purpose,

FIRST PUBLIC MEETING

which ultimately led them to come together on Lord's Day morning for the breaking of bread and prayer in Mr. Wilson's house. They were joined by the two Misses Drury, cousins of Dr. Cronin, and later by Mr. Tims, a bookseller in Grafton Street. On Mr. Wilson's departure for England several others were added, and the little company met in the back parlour of Dr. Cronin's house in Lower Pembroke Street. "It then became noised abroad," says Cronin, "and one and another became affected by the same truth, which really was the Oneness of the Body and the presence of the Holy Spirit, also seen by us very clearly. Here Francis Hutchinson found us and, as we were becoming numerous, offered us the use of his large room in Fitzwilliam Square."

Although constantly in touch with what was taking place in Dublin, Darby was still ministering to his flock in the mountain parish of Wicklow, while Bellett had not yet severed his connection with the Established Church. But events were moving quickly, and it would appear that it was about this time that the two joined the little company of believers. This fresh infusion was to bring about decisive action on the part of those faithful Christians, culminating in an entire separation from ecclesiastical systems and owning no other than the presence and Sovereign action of the Holy Spirit in their midst.

The Movement received a distinct stimulus in the publication of what may be regarded as the first Brethren pamphlet: *Considerations in the Nature and Unity of the Church of Christ*. This was the forerunner of many others which, before a generation had passed by, were to become such an outstanding feature in the prosecution of the Movement's widespread activities, and the deciding—or perhaps, alas, aggravating—of many momentous issues, which had such far-reaching results. The author was J. N. Darby. The tract forcibly set forth what those early brethren believed and practised, and the divine ground on which they acted. It contained in a large measure those paramount truths which are held by and characterise so-called Brethren to-day.

"If the view that we have taken of the state of the Church be correct," writes Darby, "we may adjudge that he is an enemy to the work of the Spirit of God who seeks the interests of any particular denomination; and that those who believe in the 'power and coming of the Lord Jesus Christ' ought carefully to keep from such a spirit: for it is drawing back the Church to a state occasioned by ignorance and non-subjection to the Word. . . . Christians are little aware how this prevails in their minds; how they seek their own, not the things of Jesus Christ; and how it dries up the springs of grace and spiritual communion; how it precludes that order to which blessing is attached, the gathering together in the Lord's name. No meeting, which is not framed to embrace all the children of God, on the full basis of the kingdom of the Son, can find the fulness of blessing, because it does not contemplate it—because its faith does not embrace it. . . . Accordingly, the outward symbol and instrument of unity is the partaking of the Lord's Supper; 'for we being many are one body, for we are all partakers of that one bread.' And what does St. Paul declare to be the true intent and testimony of that rite? That whensoever 'we eat of that bread and drink of that cup, we do shew the Lord's death till He come.' Here there are found the character and life of the Church—that into which it is called—that in which the truth of its existence subsists, and in which alone is true unity."

As others were being added to the company meeting in Francis Hutchinson's house it seemed obvious that a larger room would soon be required. It is at this juncture there is introduced a young man in his early twenties whom God had designed to occupy a notable position in the gradual unfolding of His purposes. His name was John Vesey Parnell, afterwards Lord Congleton. It was he who rented a large and commodious room in Aungier Street, belonging to an auctioneer, to which the company of believers was transferred.

Alluding to what happened at the particular period to which we refer, Dr. Cronin feelingly writes: "We soon began to feel, as humbler brethren were added to us, that the house in Fitzwilliam Square was unsuited, which led us to take a large auction room in Aungier Street for our use on Sundays. And oh! the blessed seasons to my soul with J. Parnell, W. Stokes, and others, while moving the furniture aside and laying the simple table with its bread and wine on Saturday evenings—seasons of joy never to be forgotten—for surely we had the Master's smile and sanction in the beginning of such a movement as this was!"

This was in the month of May in the year 1830; and it is from this time and place that we will seek to trace the development of this wonderful Movement, in our own and other lands, when we shall view the work of the Holy Spirit carrying out through feeble instruments His own blessed purposes of grace.

CHAPTER III

AT PLYMOUTH

A NOTABLE factor which gave direct impetus to the Movement was the establishment of what was then known as Reading Meetings. Darby was quick to observe the usefulness of these meetings, and soon after the formation of an assembly at Dublin, he paid a visit to Limerick. Here with the help of a local Christian named Thomas Maunsell—who afterwards became actively associated with the Movement—he instituted a reading meeting to which considerable numbers came, and the Lord opened the way for the ministry of the Word which continues in that city to the present time.

Those gatherings of Christians sprang up almost simultaneously in many parts of the country. Usually held in the drawing-rooms of the gentry, they were attended largely by men of good position and repute including not a few members of the clergy. Thus were the Scriptures prayerfully searched and studied, and thus God raised up faithful men, who, finding no Scriptural authority for the system of things prevailing in the professing church, were led to renounce all that this world esteems; that they might take a lowly place as true followers of the despised and rejected Son of God, realising that they could no longer pursue a course they well knew to be contrary to Divine order, embraced the truth revealed to them, and left their respective denominations.

"Amongst those who separated from the various organisations," says C. H. Mackintosh, "were some men of considerable gift, moral weight, intellectual power and intelligence—clergymen, barristers, solicitors, military and naval officers, physicians, and men of high position and property. Their secession, as you may suppose, caused a very considerable stir and drew forth much opposition. Many a link of

J. N. DARBY.

J. G. BELLETT.

MEETING ROOM, AUNGIER STREET, DUBLIN,
Where the first public meeting of Brethren was held in 1830.

friendship was snapped; many sacrifices were made; much sorrow and trial were encountered; much reproach, obloquy and persecution had to be endured."

As can well be imagined the spread of this new aggression in the field of religion, which was drawing so largely from practically every Christian denomination, created no little alarm in ecclesiastical circles. Who were those people? What new creed was this? Such were the questions asked; such were the anxious fears expressed; but no one seemed able to give an intelligible answer to the queries which appeared to disturb the peace of the religious communities.

The leaders of the churches thus affected, however, appeared to console themselves with the thought that this mysterious movement, with no ordained minister or president, and having no definite organisation, would before very long come to a pitiable end. "But the Lord Himself was with them—true to His promise, 'Where two or three are gathered together in My name, there am I in the midst of them.' And there the Lord was to the joy, blessing and edification of His beloved people. If we allow Him His proper place at the table, He will not only take it, but His presence will fill our hearts with joy unspeakable and full of glory. Thus were the Brethren strengthened, and thus the good work of the Lord went on. The Gospel was preached with a clearness, fulness and power, unknown since the days of the apostles."

Having followed the course of events which led up to this important stage, we have now opportunity to observe the work of the Holy Spirit in the spread of the Movement to other spheres. Darby, whose powerfully worded pamphlet had sounded a clarion call arousing thoughtful believers to the culmination of momentous decisions, was just thirty at the time of the historic meeting at Aungier Street, Dublin. As this man of prodigious mental energy and physical endurance figures probably more than any other person in the history of the early Brethren, it may be of interest to read what his erstwhile friend, F. W. Newman, has to say in the course of an autobiographical sketch, in which the writer, referring to Darby, states: "He was a most remarkable man, who rapidly gained an immense sway over me.... His bodily presence," continues Newman, in describing the personal appearance of Darby, "was indeed weak. A fallen cheek, a blood-shot eye ... a seldom shaven beard, a shabby suit of clothes and a generally neglected person, drew at first pity, with wonder to see such a figure in a drawing-room.... This young man had taken high honours in Dublin University, and had studied for the Bar where he had excellent prospects; but his conscience would not allow him to take a brief, lest he should be selling his talents to defeat justice. With keen, logical powers, he had warm sympathies, solid judgment of character, thoughtful tenderness and total self-abandonment."

With this brief pen-picture of this extraordinary man, we will follow his activities to another part of the United Kingdom, which was destined to become, after Dublin, a place pre-eminent in the history of the Brethren. While his friends in the Irish capital sought to build up the little assembly there, Darby, his bosom burning with an unquenchable desire to carry the truth of God whithersoever the Holy Spirit might lead, looked farther afield, and after a sojourn in many isolated places in Ireland he crossed to England—and to Plymouth.

Writing to a friend some years later, Mr. Darby gives the date of his memorable visit to Plymouth as "*about* 1831." "I went to Oxford," he says, referring to the occasion, "where many doors were open, and where I found Mr. Wigram and Mr. Jarratt. Subsequently in calling on Mr. Newman I met Mr. Newton, who asked me to go down to Plymouth, which I did. On arriving I found in the house Captain Hall, who was already preaching in the villages. He had reading meetings, and ere long began to break bread. Though Mr. Wigram began the work in London he was a great deal at Plymouth." W. Blair Neatby, in his *History of the Plymouth Brethren*, suggests that the date given by Darby is incorrect, and this seems obvious for, as we have seen, it was at this time that Darby called upon his friend, F. W. Newman, and it will be remembered that Newman sailed for Baghdad on 30th September 1830. So that it is quite probable that the visit to Plymouth would be in the month of August or early September, 1830.

Thus came about the formation of a company of Christians definitely separated from ecclesiastical organisations, and gathered solely to the Name of Jesus. This gathering of believers at Plymouth, notable perhaps because of the fact that its existence gave birth to the appellation "Plymouth Brethren," by which future generations of Christians faithful to the teaching of the Scriptures were to be ungraciously designated, was to go down in history as the first assembly of Brethren in England. The place in which the assembly worships, now known as Raleigh Street Gospel Hall, was the first building erected by Brethren in Plymouth. "When the brothers began to preach the Gospel in the open-air and in the villages around," says Andrew Miller, "no small curiosity was awakened to know who they were; there was something new in their preaching and in their going to work. But as they belonged to none of the denominations they were spoken of as 'Brethren from Plymouth.' This naturally resulted in the designation 'The Plymouth Brethren,' which has been applied to them—sometimes in derision—ever since."

An important and influential assembly, it was for many years the rendezvous of most of the early leaders of the Movement, who resorted thither from various centres for the ministry of the Scriptures and the unfolding of the mind of Christ as revealed by the power of the Holy Spirit.

In a communication written by W. H. Cole to a personal friend, the writer portrays a vivid picture of those times of unsullied happiness, when the skies were cloudless and the breakers which one day would dash with ruthless energy upon the peaceful shore were as yet unknown. An excerpt from this letter, which recently came into my hands, is worthy of recounting here, for it reveals the gracious humility and godly sincerity of those brethren at Plymouth in their desire to follow the mind of the Spirit and to obey the commands of our risen and exalted Lord. "Converted to God in early youth in Plymouth my native town," writes Mr. Cole, "I was soon afterwards brought into fellowship with those who, I learnt, assembled upon principles taught in the Word of God, where no sectarian wall of division was acknowledged, and where there was the liberty of the Spirit of God, to minister the truths of Scripture by those who were gifted by Him for that purpose.

"At that time all was happiness and peace, unruffled by personal questions, and undisturbed by jealousies or ambitions. The distinctions between rich and poor were lessened by holy, loving fellowship and unity which characterised their intercourse. Their dress was plain, their habits simple and their walk distinguished by separation from the world. The meetings of the assembly were calm, peaceful and hallowed; their singing was soft, slow and thoughtful; their worship evinced the nearness of their communion with the Lord; their prayers were earnest for an increased knowledge of God, and for the spread of His truth. Their teaching showed their deep searching of the Scriptures under the guidance of the Holy Spirit, while the exercise of the varied ministry, under the power of the Spirit, testified to the blessedness of the teaching of God's Word on each important subject. It was into this scene I was privileged to enter in the year 1843."

The Church at that time had grown to a considerable number. It began in a small house in King Street, Plymouth, and finally settled in Elerington Street, where there was accommodation for one thousand in fellowship and about four hundred others. This was a large plain building erected according to their own plans, without gallery. The large table was placed in the centre, around which were ranged the seats on a gentle rise from the floor. There were no pews, but plain and comfortable benches. The acoustic properties of the spacious hall were, however, very deficient, so that those who spoke, unless possessed of very strong voices, were compelled to stand at the table.

The leading ministering brethren were J. N. Darby, B. W. Newton, J. L. Harris, H. W. Soltau, J. E. Batten, Dr. Tregelles and W. Dyer. The exhortation of these several teachers was to a holy life in fellowship with the Lord Jesus Christ, to the cultivation of love, to a walk worthy of our heavenly calling, and to animate the blessed hope of

AT PLYMOUTH

our Lord's return. "I breathed what appeared to me the pure element of love," continues the writer; "I was in the enjoyment of the liberty of home. I was enlightened by its teaching, cheered by its joys, comforted by its hallowed fellowship, strengthened by godly companionship and encouraged by those who were over me in the Lord. Those were delightful times, so sweet for their simplicity. The fruits of the Spirit were in evidence. Whatever undercurrents were at work they threw nothing to the surface. But it was too fair a scene for Satan to contemplate, and he must by some means mar its beauties and devastate its loveliness."

The devastating work, hinted at by the writer of the letter, began soon after the return of J. N. Darby from the Continent, in 1845. It is not the purpose of this book to revive the memory of those painful years of strife. Suffice it to say that the principles of Christians called Open Brethren are those originally taught and maintained by the early Brethren in Plymouth; from which Darby and consequently his followers departed, if not previously, certainly in 1848.

From small beginnings, the Plymouth Assembly at one time numbered over a thousand; and though to-day in some measure shorn of its old-time lustre, it still maintains a faithful testimony, standing true to those principles which marked the early days of its inception.

CHAPTER IV

EARLY BRETHREN

BEFORE proceeding further we will briefly introduce to the reader those men whose names have been mentioned, and who under the guidance of the Holy Spirit were used of God in the founding and development of this and other assemblies.

When J. N. Darby and his friends arrived at Plymouth to begin work, they found a young man there who had already become known in the villages round about the ancient seaport town as a faithful and zealous preacher. He was just twenty-six. Previous to this time he had resigned a captaincy in the Royal Navy, for conscience' sake, although, it is said, he could ill afford the loss of his pay. His name was Captain Percy Francis Hall—a name which for half a century was closely identified with the activities of the Lord's people, principally in the south of England.

A man of peculiarly independent inclinations, accounted by some as eccentricities, his views are propounded in a tract, *Discipleship*, which displays not only the courage and fearlessness of the writer, but his unfailing devotion to the fundamental truths, which he ever sought to manifest in precept and practice. Warmly interested in prophetic teaching, Captain Hall was a frequent visitor to Powerscourt House, County Wicklow, the residence of Lady Powerscourt, where, along with Bellett, Darby and others, he took an active part; and in the troublous times of 1848–49 his counsel was sought in the interests of peace.

George Vicesimus Wigram was about the same age as Captain Hall at the time when he formed one of the little company of believers at Plymouth. He had been brought to the Lord a few years previously, whilst a subaltern officer in the army, but soon afterwards relinquished his position to enter Queen's College, Oxford, with a view to taking orders in the Church of England. It was here that he made the acquaintance of those men whose names in years to come were destined to figure so prominently in the Brethren Movement. G. V. Wigram was the twentieth child of Sir George Wigram, a merchant and shipowner in London, and was born in 1805. A profound Bible student, he devoted many years in the preparation of *The Englishman's Hebrew and Chaldee Concordance to the Old Testament*, and a cognate one to the Greek New Testament, in which occupation he freely used the greater portion of a considerable fortune.

Wigram interested himself in the compiling of *Hymns for the Poor of the Flock*, a hymn book which to-day, in a somewhat altered form, is still in use amongst assemblies known as "Exclusives." The first collection of hymns specially compiled for the use of Brethren was called *A Christian Hymn Book*, and was issued from Plymouth from the publishing office of their first magazine, *The Christian Witness*. The name of George Vicesimus Wigram is notably associated with the founding of the first assembly in London. Commenced on similar lines to the parent meeting at Plymouth, it was the forerunner of many other assemblies, which, in a comparatively short time, sprang up throughout the Metropolis.

In Wigram, J. N. Darby found a loyal and strenuous supporter throughout the unfortunate controversy waged by the indomitable Irish leader, and during the lamentable eruption of 1845, which brought so much pain and bitterness in its train, Wigram took a prominent part. This is no place nor is it the purpose of these pages to open up old wounds, which time the great healer has sought to close for ever. Suffice it to say that though he may have erred in his judgment on matters which affected the well-being of the Church through his unwavering loyalty to an adamant leader, "his sincerity was never questioned, his motives recognised" by at least one who stood in the forefront and received the full force of the onslaught: the venerated George Müller, of Bristol, of whom we have still to write.

It was Benjamin Wills Newton who invited Darby to Plymouth. A theologian of some distinction and an able expositor of the Scriptures, Newton very soon rose to a position of influence amongst Brethren. Born in 1807, he was thus the youngest in the group of Brethren who first gathered around the Lord's Table at Plymouth. Intended for the Church his views had already been diverted from pursuing that course before his meeting with Darby and his friends at Oxford, and he readily gave up all thought of the ministry that he might more faithfully obey the will of the Lord, according to this fresh revelation in regard to the true interpretation of Church order. From its inception, B. W. Newton was actively associated with the meeting at Plymouth, until his secession from the Brethren seventeen years later.

The influence of this new Movement, despite the many fiery darts of the enemy, was making its presence felt, not only in the town of Plymouth but farther afield, and many were added to the assembly. A noteworthy adjunct was J. L. Harris, perpetual curate of Plymstock, who gave up a comfortable living in the Church of England that he might be associated with those believers who came together on the first day of the week to remember the dying love of the Lord Jesus. This fresh infusion greatly strengthened the growing assembly. Mr. Harris was a man of considerable learning, and for a number of years conducted weekly Bible readings at Plymouth, which were attended by people of other denominations and by all classes. It was under his editorship that *The Christian Witness*, the first periodical of the Brethren, was started in 1834. "J. L. Harris was certainly one of the chief men among early Brethren as to his individual and assembly connections with B. W. Newton and J. N. Darby, as to his active part in the subsequent troublous times, and as to his writings, which fortunately remain when the sorrows are gone, and continue to breathe the fragrance of the Spirit of Christ possessed by their author." He was a prolific writer and many of his books, including *Precious Truth*, *Law and Grace*, and *The Priesthood and the Cross of Christ*, held a high place amongst Brethren literature.

In the same year that the illustrious group of Brethren

gathered to remember the Lord at Plymouth, where a lamp was lighted which was destined to burn undimmed through the winds and tides of a hundred years, a young German who had lately undergone a great spiritual change, arrived in the Devonshire town of Teignmouth to occupy the pulpit of a small chapel. His name was George Müller—a name which to-day is loved and revered the world over. Previous to this, the young pastor had been powerfully influenced by the reading of Anthony Norris Groves' pamphlet, *Christian Devotedness*, and his mind was working rapidly along lines which were to materialise into the exercise of the principles now practised by Brethren. It was about this time that he made the acquaintance of a godly young Scotsman named Henry Craik, who, since Müller's arrival at Teignmouth, had become pastor of the Baptist Chapel in the neighbouring village of Shaldon. Both were only twenty-seven years of age, the former having been born in August, 1805, and the latter in September of the same year. Having much in common, the two became closely attached to each other, with an affection which has been likened to the friendship of David and Jonathan—a friendship which was unbroken through the thirty-six years that these two saintly men were engaged as fellow labourers together in work truly ordained of the Lord. It is a remarkable circumstance that while George Müller's spiritual outlook had been completely changed by the written ministry of A. N. Groves, the life of Henry Craik had been similarly transformed through the personal influence and teaching of Groves, in whose family he had for some time acted as tutor. Singular though it may appear, it was the arrival of these two strangers in this peaceful corner of Devon that sowed the seeds which were to have their fruition in the formation of an assembly some miles away in the cathedral city of Bristol. It is an interesting story and worthy of recounting here. A Christian gentleman, belonging to the Church of England, while on a visit to Teignmouth, happened one day to attend Craik's chapel at Shaldon. So impressed was he with the ministry of the earnest Scotsman, that, soon after his return to Bristol, he wrote urging

Mr. Craik to come to that city, which would afford a much wider sphere for his usefulness. Such a request came as a surprise, but seeing in it the hand of the Lord, he decided, after deep spiritual exercise, to go to Bristol. There was no settled pastor at Gideon Chapel at that time, and here Mr. Craik began his mission. So successful was the work, and so signally was the young preacher used in the edification of the Lord's children and in the conversion of the unsaved, that he was led to write, entreating his friend Mr. Müller to join him in the work.

CHAPTER V

BRISTOL BETHESDA

HENRY CRAIK had been ministering in Gideon Chapel about four weeks when his friend joined him. This was towards the end of April, 1832. Soon afterwards, so great was the interest manifested that the congregation rented Pithay Chapel in the same neighbourhood, and much blessing followed the labours of those faithful servants of the Lord in both places. Müller had not yet acquired fluency in the English language, and many were attracted to the meetings out of curiosity to hear the young foreigner preach. Cowper has well written:

> God moves in a mysterious way,
> His wonders to perform.

Amongst those who attended the services was a notorious drunkard of whom it is said that he would sell his clothes from his back in order to buy gin. He had followed the crowd to hear what the German preacher had to say, and thus it came about that on the first occasion that George Müller preached the Gospel in Bristol a soul was saved.

Before many weeks had passed the attendances had increased to such an extent that it was obvious that a larger building would be required. Besides this, as the truths of Scripture became more real, and having a sincere desire to follow the Lord more fully, it was realised that they must have more liberty of action in bringing these truths into practice. At that time Bethesda Chapel, a spacious building situated at the top of Great George Street, which had a few years previously been built by an ex-clergyman of the Church of England, stood empty; and this was rented for one year. Here, in the month of July, 1832, George Müller and Henry Craik commenced work, the fruits of which will only be revealed in a coming day.

It is well to remember that up to this time these two brethren, under the Holy Spirit's guidance, had been acting independently of what was taking place at Plymouth; and there appeared to be so many tokens of Divine approval that, after much waiting upon God, it was decided that they come together to remember the Lord's death in the breaking of bread, and so, on the evening of 13th August 1832, "at Bethesda Chapel, Mr. Müller, Mr. Craik, one other brother and four sisters—only seven in all—sat down together, united in church fellowship, *without any rules, desiring to act only as the Lord should be pleased to give light through His Word.*"

From that time forward the work at Bethesda, under the able ministry of those two devoted brethren, prospered exceedingly. Crowds continued to flock to hear the Gospel, souls were saved, and there were numerous applicants for fellowship. So that, ten years after the historic opening service the membership had increased to nearly six hundred, and ten years later the number in fellowship had reached a thousand. I cannot refrain from recounting here the personal testimony of a lady, eight years after services were commenced at Bethesda, related by Mr. E. R. Short in his interesting little brochure, *The Story of Bristol Bethesda.*

"It was in 1840 that I first became acquainted with the 'Brethren.' I had come from a well-filled, well-upholstered London chapel with grand organ, well played, and good singing, and where the élite attended. Our pastor was a gentleman of means and education and dressed as such, with knee breeches, silk stockings, buckled shoes and ample shirt front. In the pulpit he wore a large silk scarf on his shoulders. Imagine my surprise on the first Sunday morning when I entered Bethesda, a large bare chapel, half empty. A very few grave-looking men and women came in and knelt down for a few moments, then rising sat with closed eyes till the service began. The sisters' dress was grotesquely ugly. A coarse brown woollen dress with a drab shawl, a straight speckled straw bonnet with drab or brown veil, servants and mistresses all alike. Soon a brother rose and prayed. Now we were at once in the presence of God. It was a Spirit-led prayer. I forgot the dress and all else, then a pause, then a hymn, sung like a funeral dirge with closed eyes and all sitting, and very badly sung too. Another prayer and then the bread and wine were passed round; pause again, then prayer. Now Mr. Craik stood up to speak. All had their Bibles and used them. His exposition of Scripture was quite a new feature of worship to me, and it was indeed marrow and fatness. The meaning of the passage read was brought out as I never heard it before, and I found myself feeding truly in green pastures. Dr. Maclaren, of Manchester, is the only man I know to compare with Mr. Craik. His knowledge of the original language was beyond that of most men of learning, and his insight into the meaning of Scripture also. It was a great privilege to hear such a man. 'I shall come again,' I said, and I did go again and again, and never went anywhere else while in Bristol. To me it was like a new conversion. Now I heard a clear Gospel that I could understand. The Bible became a new book to me. The brotherly love shewn was such as I had never seen before. The godly and simple lives of even wealthy people who had moved in the highest society were such as to carry one back to the days of the apostles and I felt that this was indeed Christianity of a high type."

The honoured name of George Müller, of Bristol, will ever stand a monument of imperishable testimony to the infallibility of a God who answers prayer. To-day his name is a household word, while the results of his labours extend to the ends of the earth. It would be superfluous, therefore, to write at any great length, the story of his life is so well known. And yet one cannot pass it by without the mention of a few salient features relative to a Spirit-filled life, which at once marked this man of God as one of the most outstanding stalwarts of the Faith of the last century.

A Prussian by birth, Müller was born at the village of Kroppenstaedt, where his father was a collector of excise. His early years lacked proper parental care and correction, with the result that long before he had reached manhood he had fallen a victim to vicious indulgences and wanton wickedness. With this knowledge of such a record of sin, it may astonish the reader to learn that during the years of dissipation he was all the time studying for the ministry, and had actually been accepted as a candidate for holy orders in the Lutheran Church. But God in His abundant grace suddenly stopped the wild career of the wayward youth, and at the age of twenty, George Müller was soundly converted. Four years later he came to this country with a view to labouring among the Jews in London. Here his zeal and strenuous labour in the Gospel brought about a breakdown in health and he was advised to seek a change. Thus George Müller was providentially guided to Teignmouth where, in the narrative of these events, we first made his acquaintance.

Apart from the prominent part he took in the spiritual well-being of Bethesda, of Bristol, from its inception to his Home-call in 1898, the name of George Müller is inseparably associated with the Ashley Down Orphan Homes, where, during his lifetime, this man of faith was instrumental in the erection of several large homes with accommodation for over two thousand orphans, which in later years required an annual income of about £30,000 for their maintenance. This tremendous enterprise he carried through by prayer and faith alone; nor did he once depart from this golden rule. And God has abundantly supplied the needs of this institution, from the opening of the first home one hundred years ago, to the present time, without making known their needs to any man, and without a public or private request for a single penny.

Henry Craik, his beloved fellow helper for thirty-six years, was a man of great learning and rare ability. He was born at Prestonpans, East Lothian, and after a course at a parish school of which his father was master, he proceeded to St. Andrews University where he had a distinguished scholastic career. It was during his student days that young Craik became troubled about his soul, which resulted not only in his conversion but the complete consecration of his talents to the service of the Lord. As has already been mentioned, he became tutor in the family of A. N. Groves at Exeter, where he remained for two years. He had a profound admiration for his friend and employer who so mightily influenced his life, and in after years he paid this fine tribute to the memory of the saintly Groves: "It was not at St. Andrews, it was not at Plymouth, it was at Exeter that the Lord taught me those lessons of dependence on Himself and of catholic fellowship, which I have sought to carry out." On the departure of A. N. Groves to Baghdad, Henry Craik took up a similar appointment as tutor in the family of a gentleman at Teignmouth, subsequently accepting the pastorate of a small chapel in the village of Shaldon on the other side of the River Teign, and, as we have seen, it was here that he met George Müller.

CHAPTER VI

AROUND BRISTOL

So wonderfully has the work begun at Bethesda been blessed of God, that at the present time there are about twenty such gatherings in Bristol and neighbourhood, all in happy fellowship. In a small chapel in Unity Street, St. Philip's, a work was commenced by Mr. Victor which grew to such dimensions that a larger building soon became needful. He was succeeded by Major Tireman, a man of great kindliness and originality, who soon won the hearts of the people. Untiring in his labours, and with a zeal which seemed to know no abatement, it was mainly through his efforts that the spacious building known as Unity Chapel was erected in 1862.

Ten years later, the assembly worshipping at Clifton Bethesda, Alma Road, had its origin under somewhat remarkable circumstances. In the centre of Clifton there was a large and valuable triangular piece of land on which stood a conspicuous notice board, intimating to all and sundry that this piece of land might be had gratis, on condition that it was used for the purpose of the erection of a place of worship, the ground area of which should be devoted to free and unappropriated sittings. Strange though it may seem, up to that particular time nobody applied for that land. To-day, the visitor to Clifton Bethesda may observe a tablet bearing this inscription:

"The ground upon which this Chapel is erected was dedicated by the late John Evans Lunell, Esq., of Clifton, in his lifetime for the erection of a place of worship, in which all the seats on the ground floor should be free for ever; and in conformity with the known intention of the above, £1500 were given by his widow for the erection of this building."

It was in this place of worship that the saintly George

Dr. EDWARD CRONIN.

FRANCIS HUTCHINSON'S HOUSE,
FITZWILLIAM SQUARE, DUBLIN.

CAPTAIN PERCY HALL, R.N.

GEORGE VICEIMUS WIGRAM.

AROUND BRISTOL

Müller gave his last address on Lord's Day morning, 6th March 1898. On the following Thursday, after finishing his usual day's work at the Orphan Homes, he just said, "I am tired," and that night the Lord called him to his eternal rest, in his ninety-third year.

In 1875 a testimony was begun in the Bedminster district by Mr. Welchman. As the little company of believers increased in numbers, Henry J. Harris, of the Bethesda Oversight, felt led to devote himself to pastoral and gospel work amongst them. The Lord wonderfully honoured the labours of this faithful brother, and he eventually gave his whole time to this service. The assembly first gathered in the Conservative Hall, afterwards removing to the Temperance Hall. In 1889, the present building, known as Merrywood Hall, was erected, and here the good work still continues.

In the year 1874 a large tent was pitched in Great Gardens, Newfoundland Street, by J. A. Vicary, known then as the "Singing Evangelist." He was assisted by Harrison Ord and others, and God greatly used His servants not only in the salvation of many souls, but also in the upbuilding of His own people. Almost from the first considerable interest was aroused, and so manifest was the work of the Holy Spirit that in the following year the commodious building known as the St. Nicholas Road Gospel Hall was erected. Here Mr. Vicary ministered the Word for many years. "I well remember Mr. Wright's prayer at the laying of the foundation stone," says Mr. E. R. Short, to whom the writer is indebted for a narrative of so many interesting facts and incidents in this connection. "The first gift towards the cost was a sovereign found in an envelope addressed to Mr. Coultas in a room in the Y.M.C.A., St. James's Square, where a few men were gathered together in conference. The sovereign was laid on the floor and they all kneeled round it in prayer and faith." How the prayers of that faithful few were answered is revealed in an unbroken testimony of half a century.

The Stokes Croft Assembly first came together in the year 1878. Their meeting-place was a disused skating rink

C

situated in a convenient centre, which had been leased by a few brethren. The building was in a very dilapidated condition but was soon made comparatively comfortable and attractive, and as Salem Chapel was now closed, the opening of this old building as a place of worship drew many to the services. So rapidly did the Lord's work develop that additional premises were soon required. The names of E. T. Davies and D. D. Chrystal will long be remembered as associated with this assembly.

It was about this period that Mr. Vicary the evangelist pitched one of his Gospel Tents in a field at Bishopston, upon which the Jail now stands. Here services were continued throughout the summer months and much blessing was realised. During the mission there was a special work amongst the soldiers quartered at the Barracks in which Colonel Molesworth, Captain West and other brethren took a deep interest. At the close of the Tent Mission the Lord opened the way for a permanent testimony, and thus was established the present Bishopston Gospel Hall.

It is worthy of note that from the Bristol United Bethesda Church there have gone forth to other lands to preach the Word many brethren and sisters, looking only to the Lord for support and guidance; the number at present being about twenty labouring in Spain, Portugal, Switzerland, Roumania, India, China, Japan, Algeria, Central Africa, Barbados and Argentina. Surely a royal record, which is indeed honouring to the Master for Whom they left home and friends to serve in regions beyond!

CHAPTER VII

EARLY DAYS IN HEREFORD

IN the same year that the little company of believers first gathered together in Bethesda Chapel, Bristol, there passed away at Aberystwyth, at the comparatively early age of forty-four, a Church of England clergyman. His name was Henry Gipps. Strange though it may seem, it was mainly through his faithful ministry while Vicar of St. Peter's, Hereford, that seeds were sown which in days to come had their fruition in the formation of an assembly of Christians, who were to be fettered no longer by creed or ordinance of Church and State.

Mr. Gipps was a man greatly beloved, and it is said that when the tidings of his death reached Hereford, not only the members of his own congregation but the whole city were cast into mourning. His preaching had indeed been richly blessed of God, both in the salvation of sinners and in the building up of His people, which resulted in many Christians from other parishes in the city being attracted to his ministry. John Venn, his successor—who is still remembered in the city because of his philanthropy—was a man of much grace and charm, but his preaching lacked the clear and decided tone that characterised the sermons of Mr. Gipps. Besides this, his interpretation of the Scriptures did not coincide with what his congregation had come to know, by a close study of the Word, to be the teaching of the Holy Spirit. This state of affairs in the Church somewhat unsettled a number of the most intelligent and influential Christians amongst his congregation, and they began to pray for a more Scriptural ministry. Prominent amongst these were Mr. and Mrs. William Yapp, Dr. and Mrs. Griffiths and Mr. Humfrys.

During this period of spiritual unrest Mrs. Griffiths, while on a visit to friends at Plymouth, attended some meetings where Captain Percy Hall ministered the Word. So pleased was she at the wonderful unfolding of the Scriptures that she begged the Captain to come to Hereford, assuring him that there were many Christians who would gladly welcome such teaching. Captain Hall accepted the invitation, and the first meetings were held in Mr. Yapp's house in Bridge Street. These were followed by larger gatherings in various schoolrooms and chapels in the city. His exposition of the Scriptures received general approbation, and it was felt that Captain Hall's coming to Hereford was the Lord's answer to the prayers of His people. Mr. Venn, the new vicar of St. Peter's, had given them elementary truths, but here was "strong meat" indeed, and an opening up of dispensational truth such as they had never heard before. The result was that Captain Hall was invited to take up residence in Hereford. Realising this to be the will of the Lord he consented, and a suitable house was obtained and furnished for him at Breinton, three miles out of the city, to which he and his family removed. This was in the year 1837.

It was now felt desirable to commence regular meetings, and a large room at the rear of Mr. Yapp's house was soon made ready for that purpose. As these meetings became known the attendances rapidly increased, and not only were Christians from various denominations in the city attracted but large numbers came in from the country districts to remember the Lord in the breaking of bread, so that it was no uncommon sight on Lord's Day mornings to see a row of carriages lining the side of the street in which the Hall was situated. "At that time," writes Mr. W. R. Lewis (to whom I am gratefully indebted for this interesting account of those early days at Hereford), "the leaders arranged beforehand who should break the bread on the following Lord's Day, thus little by little learning for themselves the true leading of the Spirit, which, as one might well suppose, was not learnt all at once. The premises soon becoming too small had to be enlarged to seat between three hundred and four hundred, brethren and sisters selling their plate and surplus furniture to

EARLY DAYS IN HEREFORD

provide the means for defraying the cost of such extension."

As might be expected, these meetings greatly disturbed Mr. Venn. He preached a sermon against the "Brethren from Plymouth," but despite every effort to hold his flock together he had the mortification of seeing the cream of his congregation forsaking his church, to gather with those brethren whose ministry he sought by speech and pamphlet to refute.

According to the testimony of William Seward, who passed away in 1908 after seventy years' close association with the Movement at Hereford—almost from the first—it was not the apprehension of dispensational truth nor was it the knowledge of church truth which separated so many at that time from the Establishment, but rather the deep need for that spiritual teaching which many found in Captain Hall's ministry.

The striking feature which from the start characterised the Brethren Movement, in that professional men and those of high social standing were among the first to be led out of the systems around them, was notably evident at Hereford. They were men who had gift for public ministry which their ecclesiastical position had hitherto suppressed, but now being brought out into liberty were exercised either in the way as pastors, teachers or evangelists. These Brethren now found scope for the exercise of the gifts which God had bestowed upon them, and on occasions would journey by horse and trap to neighbouring towns, as well as to the country villages, to preach the Gospel.

The young assembly at Hereford was visited by such men as J. N. Darby, the Hon. John Parnell and others who sought to establish the saints in the heavenly calling and hopes of the believer. Referring to Mr. Parnell's visit to Hereford about this time, Henry Groves, in his *Memoir of Lord Congleton*, recalls one occasion when Captain Hall was confined to bed through illness and there was no one to take his place in the ministry of the Word. Mr. Parnell was asked to take the meeting, which, rather reluctantly, he did. Though possessed of some gift he was always diffident of his capabilities as a preacher. On this occasion his subject was the resurrection life, in connection with Romans vi and Col. iii. "I had heard others speak on the same subject before," relates one who was present, "and, as it appeared to me, more from the head than the heart; but when I heard him, though his style was rather peculiar, I felt at once here is something real and in the power of the Spirit; here is one who has first learnt of God and realised what he speaks in his own soul, and out of the fulness of the heart speaks to the hearts of others." Thus, with such help, the good work received God's smile and continued to prosper.

As we have already seen, amongst the company of believers at Hereford was William Yapp—remembered as the originator of the "Yapp" edged Bibles—a man of high spiritual character, whose love for the Lord's work seemed to be unbounded. So zealous was he in the spread of the Gospel that at one time he kept five horses in his stables for use of brethren engaged in carrying the glad tidings to the country districts. In this work Mr. Yapp was greatly encouraged and helped by Dr. Griffiths, who was at that time the leading surgeon in the city. For long years the good doctor was remembered as the great tract distributor, often throwing the Gospel messages out of his carriage as he went his rounds, which were by no means confined to the city. Of a kind and benevolent disposition, Dr. Griffiths had a hospitable heart of love for the people of God, and it is said that whenever a gifted brother came along he would invite brethren to breakfast to meet him; and as on Lord's Day many would come long distances—some walking miles for the purpose of remembering the Lord in the breaking of bread—the doctor would have a cold luncheon laid out in a large room in his house for any—rich and poor alike—who cared to partake of it.

When in 1848 trouble and dissension, the work of the enemy of souls, rent many a happy company of God's children, Hereford was mercifully preserved from division. Two years later, however, a difference of opinion as to the necessity of a Gospel testimony on Lord's Day evenings in preference to addresses to believers, resulted in an estrange-

EARLY DAYS IN HEREFORD

ment between Captain Hall and Dr. Griffiths. This unfortunate occurrence brought about the separation of those two brethren, the former taking with him a few who sympathised with his views. Captain Hall, who strongly advocated ministry meetings, was pre-eminently an expositor of the Word, while Dr. Griffiths was essentially a Gospel enthusiast. There is little doubt, however, that other causes were at the root of this unhappy division, but according to Mr. Seward, "this was the final cause which led to outward separation. Shortly afterwards Captain Hall adopted Mr. Darby's view in the unfortunate Bethesda division, though in 1870 he had cause to separate from Mr. Darby owing to the latter's teaching concerning the sufferings of Christ."

In those days, before the passing of the Burial Act which secured for Nonconformists the right of burial within the precincts of a parish churchyard, Dr. Griffiths, in 1851, purchased a piece of ground which he vested in trustees, to be used as a burial-ground, not only for those in fellowship at Hereford, but also for those in the county. It was upon a portion of this ground that the present Barton Hall was subsequently built, when, at its opening, those in fellowship numbered over three hundred.

About this time there came to Hereford an Irishman whom we first introduced to the reader at Limerick, in company with Darby. His name was Thomas Maunsell. Like not a few of those early brethren, he came of good family. Educated for the Law, he was possessed of a mind of remarkable clearness, so that these trained habits of thought were made use of by the Spirit of God in the ministry of His Word. For thirty years Mr. Maunsell was indefatigable in his labours for the Lord in the Barton Hall Assembly, and he lived to see a new generation brought in during his period of ministry. In those days the morning meeting commenced at ten-thirty and lasted till nearly one o'clock, thus opportunity was afforded of consecutive ministry of the Word. This was felt desirable and needful in view of the distances many had to come to remember the Lord, and since it was their only opportunity of being instructed in the Scriptures. During the vicissitudes of a hundred years, the testimony at Hereford has continued unbroken, and though time and circumstances have wrought many changes, the evangelistic spirit, a notable feature in the early days of the assembly's history, is still kept alive by those whom God has chosen to bear aloft the banner of the glorious Gospel of the grace of God. Two have gone forth from its midst to regions beyond: Mr. William George to Central Africa and Mr. John Griffiths (who is still serving in the Gospel) to Algeria.

The history of Hereford Assembly has occupied considerable space in these pages. One reason for writing at some length in this particular instance is that it may, in a measure, give the reader an insight into the birth and building up of such assemblies in those early days. Not a few of our assemblies throughout the country had their origin and subsequent development on lines very similar to those of Hereford, which shall be seen as we proceed, although, for obvious reasons, it may not be thought expedient to enter too minutely into the details of each specific instance in the narrative of events.

In point of time we are far removed from those days when men of God, faithful to the teaching of the Scriptures and with the courage of their convictions, broke away from the bondage of ecclesiastical rule and established practices, that they might assemble themselves together in simple faith and lowliness of heart, as did the followers of our risen Lord in apostolic days. And yet in recent times there have been those, not only in our favoured centres of Bible teaching but in remote parts of the earth, with no one to point the way save the Holy Spirit Himself, who have been led to see the truth of believer's baptism and the breaking of bread, as known and practised to-day by Christians obedient to the Word. A remarkable instance relative to this was communicated to the writer by Mr. A. Hamilton of Belfast, who received the story from the late Mr. T. McCall himself. Mr. McCall was an architect in Belfast and a member of a Baptist Church. Having received an appointment with the Canadian Pacific Railway, he, along with his wife, emigrated to Canada. They were situated at a lonely post many miles from the nearest place of worship. One bright Lord's Day morning, after they had breakfasted together and the things were cleared from the table, the wife turned to her husband and said, "Tom, I would like to remember the Lord's death to-day." The husband, wishing to place a difficulty in her way, replied, "You cannot do that, dear, as we have no clergyman here."

"There is no need for a clergyman," was the rejoinder; "our Lord has said, 'Where two or three are gathered together in My name, there am I in the midst of them.'"

Seeing he was defeated in this, Mr. McCall then raised the question of the wine. "There is a bunch of grapes, and I can soon make wine," was his wife's ready answer; and suiting the action to the word, she crushed the juice from the grapes into a tumbler, placed a loaf of bread on the table, saying as she did so, "You and I are two, Tom, so let us now claim His promise." And they sat down together and remembered the Lord's death. The husband admitted that for the first time in his life he realised the truth and beauty of the Lord's words in Matt. xviii, 20, and the simplicity of the order of meeting together in His name. This was the beginning of one of the largest meetings of Brethren in Montreal.

CHAPTER VIII

ROSS-ON-WYE

As we have seen, there went forth from Hereford many of the Lord's servants to evangelise the districts round about. The town of Ross-on-Wye came within the province of those frequent expeditions. How the work began in this district has been related to the writer by Mr. James Metcalfe. But ere we proceed, it is necessary to go back to the early years of last century, for, as the mightiest rivers are traceable to a tiny spring far up the mountain track, even so the origin of this meeting may be traced to a seemingly unimportant event.

In the year 1815, a promising young naval lieutenant was stationed in the West Indies. One evening, while bent on the pursuit of some worldly pleasure, he happened to pass the open door of a house where a company of negroes were assembled. Hearing the voice of a man in earnest appeal, he stopped and listened. It was a poor illiterate negro telling out of the fulness of his heart God's great love to sinners; love which reached out to all mankind, whether black or white, bond or free. What the young officer heard from that poor black man was the means of his foregoing the purpose of his evening revel, and he returned to his quarters disturbed by serious thoughts concerning the welfare of his soul.

Not long after this event, peace having been proclaimed throughout Europe, William G. Rhind—for such was his name—retired from the Navy, receiving the rank of captain, and returned to Plymouth where he took up residence. Happening one day to enter a place of worship in that town, where an aged servant of the Lord was preaching from the text: "Behold the Lamb of God which taketh away the sin of the world," he was led to the Saviour. Of the reality of his conversion, his subsequent life gave ample proof. He had a thought of entering the ministry of the Church of England, and with this object entered Sidney Sussex College, Cambridge, but after three years' diligent study there his health gave way, and he returned to Plymouth, where he took up his abode with his mother. He afterwards removed to London, and then to Ireland where he remained seven years. Returning to England in 1838, he settled in Hereford.

Having from conviction embraced the views held by those Christians who meet simply as brethren in Christ, Captain Rhind and his wife met every Lord's Day with the company of believers at Bridge Street. Conscious that he was more particularly called to do the work of an evangelist, Captain Rhind did not long confine his labours to Hereford, but frequently visited other places, especially Ledbury and Ross. Those journeys were made on horseback. He also made excursions to various parts of the Kingdom, preaching to large and fashionable crowds at Cheltenham and other places. Of this courageous soldier of Christ it has been fitly written: "A great personal soul-winner, whether by rail, coach or steamboat he would immediately present every one with a tract. This he called 'Showing his colours at once.'"

In 1843, Captain Rhind became a resident in Ross-on-Wye, and the year following, mainly through his efforts, a room in Wilton Road was rented, when ten sat down to remember the Lord in apostolic simplicity. Very soon the room became too small, and as time went on over a hundred met in happy fellowship. The evening meetings were usually crowded, and it was now considered needful to enlarge the building. Captain Hall and others from Hereford frequently gave help in ministry and in the preaching of the Gospel. Seventeen years later it was decided to build a new hall, the number in fellowship, including a few small meetings which had been opened in the neighbouring villages, being one hundred and thirty. A commodious hall was built, but as the result of building operations by a local brewery firm the hall became sandwiched between their buildings. This incongruous position arising, it was felt desirable to make a change; therefore the hall was removed and rebuilt in Henry Street, and constitutes the present Gospel Hall.

Early in the year 1870 there were brought to the Lord and added to the Ross Assembly three youths, still in their teens, who were destined in years to come to be of great help to the meeting at Ross, and the meetings in the surrounding villages. They were William Royce, Henry T. Blake and William J. Barter. An able minister of the Word, Mr. Royce was highly esteemed, not only in Bristol, where he spent the later years of his life, but throughout the West of England. Mr. Barter (the father of Mrs. Matthew Brown now in the mission field in India), possessed little gift as a speaker. His special ministry lay along other lines, and during his forty years' connection with the Ross Assembly, to the time of his Home-call in 1912, he took a keen, practical interest in the activities of the Church. Mr. Blake, the last survivor of the trio, as a boy knew Captain Rhind, and appears to have caught much of his spirit.

Soon after their conversion, Mr. Blake and Mr. Royce had it laid upon their hearts to take up Sunday School work at Grove Common. This was before the days of easy and comfortable transit such as we enjoy to-day. Walking was their means of getting from one place to another, and no doubt they enjoyed the company of each other as they "talked by the way." Having travelled some distance from their homes they were made welcome to tea at one of the cottages near the hall, spending the time between the Sunday School and the Gospel Meeting in visiting the cottages and distributing tracts.

About the year 1868 a cottage meeting was commenced in a house at Grove Common, a village about three miles distant from Ross-on-Wye, then occupied by a Christian couple named Mr. and Mrs. Minett. As numbers increased, the need of a more convenient place where the little company of believers might meet to remember the Lord, was felt, and prayer for guidance was sought. The answer came through Mr. Minett offering to provide a site for the meeting-room on ground which formed part of his garden.

The Fownhope Assembly—some eight or nine miles

distant—were warmly interested in the work at Grove Common, and several of the brethren (one of whom was a builder) came over and gave their services free in the erection of the building. The meeting-room was built at least a mile from the Parish Church, and although many professed to belong to the Church of England, it was on rare occasions they were found attending any of the services. A prominent objector to the work being carried on at the Grove Common meeting-room was the Vicar of the parish. So long as the people went nowhere the Vicar did not appear to mind, but directly he heard they were attending this meeting-room the offenders were visited and warned that unless they returned to church, they would lose the right to derive benefit from certain charities left for the poor who attended that church. This weighed with some who had families and found difficulty in making ends meet. Others, however, would not be bought in this way and they left the church.

As an instance of the opposition which confronted the early brethren who laid the foundation of such gatherings of the Lord's people, which in later days came into being through the indefatigable labours of those stalwarts of the faith, it may be of interest to recall an incident which took place previous to this time. Captain Rhind, along with his friend, Captain Percy Hall, were on one occasion holding an open-air meeting at Grove Common. Amongst those who gathered to hear what the strangers had to say were two men who had been engaged by a local farmer to collect all the eggs they could find from the Fold Yard near by, as ammunition to throw at those servants of God. So powerfully was the Gospel delivered, however, that as they stood listening, the arrow of conviction went home to the hearts of the two country men, and instead of carrying out their nefarious work, they returned to the farmer who had engaged them, and emptying their pockets of the eggs, told him to do the job himself, remarking in their broad Herefordshire dialect, "They be good words that the gentlemen speak."

An active interest is still being taken in the Grove Common meeting, not only in the Gospel but in work among the children, a large farmhouse kitchen being used for this purpose.

About two miles beyond Grove Common, along the banks of the picturesque River Wye, is the village of Hoarwithy. The meeting-room there was formerly a congregational chapel which, becoming vacant, was acquired by two brethren who took steps to commence meetings, and God blessed their labours, many being added to their number.

Ballingham is another little village two miles from Hoarwithy on one of the many roads leading to Hereford from that point. There has been an assembly of believers in this place for over sixty years, the outcome of the faithful labours of brethren from the Hereford Assembly.

CHAPTER IX

EXETER

THOUGH there are no written records of its early church history, it is known that the Exeter Assembly dates from the first days of the Brethren Movement; in fact the place of worship in Northernhay Street, now known as Providence Chapel, was where most of those whom we have come to regard as leaders of the Movement, and whose names have now become familiar, ministered on several occasions. In later years, owing to the unhappy division, this property was sold to the Bible Christians. The interior of the building has undergone very little structural alteration since its erection, and anyone visiting the chapel to-day will at once observe that the seating accommodation is so arranged that the Table can be seen by all present.

Among the many prominent brethren associated with the Exeter Assembly, in addition to those alluded to elsewhere, may be mentioned Sir Alexander Campbell, H. W. Soltau, Col. Stafford, George Brealey (Founder of the Blackdown Hills Mission), Samuel Wreford and Henry Dyer. It was at Exeter that A. N. Groves was converted through the influence of Miss Paget—a name associated in later years with R. C. Chapman and William Hake of Barnstaple—and as we have already seen, it was in this city that Mr. Groves for a number of years practised as a dental surgeon. His eldest son, Henry, one of the first editors of *Echoes of Service*, was born here.

Mention should also be made of the good work carried on by Dr. Heyman Wreford, in connection with what was known as a Kelly meeting. For a long period he faithfully preached the Gospel in what was then the Victoria Hall, Queen Street, where crowds gathered to hear him, and, according to the testimony of those who remember those stirring times, it was not unusual to see an audience of one thousand people at the Sunday evening service. The work was abundantly owned of God, and it is no exaggeration to state that hundreds were led to the Saviour through his preaching. Unfortunately, there is little evidence to-day of those times, and up to recently the assembly met in a small upper room, previous to the present new hall being built. It was in the home of Dr. Wreford at Exeter that William Kelly passed away. Mr. Kelly is remembered amongst brethren as the leader of a party which afterwards bore his name; but also, and more happily, by his writings, largely in the form of expositions of Scripture specially helpful as being at once profound and simple. He was also a textual critic of no mean order.

Previous to 1889, when the present Gospel Hall in Fore Street was built, the assembly held their meetings in a large room over the Lower Market. This building was destroyed by fire and the meeting was transferred for the time to the Athenæum.

At the present time there are about three hundred believers in fellowship at Fore Street, where an aggressive work, especially amongst the young, is a notable feature of its Christian activities. This assembly has the care of two Sunday Schools—one at Druids' Hall and the other at Cheeke Street Hall—comprising nearly six hundred children. The work in the latter hall began about seventy years ago.

Writing of those days, Samuel Blow, an evangelist whose labours in North Devon are still remembered, says in his *Reminiscences*: "It was in 1866 I first met Mr. H. W. Soltau of Exeter. I had been holding Gospel services in Bitton Street Meeting Room, Teignmouth, the old chapel where George Müller ministered before he went to reside at Bristol. Mr. Soltau used to come to Teignmouth occasionally where he conducted Bible readings in a lady's house, and it was there I first met him. He gave me a cordial welcome to Exeter and believing it to be the will of God I went. We had meetings in the Athenæum, Bedford Circus and in Cheeke Street Schoolroom. The latter place had been recently secured for Gospel testimony. It had been used as a kind of low casino, and was the resort of the most vile and

Yours affectionately,
George Müller

HENRY CRAIK.

BETHESDA CHAPEL,
BRISTOL.

profligate. There was still at the farther end of the hall a small gallery where the musicians used to sit and fiddle while the company danced. Mr. Soltau secured it for the Gospel and a quick end was thus made of all the work of the Devil. In this place we had frequent free teas, preaching the Gospel to those gathered, and it became the birthplace of very many precious souls."

Since then these activities have continued steadily almost without a break, which has resulted in many young people being brought to the Lord, who afterwards were received into fellowship at the Gospel Hall. Thus to a great extent the work amongst the young at Cheeke Street Hall has resulted in this testimony becoming the main artery which has, during those years, fed the parent assembly.

Soon after occupation of these premises a baptistry was placed in this little hall, and here, previous to the erection of Fore Street Hall, many hundreds of believers passed through the waters of baptism.

It was in this hall, in 1872, that George Müller opened a day school which was continued for over twenty years.

Amongst the pioneers in Cheeke Street Assembly were Mr. Soltau's family, who laboured earnestly until they left Exeter in 1870. During his residence at Exeter Mr. Soltau was a tower of strength, not only to the little assembly at Cheeke Street, which ever claimed his constant thought and care, but to the many gatherings of the Lord's people in the neighbourhood. Trained for the Bar, Mr. Soltau relinquished his profession soon after his conversion (which came about through the preaching of Captain Percy Hall), and went to live at Plymouth, where he became associated with the company of Christians who, as we have seen, came together under the guidance of the Holy Spirit five years previously.

As in the case of not a few men of good family and position who at that time left the Established Church to cast in their lot with the despised Brethren, Mr. Soltau suffered much in the severing of many family ties, but though the loss and pain sustained were considerable, yet he esteemed "the reproach of Christ greater riches than the treasures of Egypt."

He was indeed a Valiant for the Truth, and there were few villages in Devon and the adjacent counties which did not hear the sound of his voice proclaiming the glad tidings of the Gospel of peace.

In 1851 Mr. Soltau left Plymouth, and for some years he and his wife resided at Exmouth and Northam, near Bideford. It was in 1861 that he went to live at Exeter, and it was from here that many of his writings, by which he is more widely known, went forth. In 1870, when his health was failing, Mr. Soltau removed to Barnstaple, where the closing days of his life were spent in sweet fellowship with his devoted friend, Robert C. Chapman. Mr. Soltau was a diligent Bible student, a fearless Gospel preacher and an able expositor of the Word. His addresses were not only concise and full of suggestive matter but remarkably trenchant and effective. "As I listened," wrote one who sat under his teaching, "each word seemed to fall like a hammer, leaving a lasting impression. . . . I frequently came across persons who had been converted while listening to him preaching in the open-air or at river-side baptisms."

Besides Fore Street meeting there are now three other assemblies existing in Exeter, the result of the work of the parent assembly, the first to be established being Buller Road, St. Thomas.

About the year 1883, a number of Christians residing in the St. Thomas district, and who attended Market Hall, Fore Street, were led to commence a Gospel testimony in their own locality, so they hired a small meeting-room known as Gray's Buildings, Cowick Street. The work began with Gospel Services on Lord's Day evenings and Bible Readings in the afternoons. A few years later it was decided to gather on the first day of the week to remember the Lord in the breaking of bread, and to establish an assembly in that neighbourhood. Amongst those who came together were some who had a heart for the young, and whose special ministry lay along these lines. Thus a Sunday School was commenced, with encouraging results. Meanwhile the numbers attending the services increased to such an extent that the meeting-place at Gray's Buildings was found to be

EXETER

too small, and after much prayer the present Gospel Hall in Buller Road was built. This was about the year 1896.

Simultaneous with the first meeting held in Gray's Buildings about fifty years ago, a few believers had a desire to witness for the Lord in the district of Heavitree, and a small house in Alpha Street was converted into a meeting-room. Regular meetings were commenced, followed by aggressive work amongst children and believers met for the Breaking of Bread until 1906, when the assembly removed to the building which it now owns and occupies, known as Ebenezer Gospel Hall. At the present time there are over seventy believers in fellowship, with a Sunday School of a hundred, and a weekly Mothers' Meeting of about a hundred members.

Whipton is a village which is now linked with Exeter, and Christian work has been carried on there intermittently for many years. At the beginning of the present century H. E. Marsom and his wife, then in fellowship with the Fore Street Assembly, conducted weekly meetings for children in the farmhouse of A. G. Alford. After an interval of some years, children's work was again begun in the village by the formation of a Sunday School. After the War, when council houses were built in the district, the school greatly increased in size and the farmhouse became unsuitable for the work, so the meetings were held in a hired public building called the Institute. In 1928 the Chapelfield Hall was built by Mr. Alford and the work was transferred from the Institute to the new hall. Here the little assembly meet on the first day of the week for the celebration of the Lord's Supper and for the ministry of the Word. A notable feature of the assembly's activities is the continued interest among the young people of the district, there being a prosperous Sunday School of two hundred children.

CHAPTER X

ROBERT CHAPMAN AND BARNSTAPLE

IN the narrative of events relative to the early days of Barnstaple Meeting, one name will always be associated not only with its beginnings, but with the subsequent history of this assembly of Christians—the honoured name of Robert Cleaver Chapman. It was a visit in 1831 to this old-time Devonshire town that led to Mr. Chapman, the following year, taking up his abode there. He had not yet reached his thirtieth birthday when an invitation came, desiring him to leave London—where ten years previously he had found the Saviour through the preaching of James Harrington Evans—to minister the Word in Ebenezer Chapel, a place of worship at that time occupied by a community of strict Baptists. Conscious of the Holy Spirit's leading, and with a desire to serve his Master in this new sphere, Mr. Chapman consented, naming one condition only—that he should be quite free to teach all he found written in the Scriptures.

That Robert Chapman had by this time closely studied and faithfully sought to follow the teaching of God's Word is shewn by an incident which occurred early in his Christian experience. Soon after his conversion he was led to see that it was the will of God that believers should be baptized, and he at once called upon Harrington Evans expressing a strong desire to obey the Lord's command. Mr. Evans, happy in the thought that the young convert had been studying his Bible, and no doubt seeking to test his sincerity in the step he was about to take, advised Mr. Chapman to wait a little while and further consider the matter. "No," was the ready reply, "I will make haste and delay not to keep His commandments."

When Mr. Chapman was led of God to take up service for Him in the town of Barnstaple and the district around,

ROBERT CHAPMAN AND BARNSTAPLE 53

there was no assembly of Christians known as "Brethren." A small company of believers had separated from the Baptists for some unknown reason, led by a Mr. Miller, owner of a lace factory, and a man of considerable wealth, who was largely responsible for the building of the Ebenezer Chapel in Vicarage Street. To this assembly of Christians known as "Close Baptists" Mr. Chapman found his way, and was welcomed for the spiritual help he was able to give through the ministry of the Word of God.

The charm and grace which characterised this saintly man—a charm and grace which we might well strive to emulate—up to the closing days of his long life, were unmistakably manifest at the very commencement of his Christian career.

It is a remarkable circumstance that the very year in which Robert Chapman went to Barnstaple with one purpose in view, and that to seek to learn and carry out what he found to be the will of God, George Müller and Henry Craik, who had just arrived in Bristol, were pursuing almost similar lines of thought which, as we have already seen, had such far-reaching results. Thus, though acting independently and unknown to one another, these brethren were being led in the path of obedience and in humble subjection to God's will according to the Scriptures.

As might well be supposed, this new form of things at Barnstaple, which ran counter to the most exalted ideas of church usage, though unpalatable to a few, had the effect of sending thoughtful Christians to their Bibles. The upshot was that the Christians meeting in Ebenezer Chapel found they could no longer continue to remain in association with the Close Baptists, the trust deeds of the chapel also would forbid such action. This led the way to the erection of the hall in Grosvenor Street, a commodious building with seating accommodation for over four hundred people. Nor did the Lord forget His faithful followers, for in a remarkably short time all the money necessary for the erection and equipment of the hall came directly in answer to prayer.

A letter written by Mr. Chapman sixty years later gives some insight into the early days at Barnstaple, and reveals to the reader the grace and patience which characterised his every action. "When I came to this place," he writes, "I waited for unity of heart and judgment among the company who called themselves Baptists; and when, by the power of the Scriptures, the greater part of them were minded to throw down their wall, we waited on in patience for fulness of unity and judgment. For this I was blamed by men of much grace, who at that time were endeavouring in the South of Devon to bring about a joint testimony of saints to the full truth of God. What we now enjoy here of mutual love and the Spirit's unity would never have been our portion had any other course been taken."

It was at Grosvenor Street Hall that Robert Chapman ministered the Word with the assistance of others, especially in those early days by Henry Heath and William Hake, the latter being Mr. Chapman's yoke-fellow for many years. The able ministry of these gifted brethren drew together a large number of people, several coming in from various denominations in the town and district. Thus many conversions took place, and believers were added from the Established Church, with the result that a membership of about four hundred continued for some years.

The meeting for ministry and Gospel testimony was held each Lord's Day morning, when the building was usually filled to its utmost capacity. In the afternoon, Sunday School and Bible Class work was carried on, and in the evening believers gathered to remember the Lord in the "Breaking of Bread," the meeting lasting from six-thirty to eight o'clock. "On those memorable occasions," writes E. S. Pearce, the intimate friend and companion of Mr. Chapman in his later years, "the hall was generally crowded, and the power and presence of God deeply felt."

From many parts of the world servants of the Lord were drawn in a peculiar way to Barnstaple and the humble abode of Robert Chapman at No. 9 New Buildings, where there was ever a loving welcome. An entry in the diary of A. N. Groves, under date 4th October 1852, refers to a visit to Barnstaple, which proved to be his last, for this saintly man, who had just returned from his life's work in the foreign field broken in health, died a few months later. He writes: "There was a meeting at Bear Street, and I accompanied her (Miss Paget, an old and devoted friend) though tired and shaken with my journey from Ilfracombe. I slept at dear Robert Chapman's, and they were all most affectionately kind. This morning we had a nice meeting . . . 7th October —I went out to breakfast with the Soltaus, and there I met with T. Hull, full of affection and kindness, and we had a most happy morning. I do trust the Lord was with us to desire a fuller measure of Christian communion, and a *temper* to bear with one another in our individuality of judgment. We had a most happy prayer meeting before we parted."

The work in Barnstaple town continues, but owing to various causes, principally deaths and removals, the assembly membership has decreased in recent years. There has, however, emanated from this meeting, mainly through the ministry and Gospel testimony of Robert Chapman and Robert Gribble, a large number of gatherings of the Lord's children in the villages of North Devon. Many interesting accounts associated with those days have been left on record, of which the following is an instance worthy of recounting here. It is the story of how the assembly at the village of Chittlehamholt, eighteen miles distant from Barnstaple, came into being. Mrs. Crawford, a Barnstaple woman, whilst listening to Mr. Chapman's preaching in the old Ebenezer Chapel, was convicted of sin and led to the Saviour. The husband of this woman was greatly opposed to the Gospel and threatened that should she go back to these services he would come and fetch her out of the chapel. He came, but could go no farther than the entrance, where he remained and listened while Mr. Chapman was preaching. Arrested by what he heard, the man went home deeply concerned about his soul. On the return of his wife from the meeting he demanded to know what she had been saying to Mr. Chapman about him. "About you!" was the surprised reply, "Why, I said nothing, of course." "But you must have," the husband insisted, "for I listened outside and Mr. Chapman was talking about me all the time."

This ended in the man's conversion to God. Soon afterwards, on hearing of Mr. Chapman's desire to walk the eighteen miles to the village of Chittlehamholt to preach in the open-air, the new convert begged to accompany the preacher, so that Mr. Chapman might not be molested by those whom Crawford knew were bitterly opposed to the Gospel. Being well-known through his constant visits on business in his unconverted days, Crawford proved a living witness to the power of the Gospel in changing his life.

The outcome of this visit, with others that followed, was the conversion of a number of those men, who were eventually baptized by Mr. Chapman in the River Taw. Not long afterwards a hall was built and an assembly formed which continues to this day.

CHAPTER XI

WESTON-SUPER-MARE

THE story of Weston-super-Mare goes back to the early 'sixties, or perhaps earlier, when a few Christian believers gathered together on Scriptural lines in a small hall in Meadow Street. It was not, however, till the year 1866, following an evangelistic mission by Lord Radstock, that any real development took place. Earl Cavan was residing in the neighbourhood at this time, and it was on his invitation that Lord Radstock came to Weston. The meetings were held in the Assembly Room, and continued for several months, resulting in a remarkable work of grace such as had never before been experienced in Weston.

Almost from the start of the mission, people in considerable numbers flocked to hear the preaching nobleman, and many, including men belonging to the professional and educated class, were brought into the Kingdom. Among the converts was one who, in after years, was notably used in carrying the Gospel into almost inaccessible places in Eastern Europe as well as to isolated posts across the vast continent of Asia. His name was Frederick W. Baedeker. Through the influence of a Christian military officer, Dr. Baedeker was prevailed upon to attend the Gospel services. Alluding to that never-to-be-forgotten night of his conversion, the Doctor afterwards said: "I went in a proud German infidel, and I came out a humble, believing disciple of the Lord Jesus Christ."

Dr. Baedeker made Weston-super-Mare his home, and except during the periods of his long and arduous excursions across the two continents he was to be found diligently sowing the seed and feeding the flock on the green pastures on the southern shore of the Bristol Channel, where he continued until his Home-call in 1906 at the ripe age of eighty-three.

In addition to the Earl of Cavan and Dr. Baedeker, brethren associated with the assembly who contributed to the spiritual development of the Church, were: Thomas Newberry, Colonel Minchen, General Rice, Judge Wylie, General Cookson, Douglas Russell, John Orr Ewing and others whose names, though unrecorded here, shall receive a worthier record more durable than the printed page.

The name of Thomas Newberry is remembered in association with his monumental work, *The Englishman's Bible*, the result of many years' diligent study and searching of the Scriptures in original Hebrew and Greek languages. Newberry's Bible—as it is known—is highly prized by Bible students, and is regarded by some as an inestimable "help" for enabling the ordinary reader to discern the beauties of the original Scriptures.

In the history of Weston-super-Mare Assembly many notable men, prominent amongst people called Brethren, sojourned there, bequeathing to this treasure-house of God spiritual riches, the fragrance of which still lingers around the memory of those stalwarts of the faith.

An unbroken testimony, attended by the ingathering of many souls, has continued these seventy years, and at the present time the assembly, now gathering in the Gospel Hall, Waterloo Street, has a membership of one hundred and thirty believers.

CHAPTER XII

EARLY DAYS AT TEIGNMOUTH

THE assembly at Teignmouth must surely date back to the early days of Brethren, for it was here in the same hall in which the believers still gather to remember the Lord that George Müller preached previous to taking up the work in Bristol, to which he had been so signally called of God. To-day, after the passing of more than a century, there are over a hundred Christians who meet in happy fellowship around the Lord's table.

The long span of a hundred years has passed by leaving behind a record which is marked by its loyalty to the Word, amid the trials and vicissitudes of its eventful history. The mention of Teignmouth recalls the labours of those whose names are inseparably associated with the early days: Dr. Cronin, J. L. Harris, J. G. Deck, George Müller, Henry Craik, Sir A. Campbell, Captain Rhind, Captain Percy Hall, William Yapp and others.

It was in the year 1838 that John Parnell (afterwards Lord Congleton), made his home in this peaceful South Devon town. He had the year previously returned from India, whence he had gone to join his friend Anthony Groves in the perilous undertaking of pioneer missionary work, an enterprise which laid the foundation of a great missionary structure. Begun in the fever-stricken Godaveri district, the work of those faithful brethren ultimately extended, not only across the parched plains of heathen India, but to many distant parts of the world.

The sojourn at Teignmouth of Mr. Parnell very soon gave evidence of the experience he had gained during the period of trial and privation through which he had so recently passed, and he not only greatly assisted the assembly by his ministry, but the missionary spirit led him out to the neighbouring districts, where he was constant in stimulating and encouraging similar gatherings of the Lord's people, and establishing meetings where they had not previously existed.

For a considerable time it was his custom to take the circuit of Teignmouth, Torquay and Newton Abbot on each Lord's Day. In the morning he would meet with the believers in Teignmouth, with those at Torquay in the afternoon, and arrive at Newton Abbot in time for the evening meeting, afterwards returning home to Teignmouth often late at night, tired in body but unwearied in soul. The quaint little town of Dawlish, three miles away, did not escape the attention of this man of inexhaustible energy, and one residing in that town in later years recalled the coming in to tea of two brethren who had walked over from Teignmouth, dusty and weary. They were John Parnell and J. N. Darby. The two had been much together in the early days in Dublin, and the Irish leader was at that time on a visit to his friend. Writing of those far-off days in the history of the Teignmouth Assembly, Henry Groves, in his *Memoir of Lord Congleton*, says: "Those few years in Devonshire were years of peace and blessing and, except to a very few, the elements of future troubles were as yet unknown and unfelt. They were to many as days of heaven upon earth."

Though possessed of ample means, the future Lord Congleton was simple in his habits and scrupulously careful withal. The house in which he lived was of the most ordinary type, for which he paid an annual rental of £12. The floor was carpetless and the furnishings were primitive in the extreme: ordinary wooden chairs, a plain deal table (which by concession to the housemaid was afterwards stained, because of the trouble it gave in constant scouring to keep clean), steel forks and pewter teaspoons, and all else to match. "Around that table," writes a friend who was a frequent visitor to the humble abode, "I often sat with others, thick as bees, while he drew us out in the study of the Scriptures which he happily and usefully unfolded—an office for which he was eminently qualified. He had a happy faculty of setting every one at ease, fostering any little remark,

EARLY DAYS AT TEIGNMOUTH

encouraging and rectifying it—a rare qualification in a teacher, which in after years I often urged him to exercise." When in 1842 Mr. Parnell's father died he succeeded to the title, and not long afterwards removed to London where for a time he met with believers at the Orchard Street Meeting.

Amongst others who assembled to remember the Lord in the meeting-room at Teignmouth in its early days was Count Guicciardini, an Italian nobleman, who for the cause of Christ had been compelled to leave his own country and seek the sanctuary of Protestant England.

It was while walking along the shore one day during his residence here that he met a fellow exile, Teodoro Rossetti, whom he led to Christ. In later years both these brethren were prominently associated with the Lord's work, not only in the land of their exile but in their own country, where they did much in the proclamation of the Gospel and in establishing assemblies of Christians faithful to apostolic teaching.

About the year 1875 there came to Teignmouth Frederick Bannister, a man whose testimony is still a fragrant memory. Of him it is said: "He was a burning and a shining light," a man of great grace, unwearied in serving the saints, diligent in spreading the Gospel, faithful in the truth, and uncompromising in all that concerns the honour of the Lord.

Mr. Bannister's father was Headmaster of Bedford College. Thus the early years of his son were spent amongst scenes which, two hundred years previously, had inspired John Bunyan to write his immortal *Pilgrim's Progress* as he lay confined in Bedford Jail. Brought to the knowledge of salvation in his early years, the young convert was not ashamed to confess Jesus as his Lord to his fellow students at Cambridge, whither he had proceeded with a view to entering the ministry of the Established Church. Having taken his degree he was shortly afterwards appointed to a curacy in Bedfordshire, and some years later became Vicar of a Hereford parish. It was while there that he, through a close study of the Bible, became deeply exercised in soul as to his position in the Church of England with the light he had received from the Word. Mr. Bannister found it impossible thus to continue, and it was not without counting the cost that the young clergyman, while yet in the vigour of life, with all that men regard as good prospects before him, relinquished his "living" as Vicar, and severing his connection with the state Church, went forth from all denominationalism to serve the Lord, as He might guide, in simple dependence upon Him for the supply of all his need.

Thus did Mr. Bannister continue steadfastly from that time until the Spring of 1919, when he was called Home, at the advanced age of eighty-two. Previous to his coming to Teignmouth he went through the Midlands with John Hambleton, the converted actor, preaching Christ. At a later period he was joined by Charles Morton who, for a number of years, laboured with him among the villages of Bedfordshire in tents and with Bible carriages, until he went south to Devon. Frederick Bannister's faithful work among the smaller assemblies of Devonshire, and his constant spread of the Gospel by word and printed page, was wonderfully blessed. He was, indeed, a true helper of the saints, a man full of grace and specially gifted as a shepherd to tend and care for the flock of God. With such stalwarts of the faith, the assembly at Teignmouth, ever faithful to the Truth and seeking only to magnify the grace of God, has been guided into channels of usefulness and blessing.

CHAPTER XIII

THE FIRST GATHERING AT TORQUAY

THE light of Truth which in the early 'thirties of the nineteenth century at first projected a doubtful gleam, casting its uncertain rays here and there, had before the passage of many years become a bright illuminant, shedding its beams farther and yet farther afield, captivating and embracing many of His scattered and oppressed people, who, at this particular period of the Church's history, were groping in spiritual darkness. While in most instances the birth of an assembly of Christians was unaccompanied by what might be likened to the loud sounding of trumpets, it was rather the contrary in the case of the ancient seaport of Torquay (or Tor as it was then called), on the coast of Devon. According to "The Records of the Christian Church of Tor," a faithful few in face of much opposition came out from the Established Church led by a stalwart, John Vivian by name. Belonging to an influential family in the neighbourhood, he was a man of high spiritual character and unbounded courage, holding fast by the written Word. His passionate appeals, ever forceful and convincing, are reminiscent of the rousing words of that valiant for the Truth, Alexander Peden of Scottish Covenanting days. "The Lord grant to His dear people," wrote Vivian, "that they may unite as one man in this work of the Lord; and though many who are fainthearted, and many who are not chosen, turn back and walk not with us, may there yet be found many who, when 'I and all that are with me blow a trumpet,' shall also 'blow the trumpets on every side of the camp, saying: Thou hast given a banner to them that fear Thee, that it may be displayed because of the Truth.' Brethren, there be many enemies of God's people now, by whom Israel is much impoverished in the treasures of Faith, Hope and Love. Break, I beseech you, the empty pitchers of prejudice and ignorance and let your light be seen shining on all sides, in obedience to the command of the blessed Captain of our salvation, the Gideon of a backsliding people. And may He of His infinite mercy lead us on to that victory which overcometh the world, and shall make us more than conquerors through Him Who loved us and gave Himself for us."

Such was the prelude which culminated in a meeting being held in the Christian Assembly Room at Torquay on Thursday, 9th October 1834, when, after waiting upon God for guidance, it was resolved that by His help, those now assembled before the Lord in humble submission to the teaching of His word, and being sincere believers in the Lord Jesus Christ, thus regard themselves as members of His body, acknowledging Him as their Head and as being present in the midst of them, according to the Scriptures, constituting them a Christian Church, ruled only by the Word of God, and rejecting every name but the name of their God and Saviour.

Their meeting-place was where the Secondary School now is, in the parish of Tor (Torre). Later the assembly met in what is now known as Laburnum Street. As numbers increased it was found needful to remove to larger premises, in order to facilitate the increasing activities of the growing assembly, and in the year 1887 the company removed to the present building known as Torre Gospel Hall. The hall was enlarged in 1890, and again nineteen years later. In 1932 the building was demolished and a larger one containing a gallery was erected in its place, without any appeal outside the assembly for funds.

The work among young people is a notable activity, and until recently the Torre Gospel Hall possessed the largest Sunday School in the town, but a township having sprung up in a suburb, many of the children went there to live. To meet this contingency the Torquay brethren built a hall in the new district, and an assembly was established. There are now seven assemblies in Torquay.

That God has abundantly blessed the testimony begun in the little fishing village of Tor a hundred years ago is

CAPTAIN W. G. RHIND, R.N.

HENRY W. SOLTAU.

LORD CONGLETON.

THE FIRST GATHERING AT TORQUAY 65

manifestly evinced by the fact that as the old-time seaport developed into the present town of Torquay with its fifty thousand inhabitants, so the work of the Lord increased in a very remarkable way. And there may perhaps be few other towns (if any) in England, of similar size, where there are six active assemblies of believers all in happy fellowship with each other. A contributing factor to the unity of believers is a quarterly united meeting for prayer, after which the elders in all the meetings remain for further waiting upon God in prayer, and for consultation on matters pertaining to the well-being of the various assemblies over which they have the oversight.

About the year 1850 Leonard Strong of Demerara came to reside at Torquay. The parent assembly had then been in existence sixteen years, and the Lord was richly adding to the Church. As the town was growing and its popularity as a health resort becoming known, the need of other accommodation for the furtherance of the Gospel was realised. Mr. Strong with true missionary spirit at once set to work, and the erection of the Warren Road Gospel Hall, where an assembly was formed, was the result. For some time the meetings were held in a room off Union Street, on the site of the present Electric Theatre. Some years later, as the meeting prospered, Mr. Strong with others from Warren Road Gospel Hall became interested in the needs of a neighbouring district, and a meeting for the Breaking of Bread and the edification of believers was commenced in what was then known as the Parish Room. This was the beginning of the St. Marychurch Assembly. Soon afterwards the little company was strengthened by there being added to their number Philip Gosse, a man who was greatly used of God in ministering to the spiritual needs of His people and in the proclamation of the Gospel.

The mention of Leonard Strong in connection with the Brethren Movement recalls the interesting circumstance that he was "breaking bread" in far-away Georgetown in British Guiana some time before the first public meeting of early brethren at Dublin in 1830. Previous to this time he was holding the position of Rector of a parish in British Guiana,

E

with a salary of £800 a year. A diligent study of the Scriptures entirely changed his outlook, and acting independently, with no other guide save the Word, he left the Church of England, giving up a stipend which was his sole income, together with a comfortable Manse, that he might meet simply for worship with those who, through his faithful ministry, had embraced the Gospel of Christ. Considerable numbers followed him, and it is said that at the first meeting, which was held in a large shed used in connection with the process of coffee-drying, nearly two thousand believers were present. From that meeting other assemblies were formed which continue to the present time.

Born in 1792, Leonard Strong entered the Royal Navy before reaching the age of thirteen. He served as a midshipman, and during the French and American wars saw much active service, being present at several engagements. It was the upsetting of a shore-going boat in the West Indies, when he narrowly escaped being drowned, that brought before the youth his lost condition as a sinner before God, and ultimately led to his conversion. He relinquished his position in the Navy soon afterwards and returned to England. With the desire to become a missionary Mr. Strong entered the Church of England and, after studying at Oxford, was ordained as curate of Ross-on-Wye, but he was unable to settle down in this quiet parish. What Leonard Strong had seen of the West Indies' urgent need of the Bible filled him with an unquenchable longing to carry the Gospel across the seas. He therefore made application, and on receiving an appointment the young clergyman set sail for British Guiana, where he was installed as Rector of a parish there. That was in the year 1826. An ardent Bible student and a fearless preacher, his ministry was used of God in pointing large numbers to the Saviour, and in drawing many of the native Christians to his side. His work among the slaves, whom he sought to liberate from sin's bondage as well as lighten the oppression of the cruel taskmasters, brought him in conflict with the planters, who threatened to shoot him if he persisted in his preaching. This he continued without abatement, and the authorities

THE FIRST GATHERING AT TORQUAY 67

stepping in, the offending clergyman was removed to Georgetown, where, as we have seen, he began a work, the fruits of which remain even to this day. Leonard Strong returned to England in 1849.

The Babbacombe Gospel Hall is an offshoot from the St. Marychurch Assembly. Begun in the year 1887, the first meeting was held in a small room over an hotel, when seven brethren and about the same number of sisters gathered around the Lord's Table to remember His dying love. The place becoming unsuitable for the purpose of these gatherings, one of the brethren had two rooms of his own house converted into what proved to be a comfortable and convenient place where the company of believers could come together to remember the Lord. In this meeting-room, with about thirty believers in fellowship, a testimony has since been maintained in a parish which is intensely Anglo-Catholic.

For some time prior to the commencement of the work in the Ellacombe district of Torquay, the Lord had laid the need upon the hearts of a few brethren. Among those who seemed more especially exercised were John Elliott and S. C. Eales. Meetings for prayer and guidance were arranged, and in the Spring of 1908 a small cottage having become vacant, brethren from the local assemblies visited it. It was then decided to convert the cottage into a meeting-room for the purpose of Gospel work. This was done, and quite a number of people came together each Lord's Day evening to listen to the Word. Thus encouraged, the workers soon afterwards commenced services for children, which were continued in conjunction with the Gospel Meetings until 1912. In that year several Christians in the district expressed a desire for the Lord's Table to be spread, and although there were at that time four assemblies in Torquay, it was prayerfully considered among them, and eventually the little company met to remember the Lord Jesus.

The labours of those who thus set themselves to know the mind of the Lord and then act upon it, were owned of God, in that many who heard the Gospel believed and were added to the Church. In the year 1926 the meeting-room in the cottage having, through extreme old age, become unsafe for public worship, the little assembly was cast upon the Lord for guidance. The way was wonderfully opened up whereby means were provided for the demolition of the old cottage and the erection of a hall over the existing site, to accommodate three hundred people.

The assembly worshipping at Avenue Gospel Hall is of comparatively recent origin, having commenced in 1922. In no small measure this assembly owes its inception and early development to the ministry and labours of F. C. Mogridge, a resident in Torquay, who from time to time gave helpful addresses to Christians on fundamental truths, which resulted in several of those who attended these meetings expressing a desire to obey the Lord's command, and these were baptized at Torre. Thus many became further exercised as to what had been revealed to them through the Scriptures regarding the will of God as to New Testament teaching, and with the full fellowship of the five other assemblies in the town, a number of believers sat around the Lord's Table for the first time on 26th February 1922.

CHAPTER XIV

BRIDFORD MILLS ASSEMBLY

THE origin of the testimony at Bridford Mills in Devon may be traced to the conversion of William Surridge somewhere about the year 1864. Saved while listening to an untutored chapel preacher, he soon afterwards found an outlet for his zeal for the Master in commencing services in a schoolroom close to the mills. Unable to preach himself, he bought a volume of printed sermons, and these he read with evident success, for the people continued to come to the schoolroom in larger numbers. This gave him courage to take the Bible and preach the Gospel as the Lord gave him liberty. Thus he continued, and in course of time the work bore fruit as one and another were brought to know the Lord.

With no one to point the way, William sought guidance from the Scriptures, for the young converts required to be fed and tended. Thus he was awakened to his responsibility of not only preaching the Gospel but also to care for the flock. So he sent for the creeds of the different religious denominations, that he might decide for himself which was the proper course to take. But the more he compared each with the Word of God, the greater appeared his difficulty in arriving at a solution to the problem which exercised his soul.

Eventually he was brought in touch with a few Christians at a village not far distant. Here a little company had been gathered through the instrumentality of Robert Gribble, and on the first day of the week they came together, as did the apostles, to remember the Lord's death.

Mr. Surridge also discovered that there was a similar company of Christian believers in Exeter, and to his great joy he found that both of these were doing just what he had longed to do. The result was that brethren from Exeter were invited to preach at Bridford occasionally, and thus the light came to that district in Devonshire.

But it is not to be supposed that the enemy would allow this new departure to pass unchallenged, for very soon opposition to the truth for a time sought to hinder the work. Such men as Henry Dyer, Samuel Blow and others equally well known at that period, lent a helping hand in ministering to the spiritual needs of those who were faithful to the Word; so that from that time onward the work grew apace, for many hearing believed and were baptized.

On the Sunday morning when the first baptism was to take place, at which William Surridge, the schoolmistress and others were publicly to confess the Lord, Mr. Surridge was ill in bed. So eager was he to witness the ordinance that he managed to leave his bed, and arranged for an armchair to be placed by the side door leading to the orchard where the baptism was to take place. When the last person was entering the water, he said to the brother standing by him, "Give me your arm"; and with his help he walked over to where the company had assembled and was baptized, without suffering any hurt. A crowd of people had gathered along the sides of the Mill stream to see this novel sight. Among them was the owner of a tool factory, who afterwards said: "I came to laugh, but went home to cry, and the next time was baptized myself."

The schoolroom soon became too small, and in the year 1875 it was pulled down and rebuilt, the expense of the work being borne by William Surridge. Six years later a further addition was made in which the little assembly, consisting of poor working-class people, expressed a desire to have fellowship in meeting the expense. Of the gathering together of the money to pay the builder's bill, a brother relates an interesting story. In the assembly was a working man and his wife with a family of three or four young children. He was earning no more than ten shillings a week, and had saved just that amount to pay the shoemaker, who was to call the following week. They both had it laid on their heart to give ten shillings towards the building; but what about the shoemaker? The matter was taken to the Lord in definite prayer, and as the couple rose from their knees they felt constrained to give the money to the Lord,

BRIDFORD MILLS ASSEMBLY

which they did. "Next morning," writes my friend, "while following his employment, John knocked a half-sovereign out of a lump of earth with his spade. Thus, the same Lord who could guide Peter to the fish containing the required piece of money, could guide John to the lump of earth in which was hidden the shining half-sovereign. And so God was honoured, the shoemaker provided for and the family blessed."

The Lord continued to prosper the work, and in 1904 the existing building was demolished and a much larger hall erected on the same site (the position of the original schoolroom), where a faithful testimony is still maintained.

The work at Bridford Mills has really been unique, as there are not more than a dozen houses anywhere in the vicinity of this large hall, the nearest village being about a mile distant. "When I first visited the assembly, nearly forty years ago," writes Mr. H. E. Marsom, "it was indeed an interesting sight to see the country people on Lord's Day, with their carts and hampers, carrying provisions for their families who had come to worship."

A feature of the present hall, reminiscent of those days, is a kitchen range provided in the back room, for the warming up of the dinners the brethren and their wives brought with them. With the advent of the motor-car this is now a thing of the past.

During the last fifty years the welfare of the young has been the constant care of F. W. Surridge, a son of the founder of the assembly, his first Sunday School class being gathered from the surrounding district. This initial experiment resulted in a work which quickly grew up, and in a comparatively short time there was a properly arranged Sunday School with the names of one hundred and thirty children on the roll.

Mr. Surridge also instituted a Sunday School Teachers' Conference, which has been held annually with growing interest. In September, 1938, some four hundred teachers and Sunday School workers gathered at Bridford Mills to celebrate the jubilee.

CHAPTER XV

IN DORSET: EARLY MINISTRY OF HENRY DYER

THE wave of spiritual awakening which had directed thoughtful Christians to a closer study of the Scriptures regarding the true interpretation of certain New Testament passages—which up to that time, doubtless because of unquestioned usage and acceptance, had given no real concern as to their true meaning—had spread from shire to shire; so that ere a decade had passed by since the historic meeting at Dublin and the subsequent gathering at Plymouth, not a few assemblies of believers, for the most part drawn from various denominations, had become firmly established.

It was on Lord's Day, the 29th of May 1842, that nine believers met together in what was then known as the British Schoolroom, in the town of Shaftesbury, Dorset, "for the purpose of breaking bread without any reference to sectarian practices, and wishing to assume no other name than that of brethren and sisters in the Lord Jesus Christ, in Whose name it was their desire to meet to commemorate His dying love." Remarkable though it may seem, this little company came together solely under the guidance and will of the Holy Spirit and having no outward contact with any similar gatherings.

Previous to this, and in face of much opposition, cottage meetings for the study of the Scriptures were held. Amongst those who had left the state Church were two men, John Rutter and Charles Binns by name, and they accepted the care of the little flock. Under their sympathetic guidance and ministry the meeting grew both in numbers and influence, so that in a comparatively short time a larger room had to be secured. Gospel meetings were commenced, and the first convert was Thomas Lear, a well-known business man in the town, who in course of time became a pillar in the assembly.

Finding that others in different parts of the country were separating in like manner from human systems, fellowship was strengthened and increased by contact with them, and many of the Lord's servants visited Shaftesbury and ministered to the spiritual needs of the assembly. Among the first were John T. Vine, Charles Inglis, Robert Chapman, Henry Dyer, Dr. Maclean, and later W. H. Bennet, John Bragg and Ephraim Venn. Thus in the days of its infancy the little assembly, early manifesting a faithful adherence to the Living Word, was nurtured and encouraged by the wise council of such men as these at a time when the religious world, struggling amid doubts and fears, was passing through times of difficulty and unrest, accentuated in no small measure by the fascinating influence exerted by what became known as the Tractarian or Oxford Movement, with John Henry Newman—who later embraced the Roman Catholic faith—as one of its chief leaders.

From such beginnings the Shaftesbury Assembly increased in numbers and usefulness. In 1887 the Ebenezer Hall was built, to which the assembly was transferred; and through the long years has borne a faithful testimony which continues up to the present time.

We will now turn to another quarter of the county of Dorset, little more than ten miles distant from Shaftesbury, where, in a singular yet very similar way, the hand of God was moving amongst a few of His own people. About the middle of last century, in the town of Blandford, several friends who were in what are now known as the Free Churches, were associated in Ragged School Work. They were accustomed to meet week by week, for prayer on behalf of the activities associated with this particular enterprise, and used frequently to converse over the Scriptures. On one occasion the conversation took the turn of an enquiry as to the mode and significance of the breaking of bread, as set forth in the New Testament. A search into the Word of God revealed the fact that the partaking of what is known as the Sacrament, in the various denominations with which they were identified, was, in several essential points, different from what was instituted by the Lord and carried out under apostolic teaching.

They decided that there was nothing to hinder them from meeting together to celebrate the Lord's Supper in a Scriptural way, at a time in the week when no service in connection with their churches was being held. This being deemed by the ministers of their denominations an irregular and unauthorised procedure, those who persisted in following the Scriptures were excluded from membership of their congregation.

Those zealous people knew nothing of similar gatherings of Christians who, as we have seen, had already come together in the neighbouring counties in South-West England, and they were acting on simple obedience to the Word, solely as the Holy Spirit had directed. The ecclesiastical pressure which had been brought to bear upon those faithful few only drew them closer to the Lord and to His Word, as well as to one another. This led to the formation of a gathering free from human tradition, and directed according to the teaching of the New Testament.

For a time the little company continued to meet for the study of the Scriptures and to celebrate the Lord's Supper, isolated in a measure from many who, up to the time of their leaving the denominations, had been close friends; but who, following the dictates of their spiritual leaders in their passionate disapproval of the step taken by those wanderers from the fold of the churches with which they had been connected, had openly avoided further fellowship with the seceders.

Through a visit by Henry Dyer to Blandford, the company of believers were brought in touch with those who had been similarly guided by the Spirit of God in other places, to carry out His Word in like manner as they had been led. Thus an assembly was established. As their numbers increased an aggressive Gospel testimony was carried on, and there were several who used regularly to preach the Gospel in the town and the villages around. They now met together in the Assembly Rooms, where J. T. Vine conducted special meetings, the outcome of which was that many professed faith in Christ and were added to the Church. Alterations to these premises necessitated the removal of the assembly to the Town Hall, and as numbers continued to increase the East Street Hall was secured, where a good testimony for the Lord is continued at the present time.

It was during those days of pioneer work amongst the scattered remnant of God's people that many stalwarts of the faith, though comparatively young in years, came into prominence. By now the names of many are familiar to the reader. Henry Dyer, who was largely responsible in God's hands in laying the foundation of the Blandford meeting and in directing the feet of the young assembly along straight paths, was still in his thirties. Brought to the Lord in his youth, Mr. Dyer early associated himself with Christians assembling in the name of the Lord in London. He afterwards spent some years ministering to the spiritual needs of the various assemblies in the South of England, and for a time resided at Sherborne in Dorset.

The name of Henry Dyer will always be associated with the founding of a conference for ministry and the edification of believers—one of the first of its kind in the country—which was to be the forerunner of what has now become a distinctive feature amongst the activities of those known as Brethren. It was held at Yeovil. Commenced with comparatively small gatherings for the most part from neighbouring assemblies, it met for a time periodically, but as its spiritual value made itself evident, Yeovil conferences became a fixed annual event and exercised a powerful influence, drawing considerable numbers from many parts of the country.

Recalling those memorable gatherings, times that were graced with many hallowed associations in which the impelling influence of Mr. Dyer was so markedly felt—W. H. Bennet writes: "Henry Dyer's faithful and loving service of those days is gratefully remembered both in Yeovil itself and in the neighbouring towns and villages, and he loved at times to speak of one and another who were brought to God through his reading the Scriptures and speaking at street corners—a work in which he was very diligent as long as he was able to continue it. When he remained in any locality he was pre-eminently a pastor. His tenderness in visiting the suffering and sorrowful was very marked, and his earnestness in seeking the wandering showed how truly he watched for souls, while his readiness—at any cost to himself—to contribute to the breaking down of barriers between the Lord's people, gave evidence of his possession of the mind of Christ in no ordinary measure."

Mr. Dyer's counsel and considered judgment in matters which affected the well-being of assembly life was much sought after, and while gatherings of the Lord's people profited much by his pastoral visits yet his special ministry was more directly connected with conferences, not only at Yeovil and Leominster, but in different parts of the kingdom, where his ministry, ever rich in expository wealth, was much valued. Watched over and cared for by such ministering servants of God, many of the little assemblies which had come into being in Dorset and the South-west corner of England round about the middle of last century and the years immediately following were marked by their loyal devotion to the teaching of God's Word; and thus they prospered in the path of faith and obedience.

CHAPTER XVI

EARLY DAYS IN LONDON

BEFORE many years had passed by, after the raising of the standard at Plymouth, assemblies of Christians faithful to apostolic teaching were gathering in widely separated places many miles distant from the ancient seaport on the coast of Devon. Thus we find in the year 1838 a record of the first public meeting of Brethren in London being established. G. V. Wigram, Darby's faithful lieutenant, was entrusted with the commission, and the little company of believers who gathered in an unpretentious meeting-room in the locality then known as Rawstorne Street, Camden Town, ultimately became, to some extent, what Neatby in his history regards as "the nucleus of Darby's metropolitan system of organisation." That meeting became an historic centre. The good seed had been sown in virgin soil, and to that meeting other gatherings in different parts of the city own their inception and subsequent growth.

There appears to be scant documentary evidence accessible giving a reliable record of the development over the early years regarding the foundation of a movement which in time to come was to take such an important religious position not only in the Metropolis but throughout the world. Without attempting to trace through the uncertainties of time and circumstance the onward course of the steady current of spiritual activity whose source, through the guidance of the Holy Spirit, was to be found at Camden Town meeting-room, I will endeavour to gather together what has been left on record concerning the rise and spread of this spiritual movement in and around the city of London.

In a remarkably short time the Rawstorne Street meeting became the spiritual home not only of Wigram and Darby but of many other brethren whose names are now prominent in the pages of our history. Among those who took an active interest, the following, now mentioned for the first time, are remembered: Dr. S. P. Tregelles, W. H. Dorman, Alexander Stewart and —— Foley.

About this time Lord Congleton, who had recently succeeded to the title, came to reside in Islington, and into this meeting he threw all the energies of his large, loving heart in its sympathy and lowliness. Every Lord's Day commenced with a prayer meeting at 7 a.m., to which numbers came from distant parts of London. So that those who attended might not have to travel back again before the meeting at 10.30 for the breaking of bread, Wigram invited them to his breakfast-table. But as numbers increased a large room at the rear of the house, formerly used as a school, was fitted up with table and chairs, in which place tea and fellowship meetings were later established, thus making the fellowship of the family of God as much a reality as possible. Lord Congleton was largely responsible for the fitting out and furnishing of the room; and to those happy gatherings any of the Lord's people were at all times welcome, for there was no distinction between rich and poor; all were alike honoured for the Master's sake.

About the end of 1852 Anthony N. Groves paid a visit to Tottenham, where he endeavoured to interest the assembly in foreign missions. An entry in his diary at this date cannot fail to engage our attention, for it recalls the labours of those pioneer missionaries whose names are given, and clearly indicates the practical sympathy with which his appeal was received. "I went to Tottenham," he writes, "and stayed with dear Miss S—— who, with the Howards, showed much kindness. I spoke of Bowden, Beer and Aroolappen; and in the evening brought the subject before the Church, and they hope, in the union with believers in Hackney, Orchard Street and other places, to form an effectual committee to care for these things. Yesterday I was at Orchard Street in the morning. Count Guicciardini was there."

The casual mention of Tottenham and the Howards recalls the early labours of John Eliot Howard, Fellow of the Royal Society, who in his early years was used in commencing a testimony for God in that particular district

EARLY DAYS IN LONDON

of the Metropolis. Formerly a member of the Society of Friends, Mr. Howard very soon in his Christian experience gave evidence of his keen interest in the Lord's work, utilising his spare time in preaching the Gospel in the surrounding districts.

An earnest study of the Bible revealed to him his true position as a believer in the Lord Jesus Christ, and with a desire to follow more faithfully the divine order laid down in the Scriptures he resigned his connection with the Society of Friends.

In 1838, when about thirty years of age, Mr. Howard began a regular Gospel meeting in Tottenham, and in November of the same year the first meeting for worship and the breaking of bread was held in a small room in Warner Terrace. In the following year he built the meeting-room in Brook Street, where the assembly continued to meet until 1883. In that year Mr. Howard purchased the lease of the lecture hall in High Road, Tottenham, and the assembly was transferred there from the old meeting-room in Brook Street.

Faithful and fearless in his expression of what he believed to be the truth, John Eliot Howard became an outstanding figure, and for over forty years his ministry was greatly owned of God, not only in leading many to the Saviour but in the edification of believers.

He rendered eminent service both to religion and science, particularly in a volume of lectures published in 1865, entitled *Scripture and Science*. In this and other notable papers from his pen he sought to show in a learned and interesting way that there can be no conflict between science, as exemplified in the works of nature, and the Word of God. "Gifted with a powerful mind, of quick perception and rapid thought," writes one who knew him, "he eagerly made himself master of the religious and scientific literature of the day. He devoted a great deal of time and thought to the study of some of the scientific questions that in these days perplex so many minds, and his clear insight enabled him to unmask much of the scientific and religious philosophies that are now prevalent."

Mr. Howard was a tower of strength, not only in the assembly by whom he was greatly beloved but was known as an able minister of the Word both at home and abroad.

Towards the end of the same year that the assembly came into possession of the hall in High Road, Tottenham, Mr. Howard was called home after a brief illness.

The assembly at Hackney, mentioned in Groves' diary, is mainly associated with its location in Providence Chapel, Paragon Road, from the early 'fifties up to recent years, when the building was compulsorily taken over by the Post Office Department for the building of a telephone exchange. Before the occupation of Providence Chapel the assembly met in St. Thomas's Rooms, St. Thomas's Road, Hackney. Then the remainder of the lease of about fifty years of Providence Chapel, hitherto occupied as a Wesleyan place of worship, was purchased by William T. Berger, a member of the assembly and head of a well-known starch manufacturing firm bearing that name.

In the early days when the assembly met at St. Thomas's Rooms, Henry Heath, then in his thirty-third year, came to reside at Hackney. Formerly a co-worker with Robert Chapman in Barnstaple, he was largely instrumental in building up the assembly, being a gifted teacher and having a true pastoral spirit, which he devoted entirely to the Lord's work. He remained with the assembly until the death, in the early 'seventies, of Captain Towers, who had done so much to evangelise in Suffolk, and had built up a large gathering of the Lord's people at Woolpit in that county. Mr. Heath was invited to conduct the funeral service of the pioneer evangelist, and was led of the Lord to remain in that remote village that he might carry on that important work, as they much needed the help and advice he was specially fitted to give.

Before the assembly removed to Providence Chapel, thereafter known as "Paragon Road Meeting-Room," the Christians gathering there were greatly helped by the removal to London, in 1854, of James Wright, commended by the Bethesda Assembly at Bristol. He was then about twenty-eight years of age and had already been invited by

ROBERT CLEAVER CHAPMAN.

THE HOME OF R. C. CHAPMAN,
No. 9, New Buildings, Barnstaple.

Sir EDWARD DENNY, Bart.

C. H. MACKINTOSH.

EARLY DAYS IN LONDON

George Müller to assist him in the work of the Orphanage, which five years later he took up, and returned to Bristol, later becoming Mr. Müller's son-in-law by his second marriage in 1871. He afterwards succeeded Mr. Müller as head of the Orphanage.

Keenly interested in young people, Mr. Wright proved to be a great help to the assembly at Hackney, and when it was removed to Providence Chapel he established the Sunday School there, becoming its first superintendent. In the *Life of James Wright*, by Dr. Pierson, reference is made to his splendid foundation service amongst the children, esteeming the work in the infant class the most important of all. The box of movable letters which he used for teaching texts to the little ones was in existence in the meeting-room for many years, and probably is still. Some interesting memories of this servant of God are recalled by Mr. T. K. Freeman, who, in a letter to Dr. Pierson, soon after the Home-call of Mr. Wright, says: "I have a vivid recollection of the first public pronouncement of James Wright, at an assembly of Christians worshipping at St. Thomas's Rooms, Hackney. Known as the Brethren, they were not unworthy of the name, for there was an intensity of love to Christ and to His people which bound them together in holy fellowship when on the first day of the week they 'came together to break bread' in sweet remembrance of the risen Redeemer. Liberty of ministry was an interesting feature of the simple worship, and a few Sundays after Mr. Wright, his wife and two sisters had been recommended to us from Bristol, he read with much precision and pathos a few verses bearing upon the subject matter of the meeting, and for about ten minutes commented upon the Scriptures he had read. Though it is fifty years or more since then, I can in memory see his striking face, indicating great feeling and much firmness, while his eye sparkled with joy that he had such a message from the Throne to deliver."

From that date Mr. Wright became to the assembly a teacher of Divine truths that all rejoiced in, and though at St. Thomas's Meeting-Room there were veterans in the Gospel, henceforth as a follower of our Lord he manifested

His glory, and was fully recognised as a teacher sent from God.

"My association with the meeting in Paragon Road," writes Mr. G. H. Marks, who has furnished the present writer with copious notes of those bygone days, "dates from my father's removal to Hackney in 1861, until our leaving for Whetstone in 1880. During that period the number in fellowship had grown considerably, being one hundred and one in 1864, two hundred and twenty-eight in 1873 and the same number in 1878. The largest number of members was probably about 1875, when the Meeting Hall was crowded on Lord's Day morning and the gallery was used for strangers and children."

About the time alluded to in the preceding chapter, the tendency appears to have been to remove farther out of London, and many were transferred to the Iron Room, Clapton. At a later date, as numbers increased, the need of greater accommodation pressed itself upon the Iron Room Assembly, but this exigency was generously met by John Morley, who erected the substantial building known as Clapton Hall. It was opened for public worship in the Spring of 1880, many well-known brethren being present on that occasion.

Mr. Morley, to whom reference has been made, was a prominent city business man, whose untiring activities in the service of the Master, during a long and useful life, are still remembered, particularly in connection with the building up of local assemblies with which he was more directly associated. Though not specially gifted as a speaker himself, he was constant in encouraging those brethren whom God had marked out as ministers of the Word. On retiring from business Mr. Morley visited many parts of Britain and the Continent, devoting his time in the furtherance of the Lord's work. During the '59 revival he crossed to Ireland, where, having joined his friend, J. Denham Smith, he exerted his whole energies in the work of soul-winning.

Of a gracious and benevolent disposition, "his genial smile, friendly handshake, kindly enquiry after soul and body," invariably supplemented by words of counsel and

EARLY DAYS IN LONDON

cheer, left a lasting impression upon those with whom he came in contact. Though his interests were many, he ever showed an intense devotion to the work in the Iron Room, and later at Clapton Hall, where for many years he kept the assembly roll-book, which in the early days showed the names of three hundred members, rising at one period to nearly eight hundred.

Relative to the opening of Clapton Hall, I came across an interesting entry in the diary of John G. McVicker, who, during the second half of last century, laboured much amongst assemblies of the Lord's people throughout the country. He was a frequent visitor to Clapton Hall, and for some time was constant in ministration there. Under date 25th March 1880 he writes: "I baptized twenty in Clapton Hall last night. Mr. Denham Smith was to preach the first Sunday in that hall. He was taken ill and it was I who preached. Now I have conducted the first baptism and I was also used in the first conversion that took place in it. My heart is being more knit to the work and the people here, and I think I am being fitted for the work and helped in it. I believe I am where God would have me be."

A perusal of the diary he kept leaves with the reader a sweet fragrance, touching the prayerful thought and care he lovingly bestowed upon this assembly in the closing days of his life. On the last day of December, 1899, being Lord's Day, Mr. McVicker gave a brief word of ministry at the morning meeting on "A Faithful God," and in the evening preached the Gospel to a large congregation. This proved to be his last public ministry on earth. On the day following—a few days before his home-call—we find this entry: "Breakfasted in bed because of chest cold and foggy, chilly weather. Judged it safe to stay in the house all day. Spent some time in prayer to God in Christ's name— a wonderful thing to be able to do. Being detained by weather (and ill-health) from attending the prayer meeting in the evening I went over the names of all in fellowship at Clapton Hall, interceding for them as I was helped."

It was about this time, too, in the history of the Paragon Road Assembly that the outward drift increased, and the character of the neighbourhood greatly changed from being a favourite residential section for city merchants and business men by a large influx of Jewish families from the East End; so that to-day nearly all the well-known Nonconformist chapels have been turned into Jewish synagogues. This, naturally, had its effect on the assembly at Paragon Road, the membership of which declined in number to about one hundred, when the Government took over the site in 1926.

At that date the way was opened up to acquire a very suitable meeting-place in a Mission Hall which was being given up by one of the Nonconformist bodies in Morning Lane, henceforward known as Paragon Gospel Hall, and conveniently near to the old location in Paragon Road.

In those days the assembly was much helped by occasional ministry from Robert Chapman and Henry Dyer. Amongst other names mentioned in the address book (1864) is that of George Pearse, a stockbroker, who was also secretary of the Chinese Association, and later a missionary. Hudson Taylor, as a young man of eighteen, wrote to him from his home in Yorkshire expressing a desire to go out to China, and it was through this correspondence that young Taylor came to London to study medicine. Thus, through the Hackney meeting, he came in touch with Mr. Berger, who was to be such a great help in later years in connection with the work of the China Inland Mission.

"I have vivid memories of seeing Hudson Taylor at the Lord's Day morning meeting at Hackney," writes Mr. Marks. "He was frequently accompanied by a Chinese brother. Dr. H. Grattan Guinness, in the early days of his training missionaries at Harley House, was often to be found remembering the Lord with us; and I have still a clear recollection of seeing young Dr. Barnardo, who, in 1866, hoped to have gone to China but later found his life's work amongst the waifs and strays. One of the incidents that made an impression on my young mind was the second marriage, in 1867, of Lord Congleton at the meeting-room, and the stir it caused at Hackney, that such an honour should have come to the locality as the marriage of a peer of the realm."

EARLY DAYS IN LONDON

Paragon Road meeting was the centre of considerable work amongst the poor. There was a little mission connected with the assembly, and the young men were much encouraged in open-air Gospel effort, as well as being helped forward by Bible readings, preparing papers on Scriptural subjects for discussion, and meetings for extempore speaking, so that several were better fitted to take part in Gospel work and in ministry.

There has always been a keen missionary spirit in the assembly, and at the present time it is represented in the foreign field by Mrs. H. F. Marks, who went out to the Malay States in 1899, and by A. Ginnings, who went out to Spain in 1910. Looking back over the years since the first gathering took place, in St. Thomas's Rooms, three-quarters of a century ago, the assembly, as we have seen, has passed through times of spiritual prosperity and blessing; and yet has not been without its seasons of trial and days of testing, but through it all the Lord has graciously owned the testimony of His beloved people.

J. Denham Smith, to whom reference has been made, was a familiar figure in the various London assemblies, from that memorable time of spiritual awakening in the early 'sixties up to his Home-call in the Spring of 1889. He was an eloquent and convincing speaker, and whether in the proclamation of the Gospel or in the exposition of Scripture truths, it was rarely he had difficulty in securing and holding an audience. His name will long be remembered in Ireland with affection, for it was during the great Revival that Denham Smith, impelled by a desire for souls, left the pastorate of a Congregational Church in Kingstown so that he might be freed from denominational bonds, and with the help of friends of like mind to himself he engaged one of the largest halls in Dublin, where he might preach the Gospel. This remarkable work resulted in large numbers being brought to the Saviour, the outcome of which was the erection of the well-known Merrion Hall in the city.

Of high literary attainments, and possessed with the pen of a ready writer, Denham Smith, besides being the author of several expository works, wrote and published a considerable number of Gospel tracts and pamphlets, which obtained an extensive circulation during those stirring times. He also compiled a hymn book, for use at his services, called *Times of Refreshing*, which contained several of his own compositions. Denham Smith is the author of the well-known hymns, "My God I have found," and "Rise, my soul! behold 'tis Jesus."

On the invitation of John Morley he came to London, and here was begun a work which was mightily used of God, not only in the ingathering of souls for His Kingdom, but in the building up and strengthening of His beloved people. It was from this centre—notably the Iron Room, Upper Clapton—that Denham Smith launched out to the provinces, reaching many of the large towns, where he left a deep spiritual impression.

After a prolonged preaching tour on the Continent, where largely attended meetings were held in Paris and Geneva, Denham Smith returned to England and finally took up residence in London, ministering regularly in Clapton Hall and St. George's Hall.

CHAPTER XVII

BERESFORD CHAPEL AND WILLIAM LINCOLN

IT would be impossible to give any account of the commencement of the work of God at Beresford Chapel, in south-east London, without mentioning the name of William Lincoln, who surely was God's chosen vessel in this connection. It was Mr. Lincoln's own expression when failing strength warned him that his course was nearly finished, "I hope you will not talk about William Lincoln, for I am only a saved sinner." But some details must be given to render this account intelligible, and for these particulars I am indebted to Mr. W. J. Hubble, who has furnished me with the history of this assembly which, in this particular connection, takes a notable place amongst gatherings of the Lord's people in London.

Mr. Lincoln was born in London in 1825, his parents dying when he was very young. His conscience was awakened at seventeen years of age, by reading Dr. Doddridge's *Rise and Progress of Religion*, a book he studied so carefully that he could almost repeat it word for word; but it was a book he never recommended to young people, as it left him in sore bondage. He sought help from many to get relief from his bondage of sin, but it was some time ere he found true peace. A desire, soon after conversion, of going to India as a missionary was not to be accorded him, as the Council of the Missionary College at Islington, where he had studied for a year, declined to send him out owing to hereditary consumption in the family. The Lord had work for him to do at home. Shortly after this he entered King's College, London, ultimately becoming an associate. In 1849 Mr. Lincoln was ordained at Preston. After ministering in the Established Church at Preston for some years, he came as curate to St. George's Church, Southwark, London. Whilst connected with this church he preached mostly at a "Chapel of Ease," in the London Road, Southwark, drawing large numbers to hear him, and some ultimately followed him in the course he later took.

In 1859 Beresford Chapel in Beresford Street, Walworth, became vacant. Mr. Lincoln applied for the "living," and in a truly wonderful way God intervened to obtain for him the appointment. At first attendances were small, but in a few months numbers were attracted by his powerful preaching. Indeed, so much so that there was soon scarcely a sitting to be obtained in a building holding about one thousand three hundred people, and weekly the chapel was crowded to excess.

In an address given to a crowded congregation at Beresford Chapel on Lord's Day evening, 23rd November 1862, Mr. Lincoln made it known that for some considerable time he had been greatly exercised in heart about his position, from a Scriptural point of view, as a minister of the Establishment so closely allied to the world. The occasion of his secession was a very memorable one, and his action at first thinned out the congregation—many refusing to follow him in this step, much as they respected his teaching as an ordained clergyman. Immediately after his secession, Mr. Lincoln was baptized by immersion at a near-by Baptist chapel. Having a few years previously preached and written in favour of infant baptism, a course which he himself afterward deeply regretted, he was urged by friends to be baptized out of London, but Mr. Lincoln expressed determination to be baptized in the neighbourhood.

Scriptural light as to conduct of an assembly of Christians seems to have been acquired gradually, and the bulk of those who remained with Mr. Lincoln continued to follow in the path of increased light as to Scriptural worship, and as to gathering only to the name of the Lord Jesus in the way the Word of God teaches. Many endeavours were made to get Mr. Lincoln to join one of the many sects, but his expression was to the very last, "May I be kept by God's grace from joining anything," cleaving to the Lord alone. Mr. Lincoln's own idea was not for a sudden change but gradually to be led on more perfectly, just taking that step for which light had been given by God, and then to look to Him for further light and guidance as to the next step. It is owing to this course, surely, through the blessing of God, that the work went on steadfastly upon maintained Scriptural lines for many years, although the general expressed opinion at the time was that it would not last a year. At first some portion of the Established Church service was used. After about a month the Lord's Supper was celebrated every Lord's Day, but in the evening; this continued for a year or two before it took its present place in the morning. One by one the old practices were abandoned, the final stage, perhaps, in the effacement of the old arrangement of things being when the use of the large organ on Sundays was given up, and the stained-glass windows covered. But Mr. Lincoln always maintained to the very last, that it was according to the mind of God in Scripture that there should be time devoted to teaching the saints after the breaking of bread on the Lord's Day mornings. For this purpose the service was arranged to commence half an hour earlier than similar meetings, to allow for ministry of the Word for the edification of the Lord's people after the worship meeting. This practice has been maintained to the present day, and many have given testimony as to the incalculable benefit derived. It was in this ministry that William Lincoln was so used of God, but he ever earnestly disclaimed the idea of being called *the* Pastor, or *the* Minister, and was pained if anyone spoke of him as such. He only regarded himself as a teacher chosen of God to minister to His saints, and a pastor among many others. He ever showed much joy and earnestness in proclaiming and pressing the truth of gathering to the Lord's Name alone, making Him the one and only Centre and rallying point for the children of God. "Let us go forth, therefore, unto Him without the camp," we might say was continually his cry, and thoroughly did he practise what he preached. Soon after leaving the Establishment he compiled *The Beresford Hymn Book*, a later edition of which is still in weekly use at Beresford Chapel.

For twenty-six years the ministry of this beloved servant

of the Lord was greatly blessed to a very large circle, but after a period of failing health in 1888 he went to be "with Christ."

The assembly at Beresford Chapel continued to enjoy the good hand of our God for many years. One special feature was the Beresford Conferences, which will be remembered by many as times of blessing and refreshing from the Lord. As time went on, and the Metropolis reaching out to suburban districts, many members removed to outlying parts, there forming new assemblies of the Lord's people. Thus "Beresford" became, as it were, the parent of other now thriving assemblies around London, which, of course, tended to reduce the numbers of those remaining. During the years of its existence the assembly had many links with the foreign field, some of its members going out at the call of God whilst prayerful interest was maintained at home.

When the lease of the building, which Mr. Lincoln held, expired, it was acquired by a Christian who was very sympathetic and generous, and more than once reduced the rent when from time to time the membership fell. On the death of this owner the lease was sold into other hands not so sympathetic, and in 1920 notice to quit was received. This caused much anxiety to the assembly, especially as occupation of the chapel had to be given up before another suitable building could be obtained. After about two years without a building to meet in, except for the use of a schoolroom close by, the Lord wonderfully opened up the way for His people. A well-built chapel, which previous to the war had been occupied by a German Lutheran congregation, became available in 1922. This building, situated in Windsor Walk, Denmark Hill, Camberwell, having a lease of thirty years to run, was procured. The assembly has, in the goodness of God, continued to meet in this building to this day. A few of those accompanying Mr. Lincoln in his step in 1862 remained to commence the work at this new place of gathering, but during the years that have intervened almost all have been called home to be with the Lord.

One feature of the history of the work at Beresford has

been the powerful effect of the preaching of God's Word by Mr. Lincoln on the lives of many believers who remained there for years, this having noticeably moulded their character, and has been a living testimony to the correctness of the step taken in 1862.

CHAPTER XVIII

LEYTON AND EAST LONDON

WELL over fifty years ago two newly married men decided to make their homes in what was then the pretty little village of Leytonstone. Their names were William T. Bilson and Ransome Wallis. Both were earnest Christian workers, and very soon they became deeply exercised concerning the lack of testimony on simple Scriptural lines. This led them to look around for some building in which they with other Christians might gather to the name of the Lord. After much searching they found a small hall in Leyton which had formerly been a dancing saloon, and had also been utilised for Salvation Army meetings. Though not considered an ideal place, yet it was felt that a door had been opened in answer to prayer, and here a number of believers gathered around the Lord's Table for the first time. Gospel services and Sunday School work were started, and soon afterwards a weekly meeting for women under the spiritual care of Mrs. Skelton was commenced. In those early days such stalwarts as Lord Radstock, William Groves (known as "Happy Bill"), Gipsy Smith, John Jones and Sergeant Bailey were numbered among the many fellow-helpers in the Gospel.

With the opening of this meeting several of the Lord's people residing at Walthamstow, who were in fellowship with the Clapton Assembly, strengthened the little company by joining the Leyton gathering. The work prospered exceedingly, and the assembly became so large that about half the number, by mutual agreement, occupied the Y.M.C.A. premises then existing near the present "Bakers' Arms" Almshouses, where a testimony was begun. The work continued to prosper, many missions were held and souls were saved. About the year 1895 the Sunday School, which from the beginning had been under the superintendency of W. T. Bilson, became so overcrowded that it was necessary to provide a schoolroom for the infant class; this was built by the teachers and friends.

When the Livingstone College was opened, just over thirty years ago, a number of medical students during their course of study were received into fellowship at Leyton. Their presence gave an added stimulus to interest in service for the Lord in other lands, and several in fellowship felt their call from God to serve Him in the foreign field. Mr. James Teskey went to Singapore, Mr. and Mrs. Charters to N. Africa, and more recently Mr. Albert Want to Central Africa. The latter was accompanied by Mr. Conrad Lohr, who was a convert in Leyton Hall Sunday School, although he went out as commended by Southend Assembly.

In the year 1912 the assembly and the work among children had again grown to such proportions that it was decided to look for fresh premises. An old house stood on a site opposite the hall. The ground was secured, the house demolished, and the present hall and classrooms built, the opening services being conducted by James W. C. Fegan.

About this time several of the friends living at Leytonstone decided with others to form an assembly in that neighbourhood, which resulted in about thirty going to form the nucleus of the testimony of Grove Green Hall. Notwithstanding this depletion of numbers together with the possession of larger premises, the efforts continued to be blessed and the assembly found themselves in urgent need of a separate classroom for the young men. However, the young men themselves rose to the occasion, and under the supervision of George Offord (a builder in fellowship) they built a brick structure large enough to accommodate sixty people. And thus the testimony at Leyton continues.

The neighbouring assembly of Folkestone Road Hall, which is one of the largest assemblies in London, commenced in the early 'eighties in a very unpretentious manner at a time when Walthamstow was rapidly developing from what had been a small outlying town to a large and important London suburb. The moment was ripe, the growing population came under the sound of the Gospel when and where it was needed, and God blessed the effort. How the work of grace began is recalled by Mr. G. J. Hyde, who has furnished the writer with the story of its rapid and remarkable expansion.

The late Mrs. Ransome Wallis—*née* Miss McCall—started a Bible Class for young men, which was held in a small iron hall that her father had erected in a field belonging to him close to Hoe Street. Several of these young men were converted, and to provide an outlet for their zeal and energy Mr. McCall and his daughter sought the aid of Thomas H. Morris, who later laid down his life for the Lord in Central Africa. A tent was procured and was pitched at Whipps Cross Corner, adjoining Epping Forest. Mr. Morris was a good evangelist and a capable organiser. Many were, through his instrumentality, brought to the Lord, and the problem immediately arose as to where the meetings could be continued. Mr. McCall offered his little building, and throughout the winter, meetings were carried on there with further signs of blessing. As at that time there was no assembly at Walthamstow, those desiring baptism and fellowship went either to Clapton Hall or Leyton Hall.

In 1884 another tent was pitched at the corner of Boundary Road and Hoe Street, with the result that many were brought to the Lord. As the tent was on the borders of Leyton, a meeting was held between the brethren then gathering in the old Leyton Hall and those who had been going to Clapton Hall, to discuss the question of securing a central place where the believers of Walthamstow could break bread instead of having to make the journey to Clapton. A site was obtained in the garden of a house in the vicinity, and the small building was removed thereto from Mr. McCall's premises. There the united Leyton and Walthamstow brethren first met to remember the Lord in the breaking of bread. A Sunday School was started here whilst other meetings were carried on at Leyton Hall. Numbers increased, outgrowing the accommodation, so a dismantled Iron Hall, which had formerly stood in the Mile End Road, was purchased and rebuilt in the Queen's Road. The Walthamstow Assembly was then duly constituted.

From the beginning the Lord greatly blessed the testimony of the Gospel; souls were saved each week, many Christians from various places of worship in the town were attracted, and, being helped, sought fellowship. After a time, so great was the interest manifested, the question arose as to providing further accommodation. Minerva House in High Street was taken and a work amongst children begun. The little Iron Hall was removed from Leyton to the Higham Hill district of Walthamstow and a mission commenced, of which Mr. B. R. Mudditt was the first superintendent.

Alluding to those early days of which we write, when open-air meetings and personal dealing with the unsaved were pleasing features, I cannot refrain from recounting here what another writer, who himself passed through those times of refreshing, has set down, for it gives us a happy glimpse into those not very remote days. After describing the speakers, whom he assures us were not giants in oratory and argument, he says: "The one who drew and held the biggest crowds was 'Daddy' Kenyon, and many a person who never entered a place of worship would go down High Street on Sunday night to hear the old man speak. He was indeed a bit of old Walthamstow, and I visualise him even now: a tall man with white hair and beard, dressed in the long frock coat of the later Victorian age, standing on a portable rostrum telling the people the number of years he had proved the Lord Jesus Christ to be the Friend that sticketh closer than a brother.

"At the close of the meeting, the Doxology having been sung, quite a number of people would move to where 'Daddy' was standing, as, with tears in his eyes, he would say, 'Now, lads, why don't you come to Christ?' And there, with open Bible in hand, he would seek to point them to the Saviour.

"At the Sunday evening Gospel meeting Mr. Kenyon was the doorkeeper, and right well did he perform the task. As the choir sang on the platform he sang at the door, and as the people came in he not only gave them a hymn book but found them a seat, and with his infectious smile made the newcomer feel at home. He then returned along the aisle still singing. On Lord's Day morning when he wished to lead the praise or prayers of the assembly, he would invariably come forward and kneel at the Lord's Table. During the week, after finishing his rounds in the performance of his duties as postman, his spare time was spent in giving away tracts to the passers-by, and in this way he became widely known; hence it was that people liked to hear him speak in the open-air, for every word he spoke was backed up by the ripe experience of a man who walked with God."

To cope with the needs of the Queen's Road work, some structural alterations to the building were carried out, which provided additional accommodation for a hundred persons. The attendance continued to increase, when unhappily the adjoining owner brought an action to restrain the premises being utilised for religious meetings. Owing to a flaw in the title deeds on a technical point, the plaintiff won his case, and the assembly was compelled to pull down the hall. The result was the erection of the larger premises where the assembly still meets, and in the present building the work has been carried on for nearly half a century. Many memorable gatherings have been held in this place, and it is associated with times of gracious revivings, for many have been saved under its roof. At the present time the number on the Church register of Folkestone Road Assembly is about three hundred and eighty. The Sunday School enrols three hundred and fifty scholars; there are in addition ninety members of the young women's Bible Class, and about forty in the young men's Bible Class.

The history of Folkestone Road Assembly is an illustration of the proverb, "There is that scattereth but yet increaseth," for there have been two new assemblies formed in the district from it. About thirty-six years ago the brethren who laboured at Higham Hill, before referred to, felt the time had come to start a meeting. A new hall, known as Higham Hill Gospel Hall, was built, and a number transferred from Folkestone Road Hall. The work has continued happily, and there are at present nearly a hundred in fellowship.

JOHN MORLEY.

HENRY DYER.

JAMES WRIGHT, BRISTOL.
(as a young man).

PARAGON ROAD MEETING ROOM.

Following a period of spiritual prosperity, the Mission in the High Street, to which we have already alluded, underwent some considerable change about ten years ago. The Minerva House work had been transferred to a Workman's Hall in 1889, and a thriving work maintained among the children and young people. The tenure of the premises was becoming somewhat precarious, when a large mission room in Markhouse Road, belonging to a Congregational Church, was secured and the work re-established there. The new premises, known as South Grove Hall, being more commodious, and no restrictions being placed upon their use, naturally gave an impetus to the work, several tent missions being held on the land in front of the hall, adding to its interest and increasing its blessing. The result was that in 1928 the workers considered that it would be honouring to the Lord if a fresh assembly were formed there. After prayerful waiting upon God, in full fellowship with the parent meeting, an assembly was established in the autumn of that year, sixty-one being commended from Folkestone Road Hall to South Grove, consisting of those who were engaged in the work there or living in the neighbourhood.

CHAPTER XIX

THE OLD CLOCK FACTORY AT WIMBLEDON

OF the three assemblies at Wimbledon, Haydon Hall, in the North Road, is some few years the senior in point of time, although Central Hall, or its predecessor, the Old Alexander Rooms Meeting, would represent the original assembly, it having been first housed in the drawing-room of that beloved Christian brother, John Churchill. It was afterwards transferred to the Old Alexander Rooms and finally to the present Central Hall, which was erected by Mr. Churchill.

In his early Christian course, Mr. Churchill manifested a desire not only towards the furtherance of the Gospel, but in teaching and the pastoral care of the flock of Christ. He was greatly helped and encouraged in this through his close friendship with Sir Arthur Blackwood, a prominent Christian, in whose house Bible readings were regularly held to which all who had a love for the Scriptures were welcome. A number of years were happily spent with believers at Malden Hall, Kentish Town, where Mr. Churchill found ample opportunity for service. On his removal to Wimbledon he found no company of Christians assembled together with the desire to be guided by the Word of God, and it was thus that Mr. Churchill, with a few others of like mind, commenced to break bread in his own house.

In this way began the testimony at Wimbledon which, in the goodness of God, very soon developed in a remarkable manner.

"In looking back on his life," one who knew him well wrote some time ago, "I am greatly impressed with the amount of time which he, a man of considerable responsibility in business, gladly gave to God and His people. He generally had nearly two hours before breakfast for reading and prayer and would often read his Bible in the morning train, and, in addition, would read in the evening his Hebrew

OLD CLOCK FACTORY AT WIMBLEDON

Bible or Greek Testament. At one time on Sunday he would gather his children around the Word after breakfast, then go to the morning meeting, conduct a Bible reading in the afternoon, visit some lonely neighbour, and preach the Gospel in the evening. This surely was a full day for a man hard at work all week, and who would usually go to three week-night meetings. In looking back on this life of active service one must heartily praise God, too, for Mrs. Churchill, who, though very delicate, was always willing to spare him for these manifold calls upon his time."

From its inception in 1879, the work carried on at Haydon Hall is inseparably associated with the names of two brothers, Edmund and William Iles. In early life both were wild and dissolute men, but God by His grace touched their hearts and ultimately called them to serve Him in the Gospel. From living a prodigal life of waste and extravagance, the brothers very soon proved that their new Master not only provided them with brighter homes to live in but paid them better wages, and being good and efficient tradesmen they were able in course of time to commence business on their own account. And while the brothers built up a thriving business they laboured diligently for the Lord, praying that He would open up the way for a Gospel testimony in their midst. Their prayers were answered in a singular way.

There being a need for stabling accommodation in connection with their business the brothers purchased a site in North Road, containing a wooden building of two storeys which had formerly been used as a clock factory. This was regarded as likely to make very suitable stables, but as Edmund was one day ascending the stairs to the upper floor (as he afterwards related), he seemed to lose sight of the floor above him and see the large building as it would be were the stairs and floor removed. At that moment it was as though a voice said, "Would not this make a splendid hall for the preaching of the Gospel?" He at once replied, "Well, Lord, if Thou dost want it for that purpose, Thou shalt have it." And realising that God had spoken, Edmund Iles and his brother William at once set to work upon the conversion of the one-time clock factory into what proved to be quite a suitable place for worship. They named the building Haydon Hall, after Haydon's Lane, the then old country lane now known as Haydon's Road. The next concern was to find a preacher who would draw the people together and proclaim the Gospel faithfully. Their choice fell on William Groves, who at that time was stirring up the east end of London. Possibly the novelty of religious services being held in the old clock factory, together with the captivating personality of "Happy Bill" (who was ably assisted by his wife), drew large numbers to those meetings, and from the first souls were saved. God had indeed set His seal to the preaching, strong men being broken down and melted to tears by the preacher's impassionate appeals. So great was the Spirit of God manifested that in many cases the awakened and anxious ones would not leave the building until they were brought into peace with God, and often in those early days the workers were dealing with the anxious until midnight.

"But those were glorious days," a brother writes; "times when the Holy Spirit was manifestly felt amongst us, breaking down and ploughing up so that men and women in soul agony were continually crying out, 'What must I do to be saved?'"

It was not long before those who found the Saviour came together for the study of the Scriptures. Thus there was revealed to those simple believers the truths of baptism and the Lord's Supper. Accordingly, provision was made for the carrying out of the Scriptural command of baptism by immersion, and almost simultaneously the Table was spread that the little company of Christians might come together on the first day of the week in remembrance of their Lord and Saviour in His dying love. It was in this way that an assembly of believers was established.

But it was not to be expected that the old wooden clock factory should stand the stress of time indefinitely. It was about the year 1884 that the main wooden support showed an advanced state of decay, so that the building became dangerous, and it was determined that another hall be

OLD CLOCK FACTORY AT WIMBLEDON

erected, the present brick structure being the result. The removal into the new hall was signalised by a season of much blessing. Since then the work has been continuously progressive, and with such evangelists as Richard Weaver, W. R. Lane, Charles Inglis, E. H. Wells, George Hucklesby, Russell Hurditch, Ephraim Venn and W. H. Dunning, God has been pleased to save and add to the Church.

Sunday School work was carried on from the early days, the first school being held in rooms over a five-stall stable, which had been adapted for the purpose; but this soon became too small and produced the problem of the provision of greater accommodation. In the course of time, additional land at the rear of the premises, with a frontage to Garfield Road, was purchased, and the present substantial Sunday School building erected. In these successive schoolrooms have gathered hundreds of scholars, in many cases reaching down to the third generation from those people who formed the original gathering, and the majority of those now in fellowship are those who have been scholars in the Sunday School.

About the year 1885 two brothers, Henry and Tom Poulton, became exercised regarding the lack of testimony in the Cross Road neighbourhood of Wimbledon, and after a time of prayerful waiting upon God for guidance, they, with others, were ultimately led to build the present Cross Road Hall, where for several years Gospel services were continued. God graciously honoured the labours of His servants, many of those who attended the meetings being led to the Saviour, which resulted in an assembly being formed. Thus from small beginnings in Mr. Churchill's drawing-room, over half a century ago, there are to-day in Wimbledon three assemblies of believers all in happy fellowship with each other.

CHAPTER XX

THE ARCHWAY ASSEMBLY

COMMENT has already been made upon the rather odd places which have been brought into commission for the holding of Gospel meetings and assembly gatherings. And yet, as we have seen, from small and not always dignified beginnings, God has been pleased graciously to give His blessing upon those who have sought in simple faith to carry out His will according to the Scriptures. Thus, as has already been observed, to such primitive beginnings not a few assemblies date their origin.

It was in a Dancing Academy which stood upon the site now occupied by the Highgate Tube Station, London, that the Archway Assembly was formed between fifty and sixty years ago. A few friends, keenly interested in the needs of the Gospel in that neighbourhood, hired the premises for use on Sunday evenings. From the start the effort received God's smile, and before many months had elapsed numbers who attended these meetings were led to trust the Saviour. This resulted in the workers and converts coming together for divine guidance, as many of those who had recently professed faith in Christ expressed a desire to follow the Lord in baptism and in the breaking of bread. Their prayers were signally answered, and in the month of November, 1883, a little company of believers assembled around the Lord's Table for the first time. For twenty-eight years the activities of the meeting continued in the old Dancing Academy in Junction Road, when, through the assistance of Arthur Garstin, the hall came into the possession of the assembly. Later, when the property was acquired by the Underground Electric Railway Company, the handsome compensation given by the directors was used to purchase a new site and build the present hall.

In its early days the assembly received much spiritual help from such brethren as Henry Varley, R. C. Morgan and Ned Wright, besides others whose names are familiar to the reader.

CHAPTER XXI

THE TESTIMONY AT WOOLWICH

IN our survey of the work of the Holy Spirit it is of more than passing interest to observe that not a few assemblies throughout the country can trace their origin to a tent mission. It was at the conclusion of a Gospel campaign conducted by John Vine at Lewisham in 1874, that Captain Orde-Browne, a retired officer of the Royal Artillery, who had become keenly interested in the work, got the idea of having the tent pitched at Woolwich. Thus in the autumn of the same year the tent was erected on a piece of waste ground on Hanover Road, about five minutes' walk from the site of the present Gospel Hall, Nightingale Vale.

The Lord mightily used this effort, and between seventy and eighty people were led to the Saviour. To this work Captain and Mrs. Orde-Browne devoted themselves with untiring energy of heart and soul, not only in visiting almost every house in the district but by their consistent Christian influence. The tent mission continued every night for about two months and conversions were followed by many being led to see the truth of believers' baptism, opportunity being afforded for the carrying out of this Scriptural ordinance at Lewisham.

With the removal of the tent a pressing need to consolidate the work presented itself to the few Christians who had a spiritual care for the young converts, many of whom having already expressed a desire to gather together once a week that they might remember the Lord's death. Bible readings and prayer meetings were convened, and as the interest continued and numbers increased it was realised that a suitable meeting-place would soon be required. This presented some difficulty, but the Lord wonderfully opened up the way by laying the matter on the heart of Captain Orde-Browne, who, with the help of others, purchased a piece of land in Nightingale Vale, upon which was erected the present Gospel Hall.

At the first special services held in the new hall Lord Radstock was instrumental in the salvation of souls, and fresh numbers were added to the assembly. In later years, among those who were used in the building up of believers and in preaching the Gospel, the names of F. C. Bland, A. J. Holiday and J. W. C. Fegan are still remembered. Towards the close of 1879 God had prospered the work so greatly and the numbers had increased to such an extent that an addition to the hall became necessary. The building was extended to the present dimensions, and the Nightingale Vale Gospel Hall became the largest assembly meeting-place in south-east London.

"The outstanding features of the work in those early days," writes one who was actively associated with the fruitful times which are now recalled, "seem to have been intense love to the Lord and a longing desire for the salvation of souls; and these traits were common to all members of the assembly, which was composed for the greater part of young believers."

Subsequent years proved how signally the Lord blessed the testimony begun in the Woolwich neighbourhood, a distinctive feature of Gospel evidence being open-air work in Arsenal Square. In connection with aggressive Gospel effort, mention should specially be made of the labours of Lieutenant H. A. Mandeville, who relinquished a commission in the Navy that he might devote himself entirely to spiritual work, particularly amongst the people of this neighbourhood; also of S. Trevor Francis—remembered as the author of many beautiful hymns—who helped the assembly very constantly by preaching and singing.

Captain Orde-Browne, who was mainly instrumental in the founding and development of the testimony at Woolwich, had a distinguished career as a soldier, and in his day was recognised as the greatest living authority on armour and ordnance. Entering the army before reaching the age of seventeen he took part with the siege train in the attack on Sebastopol during the Crimean War, and was mentioned

THE TESTIMONY AT WOOLWICH

in dispatches for his gallant conduct in the trenches. He was an intimate friend of General Gordon. These two undertook ragged school work in London, for which their names will long be remembered. When Gordon went to the Soudan for the first time he asked Orde-Browne to go with him, but his heart was in the school work and he refused to leave it.

Shortly after his conversion Captain Orde-Browne became keenly interested in the spiritual welfare of the men under his charge. He saw the sin and trouble that drink brought to the men of his troop and he set himself to lead them in cleaner paths. Quite a revival took place among them. Drawn away from the public-houses, the men were ready to come to a room he had fitted up in barracks, where he and other Christians held Bible readings. On one occasion, after a march from Newbridge to Dublin, the major commanding complimented him on his troop. "Not a man under arrest—not a sore back among the horses!" It is said that the men pursued their route along the country roads singing hymns.

On his appointment to the Royal Arsenal, Captain Orde-Browne and his wife began a work in the ragged schools and among the tramps' lodging-houses. For years he visited and preached in the kitchens. His manner was so genial and kindly that even in Roman Catholic houses the good Christian soldier was heartily welcomed, and some remarkable conversions took place through his influence. Amidst all his Government work he never allowed the work of the Gospel to suffer, but made it the primary object of his life.

Woolwich and Plumstead grew considerably in population as time went on, and it was felt that two new halls were needed in different parts of Plumstead. These, through the blessing of the Lord, were erected in due course, and in perfect harmony with the mother assembly.

UNUSUAL MEETING-PLACES

There is still imprinted on my mind an early recollection of attending, as a very small boy, a Gospel meeting up a rickety old wooden stair, which led to a long narrow room over a stable, where, during the service, the ceaseless crunching of the bit and the erratic movements of restless horses below could be distinctly heard as the preaching proceeded.

It was indeed a primitive and unpretentious meeting-place. The walls were coloured pink and the ceiling whitewashed, the only attempt at decoration being a few modest-looking card texts displayed here and there as if to break the wearisome monotony of this bare, uninviting meeting-room. Those were the days of what is now regarded as old-fashioned Gospel preaching; but preaching which drew many a lost one to the Saviour, and where, at those hallowed meetings, even the most lukewarm soul could not fail to perceive a truly spiritual atmosphere.

In my search for data in connection with this work I have been struck as I have noted the number of assemblies of Christians which first came together for the breaking of bread in a room above a stable, or in some such apartment, where believers, faithful to the Word of God, sought in all sincerity to worship the One they adored. And there have they continued until circumstances led them into premises more fitted for the purpose, where they might meet in a manner honouring to Him Whose name they were not ashamed to bear.

It may have been observed, as we have sojourned together in thought from one assembly of believers to another, that I have carefully avoided indulging in any form of criticism, particularly in what may be assumed as that pertaining to the various meeting-places chosen for the remembrance of the Lord's Supper. Nor would I even now dare to cast a stone. Nevertheless, it has often occurred to me, as it must have been obvious to most, that there are occasions in the early life of an assembly when its transference to a more suitable room or hall would have been more honouring to the testimony. In clinging to the old place, doubtless actuated in a measure by sentiment, there may be just that subtle danger of unconscious pride having a semblance of feigned humility, which surely cannot be in accordance with the will and purpose of God.

THE TESTIMONY AT WOOLWICH

A good number of years ago I had occasion to stay over the week-end in a small town in the Midlands. Not having had the opportunity beforehand of ascertaining the address of an assembly of believers, should there be one, I set out on the Saturday evening to make enquiries, and, after some considerable search, I was eventually directed to the proprietor of a prosperous-looking business establishment in the town. Having placed me under some cross-examination as to my credentials, he rather reluctantly gave me the address and time of the meeting. Next morning I sought out the address given, which was in a poor locality, and, after passing through a lane and up a badly lighted stair, I found myself in a mean apartment over a stable where the table was spread for the celebration of the Lord's Supper. There was but a handful of people present, the brother whom I had met the previous evening taking the leading part throughout the meeting. I was young in the faith at that time, and while I did not lose sight of the fact that the real object of that little gathering was to meet our Lord, nevertheless I could not help inwardly contrasting the apparent affluence of our brother who owned the big store in the town, with the cold and uninviting room above the stable—all that was provided in which to meet for the remembrance of our Saviour's dying love. This may have been an isolated case, but the circumstance is indelibly imprinted on my memory.

STABLE LOFT AT HARLESDEN

It was in some such place as the one to which I have alluded that a number of Christians met to remember the Lord in Wendover Road, Harlesden, in north-west London. For a time the little company came together in a room immediately over a stable, but eventually the unsuitable character of the place for the gathering of God's people, and for the testimony of the Gospel, led them to seek other premises. In this the way was wonderfully opened up. Previous to the time of which we write Edward Stevens came to Harlesden. This was in the year 1880. Having learned Scriptural truth regarding the gathering together of believers for the breaking of bread, he found no one in this quiet little village—as it then was—of like mind to himself. He commenced Gospel meetings in his house, afterwards holding open-air services on the village green. This continued until the following year, when Mr. Stevens with another brother and their wives came together to remember the Lord for the first time. Others were added until, as we shall see, the way was opened up for removal to better adapted premises. Negotiations were entered into with Robert Bilke, the director of what was then known as The Union Hall Mission, for the renting of a hall which, owing to lack of funds, had been closed. This resulted in a hall eminently suitable for the purpose being secured at a moderate rent. In the days that followed, the Lord graciously helped, the assembly receiving much spiritual assistance from the fellowship and ministry of such well-known brethren as Dr. Neatby and John Jewell Penstone. "They and others," says Mr. G. Radwell, who was closely associated with the founding and building up of the assembly, "frequently came and remained in the afternoon to take a homely cup of tea in the hall with fellow-believers who stayed between the Sunday School and evening meeting. On such occasions we had never-to-be-forgotten conversational ministry, and at the evening meeting which followed there was on many occasions an increase of the Body of Christ through souls being born again by the Holy Spirit."

After a period of spiritual prosperity the assembly was unexpectedly called upon to pass through a time of testing. The trustees of the hall, finding themselves in a precarious financial position, decided to sell the place. This seemingly dark cloud, however, had its silver lining, and proved to be a blessing in disguise, for not only did the Lord give the assembly the ownership of the hall, through the generosity of John Pike (who with his wife had been much helped spiritually by the ministry in the assembly), but the whole of the premises, which were in a rather dilapidated condition, were thoroughly renovated when the building was handed over. In later years the freehold of the hall was purchased by their son, Charles Pike; thus the present Kenmont Hall

THE TESTIMONY AT WOOLWICH

was provided without the necessity of appealing to any outside source.

From this assembly there went forth those seeking to lend a helping hand to Christians in neighbouring parts, who had expressed a desire to follow in paths revealed to them by a closer study of the Scriptures. Thus a testimony was commenced at Leighton Buzzard, where the large Victoria Hall was hired for a Gospel mission, in which those engaged in the effort had the co-operation of the veteran brother, Mr. Ashby. The lesser hall was afterwards rented, and regular meetings on Lord's Day were instituted and continued with the happy fellowship of believers from neighbouring assemblies.

CHAPTER XXII

EARLY HISTORY OF WELBECK ASSEMBLY

THE history of Welbeck Assembly goes back to the early days of the Movement in London, it being one of the first to be established after the start at Rawstorne Street. Originally meeting in a room in Orchard Street—a name which figures largely in early Brethren records and correspondence —the assembly in the year 1860 removed to premises in Welbeck Street, from which it took its name. Lord Congleton was in fellowship here for thirty years, a period marked by seasons of blessing and spiritual calm, following hard upon anxious and disturbing times. A brother, who for many years was associated in the oversight at Welbeck Hall, has left behind remembrances which give us some insight into the life and character manifested in the assembly at that time. In this connection his allusion to Lord Congleton's care and interest in the welfare of the assembly is recalled.

"My early impression of him," says the writer, "was that he was a stranger and a pilgrim on the earth, his chief pleasure being to meet with those who were introduced to him as Christians walking according to the light they possessed; to such he had always a word of encouragement, and was always meek and gentle in his manner towards them. Usually he would take their names and addresses, in order, if possible, to shepherd them, no matter what their social position in life might be. . . . He had a large heart for Gospel and Sunday School work, in which he was always interested, and set a high value on prayer meetings and on Bible readings. When acting in Church discipline he never flinched, however painful the duty. He was ever willing to receive into fellowship any who were commended by those known as sound in the faith. Where there was a difficulty he was always ready to have it cleared up, and very slow to

HISTORY OF WELBECK ASSEMBLY

take up or to repeat any charges brought against an individual or an assembly."

Other notable names to be found in the register of those who had a powerful influence in the spiritual good of the assembly include Earl of Cavan, Mr. and Mrs. Yapp, Lady Queensberry, Lord and Lady Radstock and family, and Mr. Underwood.

It was at Welbeck Hall that the quarterly missionary meetings were held, and the names of brethren who were present at those early gatherings conjure up memories of some of the pioneers who went out from the assemblies: Arnot, Hunter, Baedeker, Hudson Taylor, Crawford, Blamire, Wigston and others. It is worthy of note that the missionary interest thus fostered has been strikingly maintained in a very practical sense, and there are many still out in "regions beyond" in the Lord's work who spent the whole of their assembly life at the Welbeck Hall meeting. In the days of which we write, there were from three hundred to four hundred in fellowship. Since then the number of assemblies in London has, as we have seen, increased in a considerable measure, but with the tendency of late years to remove to the suburbs, the present assembly now numbers less than quarter of its original size.

One pleasing instance of happy Christian unity, which other assemblies of the Lord's people might well seek to emulate, has marked in a very real way the unhindered leading of the Holy Spirit. A well-known exclusive assembly, formerly meeting at Marble Row, Oxford Street, and formed just after the first division among brethren, has in the last year or so come together with the Welbeck Hall Assembly, and now meets in happy fellowship at No. 1 Rossmore Road. The united meeting still bears the old name of Welbeck Hall.

About fifty years ago a few brethren living in the Highgate district of North London were for some time meeting with an assembly in Hampden Road, Holloway. There being no assembly in their own neighbourhood, and the distance to Hampden Road being considerable, it was thought desirable to commence a testimony nearer home.

With this in view, the help and guidance of Charles F. Bilson—who was at that time in fellowship with the Archway Assembly—was sought. He at once offered his own drawing-room, which was a large apartment over his shop, and very suitable for the purpose of worship meetings. It was here that the Cholmeley Hall Assembly, which to-day has a membership of two hundred and fifty, was formed. Soon afterwards, Robert Farie became associated with the little gathering of believers, and remained to guide the assembly almost until his Home-call in 1924.

On Sunday afternoons, when the weather was fine, a Gospel meeting was held in Highgate Woods. A public footpath passing that way, numbers of people would gather around the speakers, or remain near by, where the trunk of a fallen tree afforded seating accommodation. As interest in this effort became evident an unoccupied shop was rented, and later the premises were enlarged to meet the growing need.

About this time a women's meeting was commenced by Mrs. Cooper. It was held on Sunday afternoons, and was followed by a homely cup of tea. Thus many of the women —among them a number of servant girls in whose welfare Mrs. Cooper showed a deep interest—remained to the evening Gospel meeting, resulting in a number of them, as they came to know the Lord, being added to the assembly. In the window of the shop premises where these meetings were held, a large open Bible was placed by Mrs. Cooper for passers-by to read. These meetings have been carried on since that time, and have proved a source of much spiritual blessing. Five years after the start in Mr. Bilson's drawing-room and the subsequent removal of the little assembly to the shop premises, it became necessary to seek larger and better adapted accommodation, and the present hall was built. It received its name from Cholmeley Park, which is near by. A special window was provided in the new building for Mrs. Cooper's Bible, with an arrangement for the illumination of the pages when the nights were dark; and the Word has been displayed ever since.

Few assemblies have shown a more practical concern in

CAPTAIN ORDE-BROWNE, R.A.

JOHN CHURCHILL.

LEONARD STRONG.

JAMES W. C. FEGAN.

HISTORY OF WELBECK ASSEMBLY

the furtherance of the Gospel in foreign lands than the company of Christians meeting at Cholmeley Hall, there being at the present time eight missionaries serving the Lord who went out from this assembly. In this connection it is of interest to mention that among the number is Sidney Adams, of Malaya, one of a family of eight sons and four daughters of Mr. A. Adams, of East Finchley (one of the original brethren who met over fifty years ago), all of whom were brought to the Lord and baptized at Cholmeley Hall.

THE START AT GREENWICH

The assembly at Greenwich had its inception, in a considerable measure, through the labours of James W. C. Fegan, whose name has already been mentioned in connection with Gospel activities in the London neighbourhood. With a view to establishing a testimony where at that time no Gospel witness existed, he purchased a large public-house in the High Street, Deptford, and turned it into a Gospel Hall, which became the spiritual birthplace of numbers who were attracted by the faithful message. Following this undertaking, a Gospel testimony was also commenced by Mr. Fegan at Greenwich, where largely attended meetings were held both in tent and theatre. The converts from this fruitful effort and from the activities at the West Greenwich Ragged School were, under the guidance of Mr. Fegan and Joseph W. Jordan (whose name is also notably associated with many of the London assemblies), gathered into a room in the town, where the little company first broke bread. This was in the month of August, 1875, and marked the commencement of the Greenwich Assembly. The meeting was later transferred to the King George Street Hall, these premises having been purchased from the Wesleyan body and converted into a suitable assembly hall and schoolroom.

Though the name of James W. C. Fegan is more directly connected with the founding and maintenance of Fegan's Homes for destitute boys, yet he ever found time and opportunity to evangelise and teach amongst the assemblies in and around London, wherever a door was opened. In his early years he was brought in close contact with many prominent brethren, whose names take a notable place in the narrative of events before us. During the frequent visits of J. N. Darby to Southampton, and later to London, the Irish leader on several occasions was a welcome guest at the home of the Fegans. The mother of Mr. Fegan, who died in 1907, was wont to relate how she recalled Mr. Darby as a clergyman coming down from the pulpit of the church where he ministered and walking along the street in his black ministerial robes, to join the company of Christians who had been in the habit of coming together in apostolic simplicity each Lord's Day, for the breaking of bread.

Brought up in this spiritual atmosphere it is not to be wondered at that young Fegan, soon after his conversion, seized every available opportunity, both in hall and open-air work, that he might lend a helping hand in the exhilarating work of soul-winning. And as we have already seen, there were few assemblies in the Metropolis where an aggressive work was being carried on, that his presence was not felt in a very practical way.

Among the notable helpers associated with Greenwich Assembly, the name of Huntingdon Stone is affectionately remembered. With a heart for the propagation of the Gospel in the foreign field, he devoted both time and money that the message of salvation might be carried to the uttermost parts of the earth. Mr. Stone provided a training home for young men and another for young women going abroad, and left his fortune of £250,000 to *Echoes of Service* for the Lord's work.

In this record of assemblies of the Lord's people, formed some generations ago, it may prove an encouragement to include the experience of an assembly of more recent date.

In the year 1926 five brethren with their wives met in conference to consider the possibility for testimony in a rural district on the outskirts of London. Among them was Mr. J. W. Laing, who with remarkable foresight conceived the idea. They had recently come to reside in the neighbourhood, having previously been in fellowship with assemblies of believers in the north. At that time a new railway had

HISTORY OF WELBECK ASSEMBLY

been built, connecting the green fields with the great Metropolis. These Christian believers, all engaged in active business or home duties, visualised the day when these green fields would become fields of humanity, spiritually "White unto Harvest."

They planned and prayed, seeking a Heavenly Father's guidance as to the very best site for a place of worship, Gospel testimony and fellowship in this developing neighbourhood. At that time the most suitable site was occupied by a railway, which would be removed in the course of a year. It was thought advisable, therefore, to wait patiently until the site was available rather than hasten matters and build a hall in a less suitable position.

Then there was the problem as to what size of hall should be built. Those faithful believers visualised great opportunities, as dwelling-houses were being erected in the neighbourhood, and yet the fear was often there—would the undertaking prove a failure? A hall was planned to seat four hundred to five hundred, with a Sunday School of equal size.

At last the site became vacant and the building of Woodcroft Hall began. By the time it was ready the number of believers had increased to twenty. On the day when the hall was opened, Christians from surrounding assemblies gathered to show fellowship in the undertaking, which was a great cheer to the few who had shouldered so great a responsibility. And when, on the day following, they met to remember the Lord in the breaking of bread, how small in number they seemed and how weak they felt, but how precious was the sense of the Lord's presence.

It being virgin soil with a growing population and no competitive Christian work, the Sunday School began with a membership of five hundred and gradually increased to one thousand. The intention of the Christians at first was to keep the hall undisturbed and not use it as a Sunday School; but the needs of the work made it necessary to consecrate the Hall for Sunday School work as well as for worship and Gospel testimony. Soon afterwards seven additional rooms large enough to accommodate about eighty children in each were added.

On the first Sunday evening the Gospel meeting had an attendance of one hundred and fifty, but this number gradually decreased until the attendance numbered only seventy or eighty. It was decided, therefore, to announce a lantern talk instead of the usual Gospel service, the slides illustrating the life of our Lord. Four of the brethren, in turn, read portions from the Gospels, which had been carefully prepared for the occasion, describing the slides. This rather unorthodox form of Gospel appeal attracted quite a number, and that night seemed to mark the turn in the attendance at the Gospel meetings as numbers steadily increased from that time.

At the close of six years there were two hundred and forty in fellowship. Of this number about one-third were from churches where modernism had robbed the message of all its power, and people sought the assembly where the Lord was revered and His Word honoured; another third had moved into the district from other churches; while the remainder had been saved and received into fellowship since the opening of the hall. It was considered that the assembly was now too large for fellowship and active service. None wished to move, but it was acknowledged by all that it would be better for some of the Christians to reach out to other districts, preaching the Word in these places also. After much waiting upon God in prayer, thirty members of Woodcroft Assembly built a hall three miles to the north-west, while another hall was built by fifty others three miles to the south-west. Thus in happy fellowship they hived-off from the parent assembly and started testimonies in those places. During the following three or four years, the parent assembly had again increased to about two hundred and fifty in fellowship, and each of the infant assemblies more than doubled the number in fellowship.

"Since the commencement of this remarkable work," writes one of the pioneer workers, "there has been no outstanding revival; and yet conversions have been fairly frequent, each year about twenty believers being baptized. God has principally used the Sunday School, the Gospel meetings and the women's meetings. To these activities may be added the faithful labours of a brother and his wife who devoted half their time to the service of visiting the sick in body and the anxious in soul."

The leaders in the Woodcroft Hall Assembly have ever sought to avoid a sectarian spirit or practice, their one desire being not to follow the tradition of men but simply to follow the teaching of the Lord Jesus, as illustrated in Holy Scripture in the records of the early churches. They are persuaded that in this period of the twentieth century, God is not using the great Gospel meetings as fifty years ago, but increasingly the testimony and life of God's people among their friends and neighbours, and so leading these to the Lord, or to the regular meetings or Sunday School, where they are led to the Lord Jesus.

. . . . . .

There are at the present time upwards of one hundred and twenty assemblies of Christians known as Open Brethren in the London area. I have only been able to sketch a brief outline of the spiritual birth and growth of a few of these. To call up each assembly and tell the story of its inception and subsequent life would indeed be a formidable undertaking, even if the exigencies of time and space would permit the pursuit of such indulgence; and yet one hesitates to pass by with little more than passing reference, the many gatherings of the Lord's people, who, for long years, in times of stress, as well as during seasons of fruitful ingathering, have been faithful to the Word.

As we have seen, from small and unostentatious beginnings in London, little companies of believers, leaving behind the alluring dazzle of ecclesiastical conventionalism that they might carry out the will of God in true apostolic simplicity, have, since the earliest times of this remarkable Movement, increased with an influence which has made its presence felt in the religious world, spreading abroad in a wonderful way from the spiritual birthplace in Camden Town to the farthest suburb of the great Metropolis.

CHAPTER XXIII

THE STORY OF THE LONDON MISSIONARY MEETINGS

THE story of assembly life and spiritual activity in the Metropolis would be incomplete without some reference to what has become known as the London Missionary Meetings.

Few gatherings of the Lord's people have in recent years so powerfully influenced the work amongst the heathen as those soul-inspiring meetings, where, from the far-flung fields of labour in regions beyond, ambassadors of the Cross meet in happy concord with fellow-Christians from almost every corner of the homeland to render an account of their stewardship in the Lord's vineyard.

It was about the year 1894 that Frederick Stanley Arnot —whose name will ever live in the annals of missionary pioneer work in darkest Africa—conceived the idea of commencing a weekly prayer meeting, having as its object the remembrance before the throne of grace of those who, in obedience to the call of the Gospel, had gone forth in implicit faith, looking solely to the Lord to supply their needs. The first meeting was held at the Aldersgate Street Y.M.C.A. in the afternoon, but the hour not being suitable for business men and others who were interested, few were able to attend. It occurred to Alfred W. Fisher that a monthly prayer meeting at a convenient hour in the evening would probably be found to be more suitable for such a purpose, and after consulting Mr. Arnot, who at once expressed his full agreement with the suggestion, a meeting of elder brethren was called at the Gospel Hall, Lewisham.

London overseeing brethren responded happily to the invitation to that meeting, which was quite conversational in character. The idea of a monthly prayer meeting in the evening was favourably received, and God gave a wonderfully unanimous judgment to those present as to the

LONDON MISSIONARY MEETINGS 119

desirability of such a meeting. After further waiting upon God for guidance, it was provisionally agreed that the prayer meeting be held at the Friends' Meeting House, at Devonshire House, Bishopsgate Street, on the last Friday in the month. A circular letter giving an outline of what had been considered and proposed, was drawn up and addressed to the London assemblies, signed by John Churchill, J. G. McVicker and Joseph W. Jordan, commending Francis Stunt, Alfred W. Fisher and A. Milne Kyd as suitable brethren to undertake the responsibility entailed by such meetings. These monthly meetings, it was suggested, would afford an opportunity for Christians from different parts of the Metropolis and district to come together for the purpose of supporting by prayer those whom they knew serving the Lord in other lands. The first meeting took place in April, 1894, not in the Friends' Meeting House but in an upstairs room on the Devonshire House premises.

Recalling those epoch-making days, Mr. A. W. Fisher writes:

"Missionary brethren were not so well known in those days in the London meetings, and it occurred to a few of us to have a gathering at which some of those who had returned from the foreign field should be asked to address us. The first of these meetings—now called the Annual Missionary Meetings—was held in 1895. On that occasion we simply had the afternoon and evening of Friday. In 1896 there was a prayer meeting on Thursday evening and other meetings on the Friday."

In the year 1912 several changes took place which necessitated the appointment of other brethren to act as conveners. Mr. Fisher had gone to Canada and Mr. Stunt intimated that his age and the distance of his residence from London prevented his continuing, while Mr. Kyd, whose activities in connection with Clapton Hall made increasing demands upon his time, expressed a desire to be free for the work of the assembly with which he was so closely attached. Consequently, a meeting of elder brethren was held at Devonshire House, when the position was reviewed, and John T. Churchill, G. J. Hyde and Joseph W. Jordan were asked to act as conveners, which position they accepted, continuing to serve in that capacity until 1925. Alfred W. Fisher, W. Stunt and A. Milne Kyd then took over the work, and with other fellow-workers have discharged this important service till the present time.

During the long years since the inauguration of these gatherings, meetings for prayer and intercession continued with increasing interest, the fruits of which will only be revealed in a coming day. The prayer meetings were held at Devonshire House until the buildings were demolished, and about the year 1924 it became necessary to remove to the premises of the Sunday School Union in Old Bailey. Later, the meeting was transferred to the Aldersgate Street Y.M.C.A., where it is still held.

Whilst those seasons of intercession on behalf of the Master's business in other lands continued to occupy a prominent place in the hearts of the Lord's people, so the Missionary Meetings, the offspring of those hallowed hours of prayer, increased in number, till, in 1913, it became imperative that larger premises be secured. These gatherings had grown to such an extent that many were unable to obtain access, causing much disappointment, particularly to friends who had come up to London from the country to attend. It was decided, therefore, to remove to Kingsway Hall, which provided nearly double the accommodation. Here the meetings were held for nine years, but owing to the increased numbers of Christians attending, a still larger hall had to be found. Thus the Central Hall, Westminster, with a seating capacity of two thousand seven hundred, was secured for the purpose, and the Annual Conference has taken place there since then. Only those who have been privileged to attend the inspiring meetings at the Central Hall during recent years, and to feel the impulse of the spiritual atmosphere which pervades, can in a measure realise how mightily God has wrought through this divinely-ordained channel, since the advent of that little prayer meeting in a hired room in Aldersgate Street less than fifty years ago. And it is consistent with these gatherings having arisen out of a prayer meeting, that two hours are apportioned for prayer on Thursday, the opening day of the conference, and forty-five minutes on Friday, the time for prayer occupying the beginning of each day's proceedings.

CHAPTER XXIV

SUFFOLK AND HENRY HEATH

In the days when the unsophisticated taste for things in general and meeting-places in particular was rather less fastidious than is the case in the times in which we live, it is not surprising to find even the most incongruous and least expected building brought into use for the holding of Gospel meetings. From John Wesley's *Journal* we learn that when no public meeting-room was available in the parish where his itinerant excursions led him, he very soon had the sombre-looking barn of a kindly-disposed farmer transformed into a bright and congenial place, with a score-and-a-half tallow candle illuminants; and here the celebrated evangelist would preach to the assembled country people with a vigour and sincerity which rarely failed to captivate his audience.

We remember, too, that it was in a barn in the remote district of Codymain, in Ireland, that Augustus Toplady, who in after years wrote the immortal hymn, "Rock of Ages," heard the way of salvation from the lips of an unlettered preacher and was converted.

Nearly a hundred years ago, within the bare walls of a barn which stood on the edge of a meadow at Tostock in the county of Suffolk, a Gospel testimony was commenced which led to the establishment of an assembly in that district. Night after night the barn was filled to overflowing, numbers coming many miles from neighbouring parishes to hear the Gospel. Those were indeed primitive times, when few people of the labouring class could read, and as hymn books were less popular than they are to-day, many of the meetings were carried through without singing. To some of us a songless Gospel meeting would seem an incongruous proceeding, knowing from happy experience that on such occasions the pent-up joy of a soul redeemed

SUFFOLK AND HENRY HEATH

had but one safety valve, in the lifting up of the voice in exultant praise to Him who saved us! Nevertheless, the Lord placed His seal on the labours of those pioneer preachers, and numbers of the people who attended the meetings in the barn were saved. Many afterwards sought to follow the Scriptural command and were baptized, the only convenient place where this could be carried out being a large slate tank in the neighbouring graveyard. As the result of those meetings in the barn there are to-day a number of assemblies in the county of Suffolk, among which are Stowmarket, Fakenham and Rougham.

The adjoining parish of Woolpit, whose assembly will ever be remembered in association with the name of Henry Heath, came under the sway of the Gospel about this time, and mainly through the labour of Captain Towers many of the country people were led to the Saviour. A man of untiring energy and undaunted courage, Captain Towers relinquished the calling of a seafaring life that he might devote his time and talent in the service of the Lord; and there were few village greens and market places in the county of Suffolk in the days of which we write where his voice, proclaiming the Good News, was not heard. Nor did he and those faithful to the Truth escape the subtle attention of the enemy. But despite the bitter persecution through which they passed, the "New Lights," as the little company were satirically named, became the nucleus of a testimony which has been honoured of the Lord up to the present time.

But it was the coming of Henry Heath to Woolpit that marked in a very real way the working of the Holy Spirit in that untouched district of Suffolk. To many it seemed strange and unaccountable that a servant of the Lord, endowed with such natural abilities as a teacher and expositor of the Word, should take up the work begun by Captain Towers in that isolated village of a few hundred inhabitants, six miles from a town and two miles from the nearest railway station. Here for nearly thirty years this faithful pastor and shepherd ministered to a flock, the boundary of whose pastures extended far beyond the limits of the almost unknown hamlet of Woolpit; and it is reputed that "people from fifteen different villages—some of them six miles away—would come regularly to Woolpit Room, to have the privilege of sitting under his ministry and go away refreshed and strengthened."

Henry Heath was engaged as a schoolmaster in the Devonshire village of Tawstock when he was brought in contact with Robert Chapman, a circumstance which was to alter the whole course of his career. He was then in his early twenties. His school was connected with the parish church, and this, no doubt, led Mr. Heath to take up the study of the Scriptures with a view to entering the ministry of the Church of England. Thus his visits to the home of Mr. Chapman at No. 9 New Buildings, Barnstaple, became frequent, which resulted in an entire change coming over the young schoolmaster, subsequently transforming his outlook on life and directing his steps in other paths. To him this wonderful unfolding of the Scriptures during those memorable Bible readings was altogether a new experience. Of this transitional stage, which marked the opening of a life wholly devoted to the Master, Henry Heath revealed to a friend that "the Scriptures had become a new power to his soul, and he was learning that the Bible was a living book, not only a theological work, fitting his mental powers for study in Hebrew and Greek, but that it was the inspired Word of God given to the Church of God in all ages."

In the year 1848, Mr. Heath took up residence at Hackney, London, where for about twenty years, as we have already seen in a former chapter, he was constant in ministry, not only in connection with Paragon Road Assembly, but at provincial conferences and other gatherings of Christians where opportunity was afforded for expounding the Scriptures. It was from Hackney that he went to Woolpit, where, till called home in 1900, Henry Heath laboured with a fervent love for the One he ever sought to exalt: a labour of love which has left a sweet savour.

After Woolpit, the Gospel was carried to other parts of

SUFFOLK AND HENRY HEATH

Suffolk, meetings being held not only on available open spaces in town and hamlet, where the ear of the passer-by might be arrested, but in the kitchens of those whose hearts had been reached by the call of the Gospel. Following upon those times of spiritual revival, there were formed what were then known as reading meetings, where believers young in the faith came together under the guidance of men imbued with the power of the Holy Spirit, that they might learn from the Scriptures what was the will of Him whom they had come to know in an experimental way as the Lover of their souls.

Moats Tye Room in the village of Combs is the outer shell of an old cottage with a thatched roof, certainly unique in Suffolk as a meeting-room. Gospel meetings were begun there in 1843, followed by Bible readings which were largely attended by those who had been led into the light of salvation at the Gospel meetings, and by others who had a real desire to become acquainted with Bible truths, of which up to that time they had been in darkness. The outcome was that as they came to learn the will of God concerning believers' baptism and the Lord's Supper, many desirous of carrying out the Scriptural injunction, walked to the neighbouring town of Stowmarket, about three miles distant, on Lord's Days, to join the little company of Christians in that town who had only a short time before come together to remember the Lord's death in the breaking of bread. Two years later the way was opened up for a permanent testimony in Combs, and after waiting upon God for guidance, an assembly was formed in the old Moats Tye thatched cottage. Thus, "On the 30th day of March 1855," says an old record book still in existence, "a meeting of believers was held in the above place. It was agreed they should meet there in future, for the breaking of bread simply as believers in Christ Jesus; and willing to receive all such for His sake, according to Romans xv, 7." Then follows a list of eighty-two names, and it is interesting to observe that the grandchildren of several of them are in the assembly at Combs to-day. For many years Mr. W. M. Hewitt, an able and gracious servant of God, was constant in his care for the flock. Then followed Mr. Salmon of Stowmarket and Mr. Tidmarsh of Bury St. Edmunds, who for a long period were real helpers at Moats Tye; and many to-day testify to the help and blessing they received through the ministry of these brethren.

CHAPTER XXV

ST. ALBANS

THE formation of an assembly at St. Albans, Hertfordshire, had its beginning in the winter of 1864 following a visit to that town by Howard Johnston. "My wife and I came to St. Albans to seek for lodgings and an open door for the Gospel. We were guided to suitable apartments, where we were comfortably cared for."

Thus wrote Mr. Johnston respecting the beginning of his labours for Christ in that town and surrounding country, which, during the three years which followed, were greatly blessed in the conversion of men and women and the upbuilding of the Lord's children. He called on a friend who owned a large iron room which was capable of accommodating upwards of a thousand persons, the use of which was readily granted for the preaching of the Gospel. Sunday afternoon services had been held there previously, but few, with a heart for the Gospel, could be found to proclaim the unsearchable riches of Christ, so that the hand of the Lord was fully acknowledged in leading Howard Johnston to St. Albans just then.

The work continued happily until, through clerical opposition and the subtle energies of other enemy forces, the Iron Room, which had been the birthplace of many souls, was closed against those who sought to uphold the truths of Scripture with an open Bible and to spread the Gospel. But the Lord did not forsake His faithful people and suitable premises were found, so that on the following Lord's Day the usual meetings—the Breaking of Bread and Bible Class, besides two Gospel meetings—were held, the latter in the new Corn Exchange, which place was well filled both afternoon and evening.

Early in the Spring of 1865 a tent was pitched, which had soon to be substituted by a larger one. The site chosen was in Lattimore Road, and many fruitful meetings were held. Before the year closed, a hall was built in the field where the tent had been pitched, the first meeting being held on the last day of the same year, when the Lord honoured the occasion in the conversion of a soul. And thus the testimony begun over seventy years ago continues to the present time, with an unswerving loyalty to the Gospel and faithfulness in carrying out the principles of New Testament truths revealed in the Scriptures.

F. S. ARNOT.

"The harvest is plenteous, but the labourers are few" (Matt. 9, 37).

EARLY PIONEERS—WHOSE FAITH FOLLOW.

CHAPTER XXVI

EASTBOURNE—1872

THE commencement of a testimony at Eastbourne, on the English Channel, may be traced to the conversion, rather late in life, of two sons of a former vicar of that town. Lord Radstock was preaching in the public room of the Maidenhead Hotel, Uckfield, when William and Frederick, sons of Dr. Brodie, came under soul conviction, and realised for the first time, that a pious upbringing in the religiously correct atmosphere of a vicarage would not obtain for them that peace of soul for which they now sought. Although it was Frederick who, in the year 1869, first began a Gospel testimony in the Old Town district of the now popular health resort, yet it is the revered name of William Brodie which will ever shine out in bold relief in any recorded consideration of the Lord's work in Eastbourne, as it was largely through his instrumentality, both spiritually and financially, that the testimony went forward. He was born at the old vicarage, which stood opposite the Parish Church of St. Mary, and in early life the boy ran rather an erratic course. On leaving school he became a midshipman, but quitted the service a few years later and proceeded to the Island of Trinidad. Here the youth was employed on a sugar estate. He afterwards sailed for Australia, where, adopting the somewhat solitary life of a squatter, some years were spent in the bush.

Reduced in circumstances, the wanderer returned to England and took up residence with his mother at Eastbourne. It was some years later that the crisis in the life of William Brodie took place. He then, after being a member of the Church of England for fifty years, felt constrained to leave it. Let me quote his own words at that time as given in an interesting little brochure issued to commemorate the diamond jubilee of Edgmond Hall, and to which the present writer is indebted for much information:

"If ever I had a direct call from God it was when I came to this decision. When I went into —— Church one Sunday morning I had not the slightest idea of leaving the Church of England. On quitting the building I said to my wife, 'Never ask me to go into that church again; I was so uncomfortable that I will never go in there again.'"

His resolve was never broken. Such a solemn and deliberate action as this, was only decided upon by reason of the enlightened apprehension of the truth of God as touching the simplicity that is in Christ, undoubtedly a direct result of the spiritual awakening which was to effect such a resolute change in his whole life.

Following the Gospel testimony begun by Frederick Brodie, Mrs. Emma Grace his sister, along with Mrs. Benest, gathered the people together into the schoolroom of the Old Town Infant School, where they talked of the good tidings of grace revealed to them through the Scriptures, and many were pointed to the Saviour. From a diary left behind, it is pleasing to observe that the foundation of this fruitful work was firmly laid in prayer. To them, prayer was indeed a power with unlimited possibilities.

Encouraged by the evidence of spiritual fruit, William Brodie, in 1871, followed on during the winter months by giving Gospel addresses to which people in large numbers were attracted. The kind of preaching to which they listened at these services was quite different from that of the parish church, which, as they said, "was over their heads" altogether. The people crowded into the meeting-room to hear the Word of God, because, as Mr. Brodie himself said, "They understood the preaching." A year later he purchased larger premises, and so great was the interest manifested in the town, that before long it was realised that the meeting-room would require to be enlarged, so Mr. Brodie proceeded to acquire the adjoining property. This he had converted into the present hall with a seating capacity of from three hundred to four hundred, which on many occasions was tested to its utmost. In fact it was found necessary at a later date to hire another hall nearer the seaside, for the convenience of visitors and others residing in the locality. This, however, has been succeeded by Marine Hall in Longstone Road, with which the names of Steinle, Baddeley, Cummings and Hewer will always be associated.

Previous to this, a desire was expressed that the Bible truths which they had come to learn should be carried out, not as man had devised, but solely according to the Scriptures. Thus a table was set up, and on the first day of the week many came together in happy fellowship to remember the Lord.

One is so accustomed to hear what is said by ourselves about ourselves, that the view of the outsider may be worthy of recounting here. Thus we read what a writer in the local press had to say some years ago concerning the Mission Hall, as it was then called. He writes:

"This is a plain building in Church Street, in which a mission has been carried on for several years by Mr. W. Brodie in connection with the communion known as 'Christian Brethren,' who have no clergy or stated ministry, and deny being a sect or denomination but hold to the saying 'One is your Master, even Christ, and all ye are brethren.' The Mission Hall ... has been comfortably fitted up and lighted. There are no pews, but forms and chairs are used as seats and a platform serves the purpose of the pulpit. ... As we have said, there is no stated ministry, but brethren from various places give addresses at services, and in various ways, efforts are put forth for the religious and temporal welfare of the inhabitants of the Old Town. The congregations nearly fill the building, and are made up chiefly of the working-class with a sprinkling of the persons in the middle walk of life. From a conversation we had with an intelligent farm labourer who attends the meeting regularly, it seems that the services are greatly appreciated by the people of his class, and are preferred to the more formal services of the Church of England. The good man spoke gratefully of the efforts put forth by Mr. Brodie and his friends for the well-being of the people living in the Old Town."

Some of the best-known evangelists and teachers of that time, whose names are already familiar to the reader, were invited to assist Mr. Brodie in the work, among them being Shuldham Henry, Harry Moorhouse, Denham Smith, Harrison Ord, Dr. Macnutt, John Connor, Charles Inglis and George Hucklesby—the latter spending many of his early days of ministry in the assembly. Thus Edgmond Hall (or the Mission Hall, as it was formerly called) became the spiritual birthplace of many who are now with the Lord. A few years subsequent to the erection of the Mission Hall, the schoolroom was added at the rear of the building by Mrs. Grace, who also caused to be erected Edgmond Lodge, which afforded convenient accommodation for servants of the Lord coming from a distance, and those who sometimes stayed for weeks at a time during special Gospel services. These properties were eventually left by Deed of Gift to the assembly, the whole being in the control of trustees. "Of Mrs. Grace it may be remarked as it was of the Shunammite woman of Old Testament days, that 'she was a great woman,' who thought no sacrifice too large for her blessed Lord." She built and endowed several halls in various parts of the country besides fully equipping at her own expense not a few labourers for the foreign field.

It is of interest to note that Edgmond Hall was one of the earliest—if not the first—"dissenting" places of worship in Eastbourne, and those connected with it suffered much from the stand which they made against what has been termed "organised Christianity." "The assembly, of course, has experienced its vicissitudes," says the writer of the brochure already referred to; "it has had its joys and sorrows, but through them all the banner of testimony has ever been unfurled, and through the grace of the Lord an unswerving loyalty to the Holy Scriptures has been maintained."

As in the case of all healthy assemblies, the missionary spirit has been encouraged and developed, so that from Edgmond Hall ambassadors of the Cross have gone forth to India, France, Congo, Balolo, China, Central Africa, Rangoon and Switzerland. In this connection I may be permitted to quote again from the writer already alluded to, and this I do with fullest approbation. "It is our firm conviction that a Church without a missionary outlook is in danger of dwindling away through its becoming self-centred." With this end in view, missionary meetings are held annually, and have been a source of encouragement and enlightenment for some years past, to believers in and around the Eastbourne district.

CHAPTER XXVII

SHANKLIN, ISLE OF WIGHT

THE first recorded gathering to the name of the Lord in Shanklin, Isle of Wight, followed the simple pattern so frequently met with in these pages. It was in his own home, early in the year 1881, that William Brown, his wife and a few friends, began to break bread. They were shortly afterwards joined by others, and by the end of the year it was found necessary to remove to a large lecture-room over a grocer's shop. There was already an assembly at Ryde, a few miles across the island, from which the little company received much spiritual help and sustenance.

At some revival services held in the Congregational Church, large numbers professed faith in Christ, and this in a measure was the means of augmenting the already growing assembly, for many who sought spiritual guidance were led into the light and liberty found in the soul-satisfying experience of New Testament teaching. James Wright, of Bristol, was visiting Shanklin during this time of blessing, and had the joy of witnessing the baptism of twenty believers, to whom he afterwards ministered those truths so dear to the child of God. Four months later, sixteen others publicly confessed Christ in the waters of baptism.

In the year following, several other believers were baptized. Among them was Lieutenant Hoste, who afterwards became prominently associated with the China Inland Mission. At that time he was stationed at Sandown.

In 1885, a new hall, large enough to accommodate two hundred persons, was built, and the work continued to prosper. Shanklin has been privileged in its association with many notable brethren who visited the island. Among those remembered because of their faithful ministry and spiritual help in the furtherance of the Gospel, and in the building up of the assembly, the following may be mentioned:—Lord Radstock, J. Denham Smith, Col. Foster, Capt. Mitchell, James Vicary and Mr. Onslow.

From its formation in the early 'eighties, the life of this assembly has been characterised by an aggressive Gospel testimony, and a faithful adherence to the principles of truth. Nor have the widespread needs of the foreign field lacked a place in their sympathies, for, as an indication of the practical interest shown, the records of the Shanklin Assembly contain the names of those associated with the meeting who have gone forth as missionaries to Africa, India, China and the West Indies.

CHAPTER XXVIII

KINGSTON-ON-THAMES—1867

IN the recording of events which have, in divinely ordered sequence, led up to the formation of an assembly of believers, one is apt to overlook the labours of the faithful few behind the scenes; those whose names are known only to the One they seek to magnify; those whose unfailing constancy in spiritual affairs escape the attention of the public eye and, anon, pass by unseen and unsung. And yet not unseen by Him whose record, unspoilt by the fickle pen of human efflorescence, will be revealed in the light of a day yet to come. While the names and doings of men of succeeding generations take pre-eminence in the building up of the church, the honoured place of the woman, alone with God in the secret of her chamber, can never be fully estimated. It is said that the prevailing prayer of two Christian sisters, unknown to the subject of their supplications, contributed in no small measure to the coming of Dwight L. Moody to Great Britain in the early 'seventies.

In like manner it was the fervent prayer of a saintly woman in Surbiton that brought about the establishment of an assembly in the town of Kingston-on-Thames. For some time Miss Ranyards had been much concerned about the need of the Gospel in that town. Towards the end of 1865 she wrote to the Open Air Mission, London, to send someone to Kingston Fair. In response to the appeal two or three young men attended the Fair, where an opportunity was afforded for carrying the Gospel to the crowds who had come to town for the festival. Oliver Fry, one of the young preachers, was invited to remain at Kingston that he might follow up the work, and the next day was spent visiting the cottagers in their homes. This resulted in a Gospel meeting being arranged for in one of the cottages. So keen was the interest that some who were unable to gain access refused to go home and remained standing outside the open door. The Gospel message, presented in all its sweetness and simplicity by the young preacher, carried conviction to one who was leaning against the wall by the door listening. This was the beginning of a remarkable work of grace, and soon afterwards a large room was hired in the building opposite to where the old Gospel Hall was later erected. Here meetings were continued till 1867.

About this time a number of those recently saved, as well as others who had come to know the will of the Lord, walked to Hampton Court Assembly each Lord's Day for the purpose of remembering the Lord in the breaking of bread. The distance, however, rendered it rather inconvenient for some who desired to attend, and it was decided to seek guidance that the way might be made clear for commencing an assembly at Kingston. Soon afterwards a suitable room was acquired in Fairfield Place. There being no accommodation in the house a baptistry was dug in the garden, the first to carry out the Scriptural command being those brethren who had so recently come to a knowledge of the Truth. Before the close of the same year in which the little company began to break bread, the room and passage leading to it were on many occasions crowded during the Gospel meeting, and it became necessary to remove to larger premises, which were obtained in the Assize Court buildings. The old Gospel Hall was then planned, and in 1868 was opened for use.

During this time Oliver Fry, who had been prevailed upon to take up residence at Kingston, continued to shepherd the flock, besides giving much of his time to Gospel work in the neighbourhood. The testimony begun at the Fair was continued each year with evidence of blessing, and in 1868 a booth was built where Gospel services were held nightly. Whilst in the midst of active work for the Master, and when his influence for God in the town was acknowledged by all who knew him, Mr. Fry was suddenly called away from the scene of his labours and from those who loved him. On the 16th of July 1869, while bathing in the river, he was drowned. This seemed an irreparable loss, but through the mercy of God those left behind were kept together.

Mr. Grove, a brother who came to reside in the town about the same time as Mr. Fry, then saw it was the Lord's will that he should give more of his time to the work of the young assembly. For a number of years he was, with the help of others, used in piloting the assembly through years of difficulty and disappointment, cheered only by seasons of spiritual blessing, at a time when the tactful exercise of a gracious spirit was required in warding off the assiduous attentions of the enemy of the Church.

The history of this assembly is one of varied experience. Still, those who continued steadfast ever sought by God's help to keep the light burning. This they did in face of many difficulties, for the assembly was called upon to pass through yet another time of testing when, on the 9th of February 1917, the Gospel Hall was burned down. From that time the assembly met in hired premises, till in 1926, having purchased a plot of land in Canbury Park Road, the present hall was built and opened in that same year. Since then many have been added to the church, the number now in fellowship being about a hundred and fifty.

THE TESTIMONY AT BALDOCK

Allusion has already been made to the useful part played by a tent mission in connection with the formation of an assembly. Particularly is this the case in outlying districts cut off from the main arteries, and in a considerable measure away from the beaten track. About the year 1879, John Brunton, an evangelist, took his tent to Baldock, in Hertfordshire, and preached what many thought to be a new type of doctrine. Up to that time no definite evangelistic work had been known in that district, and the advent of a tent pitched in the corner of a field drew many to hear this itinerant preacher. What they did hear was not the stereotyped kind of sermon to which they had been accustomed during their attendance at the parish church near by, but an ungarnished elucidation of the Holy Scriptures delivered to them in such a way that set the village talking. This kind of preaching was quite new to those who attended the tent services, and while some scoffed at the presumption of this unordained preacher, it was evident that there were those who had come with a sincere desire to learn more concerning the Scriptures.

Mr. Brunton, therefore, asked them to bring their Bibles. And so from the infallible Word of Truth he was able not only to point anxious ones to the Saviour, but it came about that before the mission ended a little company drawn from church and chapel, enlightened by a fresh revelation of what to them was entirely new, came together simply as Christians to remember the Lord in the breaking of bread. For some time they met in a hired room, but two of their number being engaged in the building trade a suitable piece of ground was secured upon which an Iron Room, large enough to seat a hundred persons, was erected.

Henry Groves followed John Brunton, and his visit to Baldock, which was chiefly with a view to ministering to the spiritual needs of the young assembly, resulted in many more being added to the Church. Since then the assembly has continued faithful to the Word, through difficult times and in face of much opposition; and though their name, like that of numerous other such isolated gatherings of the Lord's people throughout the country, may take but a humble place, yet their testimony to the truth and power of the Gospel will not pass unrewarded by their Lord.

IN SOUTH DEVON

While the tent at Baldock was fulfilling its mission in the gathering in of souls for the Kingdom, a similar work was making itself felt in the South Devon village of Starcross. John Harris, the gardener to a local clergyman, in company with Frank Tupman, a fellow Christian, hired an unoccupied cottage, which was let to them at a nominal rent, and commenced Gospel meetings. Previous to this, the only religious evidence in the village was the parish church, whose interest in the spiritual welfare of the inhabitants appeared to extend little beyond the formalities of the Lord's Day services. Fifty odd years ago—the time of which we write—this neighbourhood, I understand, was notable for its lawlessness and utter disregard for God and of any form of religious worship. The novelty, therefore, of a cottage meeting conducted by two young men aroused curiosity and the room was filled nightly. Thus the Lord gave token of His approval at the commencement by saving souls.

About this time, two evangelists, Panting and Honywell by name, arrived in the neighbourhood with a large tent which they pitched on a vacant patch of ground. No previous arrangement having been made, their arrival was taken as an answer to prayer. Gospel meetings were continued for several weeks with a manifestation of real interest and blessing; so that before the mission ended a little company of believers came together under the canvas of the tent in apostolic simplicity to remember the Lord's death. Soon afterwards a portable iron building was erected on the same piece of ground where the tent had stood. Thus the efforts begun in the cottage, and strengthened by the coming of the tent, resulted in the formation of the Starcross Assembly.

Twenty years later a brick building replaced the iron structure, which had now become too small. Owing to local prejudice some difficulty was experienced in securing ground for the erection of the new hall, but the Lord inclined the heart of a brewer, who offered a piece of land which formed part of a publican's garden, and a building capable of accommodating about two hundred people was erected on this site.

CHAPTER XXIX

CHELTENHAM ASSEMBLY

THERE appears to be no written record of the exact date when the assembly at Cheltenham came into being. For some time in the late 'seventies of last century a little company of believers was meeting in the Old Corn Exchange —now a Cinema House—where they sought to remember the Lord on the first day of the week. Regent Hall, the present meeting-place, was opened on Lord's Day, 23rd April 1882, with an early morning prayer meeting at which forty persons were present. The circumstances which led to the commencement of the assembly have not been handed down, but among those whose names are still remembered for their labour in the Gospel and the shepherding of the flock is A. J. Cummings. He was a prominent business man in the town, and it was mainly through his efforts and influence that such stalwarts of those days as Robert Chapman, Henry Dyer, General Mackenzie, George Müller, Hudson Taylor, Thomas Newberry and Shuldham Henry were to be found on occasions ministering to the spiritual needs of the assembly. Thus the meeting was cared for and built up in a very real and practical way.

Its proximity to Leominster, where an important conference for believers was held annually, drew many of the "chief men" to the assembly; and when those memorable gatherings ceased to be held, the interest was transferred to Cheltenham, which then became the conference centre. The gatherings have continued from year to year, the meetings being held on the first Wednesday in October.

Besides the annual conference for ministry, a missionary conference has been held in the Spring of each year, this being the outcome of missionary interest particularly among the young people. This evidence of spiritual life has not ceased to manifest itself, which, in a measure is revealed, in that during recent years Cheltenham Assembly has commended three labourers for work in the foreign field: Dennis Mills, who went to China; Miss Hill, now working in the West Indies; and H. G. Young, for service in Algeria.

Half a century ago Cheltenham was noted as a place where the Gospel might at any time be heard faithfully preached from many of the church pulpits in the town, though of late years evangelical energy and zeal have been on the wane. In the early years of the assembly's testimony, a number of young men were saved under the ministry of a godly Church of England clergyman. When he left the town, his successor not being of an evangelical turn, sought to divert the activities of the young men into other channels, which led them to look around for a more congenial spiritual home where their energies would be more profitably utilised in the Master's service. They were brought into touch with Mr. Cummings and were eventually received into fellowship. This infusion of young life was a decided stimulus to the assembly, and its influence in the town may be dated from that time and circumstance. It is interesting to observe that a granddaughter of the godly clergyman referred to is at the present time a member of the Cheltenham Assembly. The fact that her father was also filling the position of a clergyman in the town, did not deter his daughter from following the dictates of her spiritual desires in taking her place with fellow-believers around the Lord's Table.

In later years among those who helped in the edification of believers by gracious ministry were: Colonel Molesworth, Dr. Owles and Mr. Stewart Henderson.

Visitors to Cheltenham Cemetery are shown what has come to be known as the "Plymouth Brethren Plot," where the graves of Exclusive and Open Brethren lie side by side awaiting the resurrection morn. Among them is the resting-place of Charles Henry Mackintosh, whose familiar initials appended to Brethren literature are known the world over. He was born in 1820 at Glenmalure Barracks, County Wicklow, Ireland, where his father, who was a captain in a Highland regiment, was stationed during the rebellion.

Converted at the age of eighteen through the tender letters of a sister, followed by a prayerful perusal of J. N. Darby's *Operations of the Spirit*, he early gave himself to the study of the Scriptures. At the age of twenty-four he opened a school at Westport, but fearing the pursuit of this vocation would altogether absorb his passionate interest in spiritual matters he afterwards abandoned all thoughts of pursuing a scholastic profession, devoting his time and pen to expository work. His six volumes containing copious notes on the books of the Pentateuch, which have passed through several editions, still occupy a readily accessible position on the Bible student's bookshelf. As a platform speaker C. H. M. was much sought after, and during the Revival of 1859–60, when Ireland came under a great spiritual awakening, he took a prominent part in the activities of the Gospel. It is as a writer rather than as a speaker that his name is remembered to-day, and in this connection it would be difficult to estimate the powerful influence of the pen of C. H. M. during the last fifty years.

The closing years of a useful life were spent at Cheltenham, and though he now very rarely appeared on the platform through ill-health and advancing years, still his pen was not idle, and when towards the end of 1896 he was called Home, his last manuscript, *The God of Peace*, was in the hands of the publishers. Though Mr. Mackintosh remained with the Exclusive Brethren to the end, his sympathies were not confined to that particular circle of believers, and he was ever ready to give expression of his unfeigned love to all brethren.

THE GATHERING AT "POUND HOUSE," ST. AUSTELL

A little over fifty years ago there gathered together a number of believers in what was known as "Pound House" in the High Street of the village of St. Austell in Cornwall. For some time previous to this, there appears to have been a sincere exercise of soul and a spirit of enquiry as to the true interpretation of several New Testament passages which had engaged their attention. Amongst those who came together was Edward Petter, a man of keen spiritual discernment. He it was whom the Holy Spirit used in revealing to them through the Scriptures, what was the will of God concerning the things which appeared to disturb their spiritual peace. The result was the sweeping aside of the irksome bondage of ecclesiastical formalities, for the simple gathering to the Name of the Lord, in implicit obedience to Him Whom they sought to remember in the breaking of bread. The meeting went on in happy fellowship and with signs of blessing for a number of years, until their testimony was assailed from without by the arch enemy, brought about by a circumstance emanating from an assembly one hundred miles distant, which had no real bearing upon that particular Church. This, unhappily, had the effect of sowing discord, and the testimony of the assembly suffered in consequence. Nevertheless, there were those who, despite the severe trial and diminished numbers, remained faithful to the trust committed to them. These brethren, therefore, decided to continue in a simple way to remember the Lord on the first day of the week, the meeting being held in the drawing-room of a dwelling-house in the little village of Charlestown, a few miles distant. In later years the assembly gathered in the home of George Wood, at Slades, St. Austell.

Early in the year 1924, when the increase in numbers and the evidence of spiritual growth was felt in their midst, the brethren who had the care of the assembly became exercised as to the need of a suitable hall and a more open testimony. By this time a Sunday School had been formed and Gospel meetings commenced, so that by the following year the Seymour Gospel Hall was opened. The last Gospel meeting held in the home of Mr. Wood was attended by thirty-three people, and the Gospel was preached by R. N. Gelder, of Westcliff-on-Sea. Following upon the vicissitudes through which the assembly has passed, it is pleasing to observe that since the opening of the hall the testimony has been wonderfully maintained, several having been baptized and added to the Church.

JOHN MARSDEN CODE.

J. DENHAM SMITH.

HENRY GROVES.

WILLIAM WILSON.

CHAPTER XXX

LEEDS—AND HARRY MOORHOUSE

THE first assembly of believers in the city of Leeds was held in the private house of George Denham at 54 Briggate about the year 1864, and consisted of nine brethren and one sister. It was mainly through the efforts of Mr. Denham, who had for some time experienced deep spiritual exercise of heart, that the little company came together. But there were other influences, incongruous though it may seem in this particular instance, which contributed to its development. About this time the last public execution at Armley Gaol, Leeds, took place, when two men named Myers and Sarget were hanged. Harry Moorhouse, one of the best-known evangelists of his time, took advantage of the occasion and in company with Gawin Kirkham and William Walker preached the Gospel to an immense crowd that had gathered to witness the gruesome spectacle. This work in the Gospel, which created some considerable stir in the city and brought about lasting results of grace, was followed some time later by a series of addresses delivered in the Prince of Wales Music Hall by William Booth, who afterwards became the founder of the Salvation Army.

During this period the believers continued to meet in Briggate, but as numbers increased, a meeting-room was rented for a time in Burley Street. Pastoral visits by A. J. Holiday and other ministering brethren resulted in many being added to the church, and in 1878 the assembly removed to the Temperance Hall, Holbeck. About this time, a young evangelist, who was destined in years to come to carry the Gospel to many parts of the world, arrived in Leeds. A year or two previous to this, at a meeting in Union Hall, Glasgow, he had been commended to the Lord for the work of the Gospel. His name was Alexander Marshall. He, in company with W. Willington, began a Gospel campaign in premises known as Adam's Circus, Cookridge Street, where the Coliseum now stands.

Later, a tent was pitched in Meadow Lane, where the two evangelists were joined by a young man, an ex-Guardsman, who, like his Scottish compeer, afterwards became prominent in the work of the Gospel, and was possibly one of the most powerful preachers of his time. The young man was W. R. Lane, whose Home-call at the advanced age of eighty-four took place at the close of 1935. These were indeed stirring times; souls were awakened, and many anxious ones were led to the Saviour. The fire and zeal coupled with a passionate love for perishing souls, which characterised Mr. Marshall as a herald of the Cross, had already become manifest. His stentorian voice proclaiming the Gospel, as he was wont to do, with no uncertain sound, was long remembered by many who attended those meetings. On the last occasion that the veteran evangelist visited Leeds (shortly before his Home-call), he delighted to recount how he and Mr. Willington, during their campaign in the early days, used to march up and down the streets, singing "Hold the fort, for I am coming!"

Soon afterwards, as a result of those meetings, the Carlton Hill Hall was opened, in conjunction with which the work of a Bible Carriage was commenced. Amongst those who were engaged in this work was Horatio Wallis, who later went as a missionary to the Shetlands. In 1883 an assembly was formed in Cookridge Street, followed by special meetings conducted by Richard Graham, when a remarkable revival was experienced. Many were converted and numbers added to the assembly, amongst them being a family of twelve named Taylor.

As the work prospered it was found expedient to commence a testimony in Queen's Square, where a hall was acquired, and before many months had elapsed there was an assembly numbering about one hundred and fifty. The Lord was indeed honouring the faithful labours of His people, and soon after this a small meeting-room, known locally as the "Shovel Shop," was opened on Penny Hill, Hunslet. A year or two later a more suitable hall was

LEEDS—AND HARRY MOORHOUSE

secured in Church Street, where a splendid work was done for the Master, and it became the spiritual birthplace of many souls.

When the "Needed Truth" trouble became acute, many from the Queen's Square Assembly came to Church Street meeting and continued there for a time, but for reasons of residential convenience this hall was closed and in 1897 the old Medical School was opened. It was to this hall, on his return from his hazardous journey across Africa, that F. S. Arnot of Garanganze came, preaching on the Sunday evening, the subject of his discourse being "How black men are made white." These premises were available only on Lord's Days, so in 1901 the Fenton Street Hall was acquired, and meetings continue to the present time, with a large and aggressive assembly. The Chetwynd Hall Assembly was formed a little over thirty years ago, following a tent mission in Elland Road, Holbeck, by J. C. M. Dawson, of Belfast. Here the meeting continued for some years, afterwards moving to Joseph Street, Hunslet, not far from the old Church Street meeting of bygone days. The Lord signally owned the testimony, and in March, 1932, a commodious hall, built at the cost of £2000, was opened for use.

As will have been observed, the testimony in Leeds since the first gathering in Mr. Denham's house in Briggate seventy years ago, had spread to various parts of the city, and the work continues to prosper. In recent years three more assemblies have been commenced: one in Cardigan Road district, another in Alpha Street Hall, where Russell Elliott and A. Widdison were for some time in fellowship (the believers now meet in a new hall in Ladbroke Place, Dewsbury Road), and another in the Headingly district.

HARRY MOORHOUSE

The name of Harry Moorhouse has frequently been mentioned in our review of the times covering the second half of last century. As he comes into the present picture in rather dramatic fashion at the very commencement of the

Movement in Leeds, it may be deemed opportune to acquaint the reader of the present generation regarding this singularly remarkable man. Born in 1840 of humble parents, the early life of this fragile-looking Lancashire lad was for the most part spent in the companionship of the lawless and profane. While yet in his teens he had plunged deep into the vices openly indulged in by evil associates many years his senior. But the downward career of sin and dissipation was suddenly arrested.

It was the period of the '59 Revival. This memorable work of God had swept across the Irish Sea, and various cities and towns of Lancashire were caught in the flood. Largely attended meetings were held in Manchester, addressed by such notable preachers as Lord Radstock, Reginald Radcliffe, Richard Weaver and W. P. Lockhart. Among those brought to the Saviour was one of Harry's companions in evil. The young convert at once sought out his friend but, despite entreaty and pleading, his appeals seemed to fall on deaf ears. But the arrow of conviction had found its mark, and after weeks of abject misery and contrition, the profligate at last found peace for his soul's distress through the finished work of Calvary.

From following the promptings of a lustful passion, Harry Moorhouse at once flung aside every weight and encumbrance that had dragged him to the depths of degradation from which he had so recently been rescued. He had become a new man and determined that his life, both in word and act, would manifest the great spiritual change.

It was John Hambleton—at that time known as the converted actor—who, in God's hands, largely influenced the future career of Harry Moorhouse. Hambleton was preaching in Lancashire when he met this puny-looking youth, and being struck with his zeal and honesty of purpose, invited the young convert to join him. Together they travelled the country, visiting towns and villages, public fairs and race meetings; wherever an open door was found they preached Christ. This first experience of Gospel pioneer work, when hardships and discouragements confronted their path, was truly preparing the young convert for the work which God had planned for him in days to come. At Halifax they were gladly received. Here a work of grace was in progress and an opportunity was given to preach in the Oddfellows' Hall. Large numbers flocked to the meetings and the hall was crowded night after night.

This was but the beginning of a life crowded with faithful and unstinted service for the Master. The governing principle in that life was to do the will of God; hence he did not hesitate to follow where God led. The visit of Harry Moorhouse to Dublin, in company with Edward Usher, where the two evangelists were warmly received by William Fry and Henry Bewley (through whose good services meetings in Ireland were arranged), was the beginning of a remarkable work of grace. Their sojourn across the Emerald Isle, preaching and distributing thousands of tracts as they went; their appearance in the drawing-rooms of the well-to-do; and their kitchen meetings in the crude apartments of the humble cottars are memories that still live.

Fruitful with blessing though his labours in Britain were, his visits to America—six in all—were productive of even greater results. Here he was affectionately hailed as "the great English preacher"; everywhere doors were opened to him; invitations came from city church and cosmopolitan mission. The labours of this untutored, unostentatious young man, whose speech bore undisguised traces of his native Lancashire, had indeed received the Holy Spirit's seal. The story of his first contact with D. L. Moody is worthy of recalling, when, in the absence of the celebrated American evangelist, Harry Moorhouse preached on seven successive nights from his favourite text, John iii, 16. On his return to Chicago, Moody was curious to hear the youthful preacher. It was the seventh night.

"He went into the pulpit," says Moody. "Every eye was upon him. 'Beloved friends,' he said, 'I have been hunting all day for a new text but I cannot find anything so good as the old one; so we will go back to the third chapter of John and the sixteenth verse'; and he preached the seventh sermon from those wonderful words: 'God so loved the world.'"

Harry Moorhouse met Ira D. Sankey in the winter of 1872 at a meeting in the North Side Tabernacle, Chicago.

"It was he who first suggested the thought of going across the sea to sing the Gospel," says Sankey, "and I remember how confidently he expressed his opinion that God would bless my singing there."

When the two American evangelists arrived in England the following year, Harry Moorhouse was among the first to welcome them at Liverpool.

"The Churches have perhaps not been aware of the effects of what may be called the evangelistic side of the Brethren Movement," writes a contemporary. "Moorhouse, moving in that circle and giving himself to ardent study, became, as the years passed, emphatically a 'Bible' evangelist and teacher; and it is no difficult matter to trace much of the revived interest in the Holy Scriptures (which, although seldom recognised, marked the later years of the nineteenth century and the beginning of the twentieth) to the boyish preacher from Manchester."

During the last few years of his life, despite incessant suffering, he continued to labour for the Master, on occasions leaving a sick-bed, so unutterable was the longing in his heart to win souls for the Kingdom. In 1880, when yet a comparatively young man, Harry Moorhouse returned to his native Manchester, weak in body, but with soul still aglow with a heavenly love. His work was done; and on the 28th of December he passed into the presence of Him whom he loved.

CHAPTER XXXI

CUTSYKE

IN the summer of 1904 a Gospel tent mission conducted by Edward Hughes and J. C. M. Dawson, was pitched at Castleford, a village near Leeds; and though no definite cases of conversion were achieved, the mission happily resulted in bringing blessing to Christians and proved to be the first link in a chain of circumstances which eventually led to the founding of an assembly at Cutsyke, a suburb of Castleford.

To arrive at the real commencement of the work in Cutsyke it is necessary to go back nearly forty years. Frank Smith, a brother whose home was at Featherstone, in his journeyings to and from Leeds on business had to pass through Cutsyke. A burdened desire came into his heart that the Lord would raise a testimony to His Name in the village, where at that time there was none. For years he continued unceasingly to pray that this would be brought about. Those prayers were marvellously answered.

God began to work, but at that time, considering the place at which He started, one would have thought that Cutsyke was not in His plan at all. Among those upon whom the power of the Holy Spirit fell were three men, associated with the Congregational Church. For some time following the Gospel work in the tent at Castleford, the desire for a deeper spiritual life grew upon them. As yet they had not learned the truths which were to be found in the bountiful store of the Scriptures. The desire continued to be manifest in the lives of these three men. They were eventually brought in contact with a believer who was in fellowship with brethren before he came to reside at Castleford. Through him they learned of a meeting for Christian believers who gathered to the Name of the Lord at Pontefract. Thither they went, and after hearing the truth ministered and the Scriptures unfolded, they each felt that here was the place for which they had been seeking so long. With souls on fire for the Master their thoughts were now directed to the spiritual needs of Cutsyke, and they sought an opportunity to carry the Gospel to that place. It was about this time, or soon afterwards, that George W. Ainsworth pitched a tent in the neighbourhood, when a considerable number professed faith in Christ and were afterwards baptized. And thus from these beginnings a testimony was established in the village.

FEATHERSTONE

The assembly at Featherstone—the Yorkshire meeting from which James Clifford went forth to the Argentine—was formed in the early 'nineties, following an intensive Gospel mission by Edward Peck in conjunction with Alfred J. Holiday.

CHAPTER XXXII

EARLY DAYS AT BATH

THE wave of spiritual awakening which suddenly swept in, unheralded, upon the old-time seaport of Plymouth, in the year of grace, 1830, had in the course of a few swift years made its way across the land, leaving in its train unmistakable evidence of a path marked out by God. To the ancient city of Bath there came one day—exactly when, no one at this distant date can say—some divinely led person bearing the savour of those primitive gatherings of God's people. Thus was the seed sown. And though neither the name of the ambassador nor the occasion which brought about such fruitful results are known, yet there are in existence old minute books and other documents indicating that an assembly was formed in the year 1837.

It is known that a house of local historic interest, still standing in the city, was for a period used as a meeting-place, but the exact date cannot now be determined. It is certain, however, that the assembly acquired the premises known as Princes Street Hall, in 1845, and continued there for forty-two years.

In the year 1840 the little company was greatly strengthened by the arrival in their midst of John Marsden Code, who ministered the Word with much acceptance in the assembly, up to the time of his Home-call in 1873. Mr. Code was educated at Trinity College, Dublin, where he took the degree of M.A., following which he was ordained a clergyman in the Church of England; but, as in the case of J. N. Darby and others about that time, he left the Church that he might more faithfully carry out the will of God, a fresh revelation of which, having been brought about by an intense study of the Scriptures. He was joined in 1846 by his friend, J. G. Bellett—a name now familiar to the reader—who had also taken up residence in Bath. These two devoted brethren shared in the ministry and gave much of their time to the tender care of the flock.

The story of the Bath Assembly is notable because of its association with brethren whose names stand out prominently in the history of a Movement, the vicissitudinary course of which we have sought to pursue. In 1848 there is an entry in the assembly book that a meeting of "Guides" was held, and that Captain Percy Hall, R.N., was one of the principal speakers. About this time also, Sir Edward Denny, the author of many beautiful hymns largely in use amongst Brethren to-day, came to reside here; and his name, with that of his sister, appears on the Church roll. The work at this period must have made rapid strides, for in 1848 we find nearly three hundred names on the assembly roll, and this number was maintained until 1873 when it was found necessary to acquire a second hall. This was a Baptist Chapel, recently vacated, in Somerset Street, and here for fourteen years there was a Gospel testimony each Lord's Day evening, whilst at the same time a meeting for believers was being held in Princes Street Hall.

About the year 1875 Harrison Ord pitched a large tent in one of the principal squares in the city, where an aggressive work in the Gospel was continued for several weeks. These services produced a lively interest in the neighbourhood and were fraught with much blessing, many of the converts being added to the local assembly, while there were also those who joined other places of worship.

"These activities," writes Mr. Frank Webb, who has made a careful record of the assembly's history, "whilst demonstrating the life and zeal of the assembly, were proving costly to maintain and inconvenient to operate, as neither hall was sufficiently large to meet all the requirements of the still growing work. The need for larger and more commodious premises became a pressing one, not only from the point of view of expense but of the efficient carrying on of the work in its many branches."

The problem which presented itself was to receive a happy solution in a remarkable way. At this juncture there came to reside at Bath, one whose name is written large in the annals of the assembly, in the person of John Lindsay Maclean, M.D., son of Gen. Sir George Maclean. He had been marked out for an army career; indeed he actually commenced it, serving first at Malta and later in the West Indies with the 69th Regiment. Whilst stationed at Malta he came under the care of the colonel of his regiment, an active Christian, through whose consistent example and personal influence young Maclean was converted. Soon afterwards he relinquished his army commission in order to study for the medical profession. He took his diploma at Edinburgh, then went to reside at Leominster, remaining there until his departure for Bath in 1873. On his arrival Dr. Maclean evinced a warm interest, entering into the various church activities with a quiet yet practical zeal. He very soon perceived the growing assembly's urgent needs, and at once turned his attention to the matter of more commodious premises. In 1887, largely through the good doctor's very practical interest and munificence, the Manvers Hall was built. Here Dr. Maclean ministered for a number of years. Though not a fluent speaker his ministry was marked by a high spiritual tone. He was a constant visitor to the bedside of the sick as well as to the homes of the needy ones, and was greatly beloved by all.

His keen interest in foreign missions led Dr. Maclean to commence, in fellowship with Henry Dyer and Henry Groves, a publication known as *The Missionary Echo*. This was in the year 1872. From this modest beginning has grown the missionary magazine we now know as *Echoes of Service*. Although several changes of name have been made in the interim, yet from earliest days Bath and foreign mission work have become almost inseparable, and to many are, indeed, synonymous terms. Dr. Maclean's Home-call in 1906 was a very real loss to the assembly and to that wider sphere of missionary work, which now had representatives in almost every quarter of the globe.

Doubtless because of its fame as a delightful health resort endowed with hot mineral springs, Bath attracted many notable families, who took up residence in the vicinity. Thus the growth of the assembly was in a measure due to this fact, while its influence and acquaintance with well-known brethren brought many such to minister to believers from time to time.

On the Home-call of Henry Groves in 1891 Robert Eugene Sparks, B.A., resigned his position as solicitor to the Bank of Ulster, and in 1894 came to Bath to assist in the ever-growing work at *Echoes* office. Besides these arduous duties, which entailed much care and anxious thought, he ever found time to render spiritual help to the assembly, his gracious ministry being of a kind that was always practical and helpful. The early demise of Mr. Sparks was lamented by a wide circle of friends, and his name is still a fragrant memory. His beloved widow was long spared to carry on a wonderful work for God, more especially in the interest of sisters in the foreign field, hundreds of whom will remember with gratitude her loving service on their behalf. In the closing days of 1937 Mrs. Sparks was called Home at the advanced age of ninety-four. W. H. Bennet, of Yeovil, who had for some time been assisting in the work of *Echoes*, whilst not residing in the city, was a frequent visitor to the meetings, where his ministry was always welcome and highly appreciated.

"The activities of brethren," says Mr. Webb in his interesting account of this assembly, "were not confined to the city only. Many villages around were visited each Lord's Day, so that to-day we find quite a flourishing assembly at Corsham Side and another at Box. Nearer home, meetings, the result of 'hiving' off, were commenced at Twerton and Snow Hill, both suburbs of Bath, whilst still later yet another was commenced at Sladebrook, following a tent campaign by Fred Glover."

It is not surprising that in an assembly whose outstanding activity appears to be the furtherance of the Gospel in other lands, there should be a lively interest manifested at home. A chart hanging in the hall records the names of those in fellowship who have gone forth. It shows, too, that while many have passed to their reward, there are at the present time those from the assembly serving the Lord in Central

Africa, China, Czechoslovakia, India, the West Indies, Morocco and Spain.

It is often said that God buries His workmen but carries on the work. Especially has this been the case with regard to *Echoes* office, for, after the Home-call of Dr. Maclean, those who shared the responsibilities incumbent upon this important work were much encouraged and stimulated by the coming of W. E. Vine, M.A., of Exeter. Later, following the passing of Robert Sparks, W. R. Lewis, of Hereford, was invited to give help, and eventually came to share with his colleagues the valuable work so long and faithfully carried on. With added responsibilities in the ever-increasing demands it was felt that further assistance was needful, and later the two brethren were joined by R. Boyd Cooper, of London.

And now just a word concerning the vehicle which in God's hands has been so wonderfully used, not only in the publishing of tidings from afar but in creating a very real and practical fellowship in this important service. Almost from the start, the interest which attended the outgoing of the little publication, *The Missionary Echo*, continued, and in 1885, a larger paper with the present title, *Echoes of Service*, took its place. Since then some desirable improvements have been effected, particularly in recent years, so that the present issue of our missionary magazine, produced under the joint editorship of the three brethren whose names are mentioned above, is indeed eminently worthy of the high object of its mission. God has been pleased to use this monthly paper to stir up interest in foreign mission work. For, since it went forth, "many were moved by reading its pages to give themselves to the work and still many more were stirred to fellowship in helping forward by their gifts, until at the present time there are about a thousand missionaries in many parts of the five continents."

No record of this assembly's activities would be complete without a reference to the Missionary Conference, now an annual event and held in July each year. On the discontinuance of the Leominster Conference the need was frequently expressed for a similar gathering in the West, and Bath appeared a very convenient centre. From the first the divine approval was apparent. Indeed, since its inception this gathering of ambassadors from the ends of the earth, together with home workers and a great company of others of the Lord's people, have in a very abundant measure shared the happy fellowship of one another, while their souls have been refreshed and invigorated by the congenial atmosphere which is ever present during these memorable gatherings.

CHAPTER XXXIII

SWINDON

THE work at Swindon, in Wiltshire, began with the visit of Charles Russell and Edward Hurditch, who arrived in the district with a Bible carriage. At that time the influence of a spiritual awakening in that part of the country was making itself felt, and on every hand there was an earnest desire for the Word of Truth. This was followed by a real work of grace and many were brought into the Kingdom. After fulfilling their brief mission the evangelists left the district, but in response to many appeals they returned to commence a more permanent work. This was in 1880. A tent was pitched on almost the same spot upon which the Regent Hall now stands. During the mission and afterwards, much valuable help was given by such brethren of repute as Henry Varley, Ned Wright, J. Denham Smith, as well as others whose names have still a fragrant memory.

Many of the young converts, along with those Christians whose hearts had been revived, eager to testify for the Master, found a ready outlet for their pent-up zeal in the open-air. Dinner-hour meetings were held near the Great Western Railway works entrance. Such new form of religious energy aroused bitter opposition, and some of the leaders were summoned by the police for obstruction. This proved a good advertisement, and as large numbers were attracted to the Gospel through the street-preaching, it became necessary that a place be sought out for indoor meetings. A hall was secured in King Street, but this soon proved inadequate. An auction-room in a good central position was afterwards purchased and named the Central Hall. In the summer of 1883 the work was transferred to this hall, where for a number of years a remarkable ingathering of souls for the Master was witnessed. Several noted characters in the town were converted. Two of these, Edward Williams and

Richard Picket, came out boldly for the Lord and were singularly used as open-air preachers.

In 1883 a young man named William Hooper was brought to the Lord through the instrumentality of Joseph Dore—one of the most active and faithful workers in the mission—and soon after his conversion was baptized with about fifty others. Mr. Hooper, in the vigour of youth, threw himself into the activities of the mission and for over half a century continued steadfast in the work of the assembly, unmoved by the vicissitudes through which it has passed. It was largely due to his efforts that both the Regent and the Kingsdown Halls came into being.

The meetings of the Evangelistic Mission, by which name it was known, were conducted much along the lines of "Brethren" at the present time. This continued very happily until early in 1889, when trouble arose over matters of a doctrinal nature, which resulted in about forty of the most active workers withdrawing from fellowship and the collapse of the Evangelistic Mission in Swindon.

Many of the brethren and sisters were now without a spiritual home. Some of them turned to the denominations, while others lost their way. A few, however, kept together under the guidance and care of Thomas Hacker, who had been a pillar in the mission. These believers, twelve in all, on the 30th of November 1889, met in Merton Hall to consider the advisability of commencing a meeting on Scriptural lines in fellowship with what they knew as "Open Brethren." It was decided to do so in that hall. The advice and help of Dr. Maclean of Bath was sought and readily given; and the first meeting for the breaking of bread took place on the following Lord's Day morning. When the object of the gathering in Merton Hall became known, many Christians who understood the truth and were feeling the dearth of spiritual life, sought out the little company of worshippers. The joy of the infant assembly was increased when the Lord owned the testimony in the Gospel in many conversions taking place.

There was now a steady increase of numbers, and in 1898 it was decided to rent what was known as Queenstown

JOHN WARDROP.

WILLIAM REID.

JOHN RITCHIE.

JAMES ANDERSON.

School. The Lord continued to prosper the labours of His people, and it now became necessary to consider the erection of a building of their own. The Regent Hall, which was opened the following year, was the result. With the establishment of a testimony and a growing Sunday School, the Gospel was now carried to the neighbouring villages, resulting in the formation of one or two assemblies. Principally through the frequent visits of Dr. Maclean to Swindon, a warm missionary interest has existed in the assembly since the early days. The assembly has for many years been represented in the foreign field by two of their brethren, George Sims and Arthur Morse, with their wives, who went out to Central Africa.

CHAPTER XXXIV

IN SOUTH WALES

MORE than eighty years have passed by since a few believers began to meet simply in the Lord's name in a private house in Cardiff. God blessed that humble beginning, the fruits of which are to be seen to-day. In Cardiff district alone there are about twenty-four assemblies, while in South Wales they number eighty-five in all, not including a number of other gatherings who meet on more or less "Exclusive" lines. Development in Cardiff was greatly helped forward by Edwin H. Bennett, a prominent business man at Cardiff Docks, and son of one of the original three who started breaking bread in 1852. A devoted and able leader of assembly life, Mr. Bennett was the mainstay of the work at Adamsdown, and proved himself a zealous worker throughout the district until his Home-call in 1903.

But let us go back to the beginning. In 1852 two brethren and one sister—William Bennett, his wife and a Mr. Bright —came to reside in Cardiff, and at once commenced a meeting for the breaking of bread in the home of Mr. Bennett, where numbers steadily increased. The commodious hall in Adamsdown was then provided, and the opening service took place in 1877. This assembly was the first known in South Wales, and some sixteen years ago there was gathered from Church records a list of over two thousand names of believers in fellowship in the district who had early association with the Adamsdown Assembly.

About the time that this assembly moved into their new hall, John Fry, a merchant at Cardiff Docks and residing at Penarth, commenced to break bread in his drawing-room with other brethren. After a period of testimony in hired premises, Plassey Street Hall was built at Penarth, and subsequently a similar-sized building, Hebron Hall, at Cogan, an adjacent parish. As a result of those beginnings, active assemblies with flourishing and comprehensive activities are progressing in these places to-day.

In the late 'sixties or early 'seventies a few Christians of the seafaring class were exercised as to gathering to the Lord's name. They had been converted in the old ship *Thisbe*, an obsolete man-o'-war then moored in the West Dock, Cardiff, and used as a Mission to Seamen. The little company acquired a large apartment, capable of seating two hundred persons, situated over some stables in Eleanor Street, near the docks. For some years there was a meeting in the morning from 11 to 12 o'clock, conducted by Mr. Gale, a missioner to seamen, which was followed by the breaking of bread. At a later period the meeting was conducted on simple Scriptural lines. A lively work among the young attracted large numbers, not only to the Sunday School but to specially convened Gospel meetings. This resulted in many being brought to the Lord, among whom were pilots, boatmen and others of the seafaring class. Those faithful brethren were known by the rather ungracious sobriquet of "Plymouth Rocks." "Oft-times the horses in the stables underneath disturbed us," says one of the brethren in a letter to the present writer, "but we look back with joy to those happy days. We may not have known the truth as fully as we know it to-day, but we knew what it was to feel the presence of God in our midst. Those were indeed times of refreshing, and we recollect how the tears of joy would fill our eyes as we remembered our Lord around the Table." In 1899 a more commodious hall, capable of seating about six hundred people, was built in Corporation Road, and in this place there have since been evident signs of divine approval, as shown by the large number who have been saved and added to the Church.

Another Church of those days was that meeting in Windsor Hall, a very commodious, hired upper room, for years blessed with an able ministry and pastorate with crowded Gospel meetings, and still continuing.

In the building up and shepherding of the Lord's people the names of notable pillars in the Church are remembered with affection: James Buck, a godly schoolmaster, was greatly used in Grangetown; Peter Evans at the Docks; Thomas Cross at Canton; John Fry, Frederick E. Hallett, William Howe and others at Penarth and Cogan; George Willie, A. McLay and W. J. Burt at Mackintosh; while visits from such honoured servants as R. C. Chapman, Henry Dyer, Henry Groves, George Müller, James Wright and others, and the pastoral work of E. J. Tapson left an impression on believers that could hardly be gauged. The Gospel platform was not neglected, and men like John Hambleton and Harry Moorhouse were brought into requisition from time to time.

A feature of the Movement in South Wales—pleasing evidence of the spiritual growth and development of the work—has been the branching off from existing assemblies. The assembly now meeting at Mackintosh Hall was started in 1885 in a little shop in Cathays by a few young men from Adamsdown, including George Willie, Thomas Brookes and Charles Pullin. Interest and numbers increased so that larger premises had to be taken, till in 1897 Mackintosh Hall was built and opened. The district proved to be a fruitful one and numbers continued to increase to such an extent that further subdivisions became essential, with the result that other assemblies were formed from time to time, including those meeting in the Heath Gospel Hall, Welcome Hall, Glanyllyn, Minster Hall and Rhubina.

Development was largely due to the fact that reaching out into the open-air, tents and neutral halls with the Gospel was ever kept before those who had a care for the Church as their duty and privilege. United missions were held with marked success, David Rea, John Brunton, Ferguson and Hamilton, Alex. Marshall, Fred Glover and other well-known evangelists taking a leading part in the proclamation of the Gospel and the gathering in of souls. During recent years large Tent Missions held in the centre of the city have been signally blessed of God. These activities have done much to keep the assemblies together, and to build up a strong, virile testimony in the district. Special attention has been given to Sunday School work, Young People's meetings, Women's meetings, Saturday afternoon tract bands and open-air meetings, which has fostered gift and a sense of responsibility amongst younger believers. Nor has the fellowship of neighbouring assemblies been lacking in the arrangement of united conferences for the furtherance of the Lord's work, as well as for the spiritual edification of believers. To all this has been added pioneer work in suburban housing estates. At Ely, in West Cardiff, a hall erected in 1930 proved inadequate and was doubled in size in 1936. Here there is a school of over one thousand two hundred held in two sessions every Sunday, a Women's meeting of two to three hundred, and an assembly approaching one hundred. The story of the assembly gathering in the Mission Room at Mumbles may well be prefaced by another story, being the conversion of James Henry Burgess and his wife Laura, who eventually formed part of the first company of believers gathered to the name of the Lord. In the year 1875, being in considerable affluence and at that time members of the Church of England and attending formally the Parish Church, Mr. and Mrs. Burgess went to a fashionable ball at Newport, Mon. While there, they received an urgent summons to return home, where they found that their eldest son, a boy of six years, had fallen into the fire. The child died a few days later. Shortly afterwards heavy losses were experienced in Mr. Burgess's business, which was that of a sailing ship owner. Reduced to poverty, the pair were compelled to abandon the large house they then occupied and take a small house at West Cross. These afflictions brought them into much distress, and Mary Dalling, wife of Captain Dalling, of Barnstaple, a relative and a woman who knew the Lord, came over to comfort them. She was the means in God's providence of leading them both to the Saviour.

Mrs. Dalling was at that time meeting with Christians in Bear Street, Barnstaple, the spiritual home of Robert Chapman, and it was not long before a few such souls in similar cases were found in West Cross, a hamlet adjacent to Mumbles. The breaking of bread first took place in the house of E. J. Grayson, at Beaufort Place, West Cross. The little company consisted of E. J. Grayson, J. H.

Burgess, S. C. Johnson, with their wives, Dr. Nicholls and one or two others. A year or two later the assembly moved into what became known as the Mission Room, the building having originally been a Congregational Chapel called "The Tabernacle." The assembly Minute Book contains the interesting record that the first baptisms took place on the 12th and 15th April 1883 at Langland Bay. The testimony continued with evident blessing, and in the year 1903, the company having considerably increased, the present hall at Castletown was erected as a testimony unto the Lord by James Henry Burgess, the story of whose conversion I have just recorded.

CHAPTER XXXV

LIGHT AT TREDEGAR

THE lamp which had been set burning in Cardiff about the middle of last century did not long remain a solitary illuminant, for scarcely had a decade passed by before the divine light, piercing the mists of religious uncertainty, found its way across the hills and through the valleys of South Wales, leaving in its course a beacon light here and another there, which to-day continue to send forth their gladdening rays.

Round about this time there was indeed a spiritual atmosphere which could be felt. Thoughtful Christians, hitherto fervent enough in the ordinary routine work of church and chapel, were now turning to the Word for a solution to the inward promptings of a conscience not wholly attuned to God. Thus it came about that many believers, enlightened by a fresh revelation, became conscious for the first time in their Christian experience as to the will of God in relation to many New Testament passages, which, up to that time, had been to them truths yet unrevealed. The result was a return to the simplicity of apostolic ways and doctrine, so clearly defined in the Word of God.

Such were the thoughts and feelings that disturbed a Sunday School Superintendent of the Church of England in the town of Tredegar. His name was Ebsworthy D. J. Tapson, and as it was mainly through the step he took at this particular time that the assembly at Tredegar was subsequently formed, it seems fitting that the story should be told here. Converted as a lad of twelve through reading Bunyan's *Pilgrim's Progress*, he began a few years later to serve the Lord in lowly spheres in his native town of Newport, Mon. In 1868 he accepted an appointment in Tredegar, where his real activity as a Christian worker began. It was while here that, through prayerfully reading the Bible and allowing its light to lead him in the paths that the Lord has marked out for His people to walk in, he saw it was his privilege as a believer in the Lord Jesus Christ to be baptized. Thus, in faithful obedience he, with William L. Hamilton, his brother-in-law, walked to Abergavenny, a distance of twelve miles across the hills, and publicly confessed Christ in the waters of baptism. This was 12th August 1876. On the following Lord's Day, at Mr. Tapson's house, Queen's Square, a few met in that Name alone, apart from all denominations, to worship God and shew forth the Lord's death according to the pattern given in the Scriptures.

As the two men held fairly responsible positions under the Tredegar Iron and Coal Company—one being the Surveyor and the other Property Agent—besides being prominently identified with Church activities, this new departure created some considerable stir in the town. Amid much opposition and no little persecution several Church members joined them, including Evan Williams the choir master. Brought together in an altogether different spiritual atmosphere, and freed from the traditional ways and formalities of the state Church, the little company seemed to feel and realise the Lord's presence in a manner never before experienced. Thus they continued, happy in the knowledge of a Father's smile as in simple obedience they sought to carry out His will.

When the numbers increased so that Mr. Tapson's house became too cramped, a room was taken in the Temperance Hall, where a company continued for some years. Later a Primitive Methodist Chapel was acquired. In 1918, because of the need of road improvements, the local Council offered a sum for the removal of the hall. Just at this time the Lord intervened in a remarkable way. A disused Congregational Chapel, seating about two hundred and fifty people with excellent accommodation, was offered for £100, and subsequently came into possession of the assembly.

David Jones, of Llanelly, an evangelist well known in South Wales, came to Tredegar in the early days, and as a

LIGHT AT TREDEGAR

result of his faithful labours in the Gospel many were led to put their trust in the Saviour. This was followed by a season of helpful ministry, when quite a number were added to the local assembly. Mr. Jones did not remain long in the district, but returned to his native Llanelly where the Lord used him in establishing a healthy assembly.

For some years Mr. Tapson continued at Tredegar, and while diligently fulfilling his daily vocation he gave himself assiduously to the tender care of the young flock. On his removal to Cardiff he became associated with the assembly of believers in Plassey Street Hall, Penarth, where he at once interested himself in the growing activities of the Sunday School. He also conducted a Men's Bible Class on Lord's Day afternoons. In this service the Lord greatly blessed him. Gospel work was carried on continuously on simple Scriptural lines, hundreds were converted and added to the assemblies and these multiplied greatly. In 1895 Mr. Tapson's health gave way, and a voyage to South Africa was undertaken. Here he had opportunities of seeing life in many forms and of visiting lone and widely sundered children of God in the rising townships of the colony. Returning to South Wales in better health he gave himself unstintingly to visiting the various assemblies, which were continually increasing in number and needed just that well-balanced ministry of grace and truth in which Ebsworthy Tapson excelled.

"Tender and gracious as a mother with her children," writes one who was associated with him in the work, "Mr. Tapson never surrendered the Truth nor lowered the claims of His Word, but clave to all that God had taught him and passed it on intact to others."

How the Lord wrought in a wonderful and what might be considered a rather mysterious way in the building up of a neighbouring assembly is worthy of being placed on record. A family from Tredegar immigrated to Scranton, U.S.A., and were instrumental in the hand of the Lord in commencing a testimony at that place, where an assembly was also formed. An Abertillery family by the name of West— Abertillery is a Monmouthshire mining town six miles from

Tredegar—went to Scranton about the same time, and among others a lad of about twelve years was saved and received into fellowship as a result of the preaching of the Gospel by the members of the Tredegar family whom they met there.

A year or two later the West family returned to their native place in Wales. Longing for the fellowship of other Christians, the young convert was disappointed and grieved to find that none of the denominational places which he visited remembered the Lord in the simple way that he had come to learn was the only true way. So he decided to stay at home on Lord's Day morning to read his Bible and give away tracts in the afternoon. One day, when handing Gospel messages to passers-by, he seemed to be drawn in a peculiar way to a lad of about his own age, with whom he entered into conversation about his soul. So anxious did his new-found friend become, that he took young West to his home, which was above a public-house. Here our young brother pointed the lad to Christ. This first fruit still remains and is to-day one of the elders of the meeting. Gradually others were added till they were ten to twelve in number. A Gospel testimony was commenced both in open-air and indoors, and it was decided to meet together to remember the Lord. So they rented a place for the purpose. That summer Douglas Perry arrived in the district with a tent, and a number were saved and brought into fellowship. Truly "the wind bloweth where it listeth, thou hearest the sound thereof, but canst not tell whence it cometh and whither it goeth." How wonderful are the ways of the Lord!

But to return to Tredegar. Baptismal meetings were an interesting feature of this assembly. The services took place at a pond called Cefn Golau, at the top of a hill 1200 feet above sea level. To these meetings large numbers of unsaved people came out of curiosity, and a favourable opportunity was presented for preaching the Gospel. "While the ministry of those days was fresh and invigorating," writes Mr. D. J. Stephens, "the need of separation from worldly principles and associations was constantly affirmed by our esteemed brother William Laurie Hamilton, who by his own separated life was a pattern to the rest of the believers." His consistent testimony in the neighbourhood, as well as his unremitting labours in the Gospel and in Church government, are still remembered.

The result of Mr. Hamilton's first step of obedience on that afternoon in August, 1876—already referred to—when he passed through the waters of baptism at Abergavenny, was a great spiritual enlargement and sense of liberty he had not previously enjoyed. On that occasion, so filled was he with the joy of the Lord that he was unable to constrain himself from openly testifying for Christ. And this he did to all he met as he walked the twelve miles to his home at Tredegar. His faithful service in the years that followed in and around Tredegar, Rhymney, Ebbw Vale, and in the villages of "the valleys," was marked by much of the Lord's blessing, and is remembered by many who were helped by his ministry. In happy fellowship with Edwin H. Bennett, of Cardiff; H. G. Lloyd, of Newport, and E. J. Tapson, many small assemblies of believers were established by means of meetings for ministry, and in gatherings of Brethren for mutual help and godly counsel as to the shepherding and guiding of the Church.

In the Spring of 1861, George Davies removed to Abergavenny from Grosmont, Herefordshire. His thoughts had been working along lines which had given some spiritual concern for a considerable time. Constant attendance at Church services brought no peace to his distressed mind but seemed to accentuate the cloud of perplexity. While in this unsettled state he found a family from Hereford of like mind to himself. With William Lewis unexpectedly coming into his life at this juncture, George Davies was directed to a prayerful study of the Scriptures. They were joined by R. H. Hill, a civil engineer, the son of a Devonshire clergyman, and William Green, both of whom were at that time engaged in the construction of a railway in the neighbourhood. The former afterwards became the first secretary of the China Inland Mission, and the latter was associated in later years with missionary work in Spain.

The first meeting for the breaking of bread was held in

the drawing-room of William Lewis, when seven sat down to remember the Lord's death. In the following year a few more having been added to the number, the assembly was removed to a building which had been used as a schoolroom; and there to the present time the company of believers meet around the Lord's Table.

CHAPTER XXXVI

MERSEYSIDE

THERE would doubtless be those in Merseyside — independent of what had taken place elsewhere — who, previous to the 'seventies of last century, were exercised regarding the true interpretation of New Testament Scripture as applied to the Lord's Supper and Believers' baptism; and yet it was forty years before the light of the great spiritual Movement found its way from Plymouth Sound to Liverpool. The first gathering of believers known as Open Brethren, at which there were present several men well known in Christian activities in the city, took place in a meeting-room in Crown Street.

Begun in a quiet, unostentatious way, it became the happy centre of believers in search of the Truth, which at that particular time of spiritual revival in Britain was gradually being revealed. The Moody and Sankey Mission to this country had startled the apathy of Christians and sent them to their Bibles with a vigorous expectation never before experienced.

It is interesting to recall that it was in the city of Liverpool that the first prayer meeting of that great mission was held. Harry Moorhouse, Douglas Russell and John Houghton met the American evangelists on their arrival, and the party made their way to the Great Western Hotel, where, in a private room, a time was spent waiting on God in earnest intercession. It is not to be wondered at, therefore, that in a comparatively short time much spiritual progress could be observed amongst those whose hearts had been drawn to the source from which there came a fuller realisation of the treasures to be found in Christ Jesus.

Dr. Owles and Dr. Eddis, who were known to have taken a notable part in the formation of the first assembly, were also actively engaged in the Burlington Street Medical

Mission, where opportunity was afforded to preach the Gospel to patients. The work spread, and Gospel efforts in small halls in the neighbourhood led to the opening, in 1878, of Boaler Street Gospel Hall. Since its formation there has been a steady and fruitful aggressive work carried on. As evidence of this, it is worthy of note that from Boaler Street Assembly there are to-day ten missionaries in the foreign field.

Radiating from this centre of activity, workers with a zeal for the Master carried the Gospel to the south end of the city, where Alexander Hall, Park Road, was engaged for meetings. This building, however, proved to be unsuitable for the purpose, and a move was made to Admiral Hall. Here the testimony continued for many years, and as numbers increased it became necessary to secure a more commodious building. The assembly now meet in David Street Chapel, Park Road.

In the year 1878 attention was directed to the north end of Liverpool, where a testimony for the Lord was established by a number of brethren from the parent assembly who built, in Church Street, Kirkdale, what was known as the Iron Room. This iron structure has now given place to a well-built brick building, where a faithful testimony to the Lord still continues. In the following year the work spread to the Cheshire side of the Mersey, and a number of Christians from the Claughton Mission joined with Rice T. Hopkins and other brethren in Atherton Hall, Birkenhead. Some two years later, another hall was opened in Ebenezer Street, Rock Ferry.

The labours of those faithful brethren in this important corner of God's vineyard, away back in the 'seventies, have not been in vain. The seed sown has borne fruit, sinners saved, saints gathered to the name of the Lord; and to-day there are nearly thirty assemblies of His people in what is known as the Merseyside district.

CHAPTER XXXVII

ISLE OF MAN

ALTHOUGH sparse documentary evidence is to be found, it is reasonably supposed that the first gathering of Brethren in the Isle of Man dates back to about 1840–1850. "My earliest recollections of Brethren," Edward C. Quine, when about eighty years old, told the writer, "goes back to the late 'sixties of last century. When a boy, I have seen some of these people, but being in a Methodist family I was taught to look upon them as very queer people indeed. At that time they held their meetings in a room in Athol Street, Douglas. Another company met in Ramsay, both being 'Exclusive' meetings."

With few, if any, gifted brethren able to take the helm and pilot the drifting vessel through troubled waters, the testimony, over a long period, owing to dissension and kindred evils, was one which bore evidence of stunted growth and senile decay. Indeed it is only during comparatively recent years that assemblies at Douglas and Ramsay have shown signs of healthy development; and this mainly through the spiritual help and guidance of Mr. Quine, who has moved amongst assemblies of the Lord's people for upwards of fifty years, nearly half that time having been spent on the Isle of Man.

CHAPTER XXXVIII

MANCHESTER

In the days when people called Brethren were little known in the religious activities of Lancashire, four Christians, members of a Presbyterian Church in Manchester, discovered through a careful reading of the Scriptures, that there was much in the doctrines of the Church they attended which was not revealed in the Word of God. They also found that it was in a very simple manner that the disciples first gathered. Thus enlightened, the four friends decided that nothing should be done in a hurry, but that they meet together one evening a week, to enquire further into these matters. With an open mind and the Holy Spirit's guidance, their desire was to search the Scriptures and see what God had to reveal to them of His will as to how they should meet. They had several such gatherings, and in due course it was made known to these men that God would have them leave the Presbyterian Church and meet together in an appointed place to obey His command: "As oft as ye eat this bread and drink this cup—ye do shew the Lord's death till He come." Search was made, and a suitable apartment over a coal-shed that could be rented at a low figure was found in Rumford Street, in a poor part of the city. This small beginning was the nucleus of a large and continuous work of God in the city of Manchester.

These four brethren, John Winn, John Pickering, James Pickering and Arthur Lorimer, not knowing at the time of any other such gatherings, were simply led to take this step, through their study of God's Word, without any thought of giving the movement a distinguishing name. They met on Lord's Day morning to break bread, in obedience to His command, and in the evening for Gospel testimony. "The meetings were of a very simple character," writes a brother whose father was one of the four, "but God

GORDON FORLONG.

JOHN STEWART.

JOHN DICKIE.

THOMAS McLAREN.

PETER HYND

SAMUEL DODDS.

blessed the testimony and some were truly saved, and added to the little company, without any question of 'The Fellowship' or 'The Church' to which we have become so accustomed these days. They were shewn from the Scriptures, that so soon as they received the Truth and were born again, God would have them to be baptized; and that it was His will they should meet together to remember the Lord's death in the breaking of bread."

After some little time, these brethren discovered that there was another meeting of the same kind in a different part of the city—in a hall in Walter Street—which had been started some years previously, and that there were quite a number of believers attending this place. The thought that they were not alone in the step they had taken seemed to give them new life, and they were much refreshed by the fellowship they had with these Christian believers.

The work at the Rumford Street Hall grew until the meeting-place was too small to accommodate the numbers coming to hear the Gospel, and it was very evident that a larger building would soon be required. "I remember," continues my correspondent, "on many occasions going with my father on Sunday mornings, an hour or so before meeting time, carrying the wood for the fire in the hall. One of these times we noticed some building operations had commenced in Warwick Street, where we had to pass along to reach Rumford Street. As the weeks went by and the building progressed, it looked to us as if they were erecting some kind of a hall, and I remember my father saying: 'Arthur, that would make a fine Gospel Hall.'"

It was later found that the building was intended for a contractor's office, with a ground floor, a business office, and behind it another room for storing timber and building equipment, while the large room upstairs was to be used as a carpenter's workshop. As the building went up, the brethren cast covetous eyes across the way. They were of one mind that such a place would be ideal for a Gospel Hall. But, of course, it was foolish to think that the new erection should interest them knowing the purpose for which it was being built. Just when the building was completed and the brethren were still searching for a larger meeting-room, a card with "To Let" appeared in one of the windows. It was afterwards learned that the owner had died suddenly and the agent was anxious to get a tenant for the premises. Soon afterwards, the agreement of tenancy was signed by the brethren, and after some structural alterations, the building was converted into a commodious Gospel Hall. From that time a testimony for the Lord was maintained for thirty years and many souls were converted to God.

It was not long before the upstairs room had to be almost doubled in size as the attendances increased, and by the time of which we write, the Assembly Roll contained two hundred names.

After long years of happy fellowship and blessing, the enemy of the Church crept in through the seed sown by the advocates of the "Needed Truth" doctrine, which brought about dissension. Many sought sanctuary in the assembly at Walter Street. Of this meeting our brother writes: "It had been used for an upper-room meeting-place for some years, but could hardly be called very suitable. The entrance was down a small dark street, after which there was a long spiral sort of staircase which had to be climbed before reaching the hall, an operation which taxed the strength of some of the elder members of the assembly. Furthermore, the downstairs portion of the building was used by a candy manufacturer—a man who also sold cough mixture in the market on Saturday nights—and often the smell of horehound and other ingredients became almost suffocating as we met in the upper hall on Sunday mornings."

The brethren decided to put forth a special effort in the Gospel. A large tent was obtained and Alex. Marshall was invited to conduct the meetings. A splendid site was secured on which to erect the tent, the ground being rented from a Roman Catholic lady. The position being central—at a point where four principal roads met, leading from the city—the ground rent was very high; but when all arrangements were made and it was made known to the lady owner the purpose for which the ground was to be used, she informed the agent that the ground was free of all rent for so long a time as it was required.

The tent was erected, and wonderful times were experienced during the time it remained at Ardwick Green corner. Crowds came to hear the Gospel, and on Sunday evenings the sides of the tent had to be let down so that the people unable to gain admission might be reached. Considerable numbers were made new creatures in Christ Jesus during the four months the meetings were held, and many were added to the different assemblies that were now in the city.

By this time the old Walter Street Hall, which had stood the test for forty years, was now in a very unsatisfactory condition. This did not escape the critical eye of the pioneer, Alex. Marshall, who ever deprecated the renting of a hall in a back street or up the proverbial "close," and it was his suggestion that the old hall be abandoned and a new building, worthy of the Gospel, be erected on the site of the tent.

Plans were prepared, and when the lady who had acted so generously on a previous occasion was again approached as to the sale of the land, she would only accept a very nominal ground rent. Thus the way was opened up, and the Hope Hall, Ardwick Green, became the centre of an aggressive testimony in the city.

CHAPTER XXXIX

WARRINGTON

THE first meeting for the breaking of bread at Warrington took place in the kitchen of Thomas Brocklehurst in the winter of 1883. Previous to this a few Christians, who had recently withdrawn from the denominations, were meeting for Bible study in a workshop. Fred Podmore, a native of Warrington, in fellowship with one of the Manchester assemblies, hearing that these friends were seeking light, came over on several occasions, and opening up the Scriptures, taught the little company the principles of gathering to the name of the Lord. They continued to meet for a brief period in the home of Mr. Brocklehurst, but the Lord wonderfully prospered the evidence of Truth in bringing many into the Kingdom through their activities in the Gospel. There are at the present time three assemblies in Warrington all in happy fellowship.

CHAPTER XL

BARROW-IN-FURNESS

TOWARDS the close of the year 1872, Thomas Robinson—who in later years was to become so closely associated with assembly life in the home of his adoption—came from London to commence business in the North Lancashire town of Barrow. His stock-in-trade included something more than the everyday commercial paraphernalia, for Thomas Robinson had a heart which at once went out to the perishing. At that time there was very little open-air preaching in the town, except by the advocates of the Temperance question, and although their opening hymn was invariably:
"Rescue the perishing . . .
Tell the poor wanderer a Saviour has died,"
it was rarely, apart from the hymn-singing, that a word about the Saviour was heard.

Thomas Robinson had a better story to tell, and lost no time in finding an opportunity of preaching the Gospel. Along with James Wharton, who joined him, he took his stand at what was known as The Fountain, where his voice was often heard as he told forth "the old, old story." The testimony in the street was honoured by God saving a few souls. Soon afterwards a number of Christians met for the breaking of bread in the house of W. B. Hargreaves, a devout Christian bank manager.

Later a room was rented, but it was soon crowded out. The provision of a portable wooden building where larger numbers could be accommodated, seemed to be the next step to take, but they were confronted with the difficulty of finding a suitable position for its erection.

John Hambleton, known as the converted actor, was holding successful Gospel meetings in the Town Hall just then, and when the Christians told him of their difficulty, he at once asked them where the land was they thought would be suitable. On being told, John went with them to the place. Arriving there they all knelt down on the ground and asked the Lord to give them the piece of land for His work if it was His will. That prayer was answered and there the work went on for twenty years, during which time many eminent servants of God such as Robert C. Chapman, Henry Groves, Henry Dyer, Henry Moorhouse, George Groves, and others ministered the Word to the edification of the saints and the conversion of sinners.

With the development of the Lord's work and the subsequent increase in numbers there came a need for a larger building, so a piece of ground was secured on the Abbey Road, the principal thoroughfare in Barrow, where the present hall was built. As evidence of the remarkable development of the work begun over sixty years ago, there are now five healthy assemblies in Barrow and district.

CHAPTER XLI

WALNEY

THE testimony at Walney Island, across the river from the parent assembly at Barrow, began in 1904 by gathering together the children of believers living there. Thus a Sunday School was formed, which continued and increased until their meeting-room in a little wooden hut, rented at one shilling a week, was filled. Encouraged by the Sunday School work, Christians living on the island commenced a Gospel effort, but few unsaved could at first be persuaded to venture into "the black hut," the name by which the meeting-place was known. Nevertheless, after-years proved that fruit was gathered. Later, the building being required by the owner for other purposes, the testimony was transferred to the old ferry waiting-room, a place which was none too attractive. At times, the tide could be seen surging through the floor, but it was the only available place within the limited means of those faithful workers.

But brighter days were in store for those who, amid trials and difficulties, had borne the burden for long years. The Lord prospered the work begun in the little wooden hut, and twenty years later the Walney Assembly entered into their own new premises with a Sunday School numbering nearly four hundred children. Surely an indication of the spiritual growth of a testimony upon which God had set His approval.

CHAPTER XLII

LANCASTER

PERIODICAL visits to Kendal in 1876 by Isaac Nelson, a Lancaster printer, led to the formation of an assembly in his native town. On the occasion of these visits, he was invited to attend ministry meetings in the Sand Area Meeting-Room. The truth learned there, led to his publicly confessing the Lord in baptism and to an enquiry along Scriptural lines towards gathering to the Name alone, apart from human systems. Following a prayerful study of the Scriptures, and being fully persuaded that the step he was about to take was in the will of the Lord, Mr. Nelson, along with a few other Christians, came together in the sitting-room of his home, where a table was spread and the symbols partaken of in apostolic simplicity.

Henry Groves, who at that time was resident in Kendal, came over to join the brethren at Lancaster during those early gatherings; and from that time until his Home-call, his honoured name was associated with the assembly's spiritual progress. The character of these gatherings was truly spiritual and edifying. A woman who happened to be present at the meeting, although not one of those who were breaking bread, was saved on the first Lord's Day morning. This happy occurrence was followed by the husband confessing Christ in the evening of the same day during a talk in the home of one of the brethren. A small hall was rented in Church Street, where morning and evening meetings were held with apparent blessing, and as numbers began to increase it was found necessary to remove to a classroom in the Palatine Hall. The well-known evangelists Weaver and Sylvester paid a visit about this time. A wave of blessing attended their activities in the Gospel, which brought much joy and gave a stimulus to the little assembly in seeing souls saved and added to the Church.

Although the assembly continued active in the work, the membership never attained to large proportions owing principally to the fluctuation in the town's industry, consequent upon which there was a constant exodus from the town of those who made up the assembly. For many years after the commencement, the small gathering received much spiritual help and edification by regular pastoral visits from W. H. Hunter, of Manchester, and A. J. Holiday, of Bradford, as well as other esteemed brethren who gave refreshing ministry, and thus contributed to the building up of a testimony for the Lord, which has since been maintained in a commodious hall of their own, situated in a large artisan population.

CHAPTER XLIII

IN WESTMORLAND

In the early 'thirties of last century, a journey of three hundred miles from Devon to the north-west corner of England, over roads which had not up to that time received the patient care and engineering skill of later days, was indeed a formidable undertaking. And yet, incredible though it may seem, in a comparatively short time from the start at Plymouth, brethren were to be found in the town of Kendal in distant Westmorland, assembling themselves together on the first day of the week for the purpose of remembering the Lord in the breaking of bread. While it is generally assumed that the assembly came into being as a result of personal intercourse with early Brethren at the very commencement of the spiritual Movement in the South, yet there appears to be no documentary evidence extant to support this. Who can say but that those believers may have come together solely under the guidance and influence of the Holy Spirit, quite independent of what had already taken place elsewhere.

About this time, or soon afterwards, what was known as the Fell Side Sunday School was started in the poorer part of the town by William Wilson, an influential gentleman of high Christian character, who was greatly respected in Kendal. It was an undenominational school, assisted in later years by teachers from Kendal Assembly, which then had and still has its meeting-place at Sand Area. Under the spiritual care and guidance of Mr. Wilson, the school became a powerful influence in the neighbourhood. Many who in after years went forth to preach the Gospel, were brought to the Lord at those primitive services. As an indication of the large numbers attending the Sunday School, it is stated that at the annual summer outing to Levens Hall, some three or four miles distant, to which place the journey was undertaken by canal boat, there were usually about a thousand passengers, including parents and friends. The present Sunday School at Sand Area was commenced by Thomas Wales, who, along with his wife, afterwards went forth from Kendal to serve the Lord in Demerara.

In reviewing the early days of the Movement, it will have been observed that in the majority of cases—strange though it may appear to readers of the present generation—those early gatherings were for the most part composed of Christians who had formerly been staunch Church members, but had left the denominations because of spiritual convictions as to what should be the true attitude of the child of God in relation to the Scriptural meaning of baptism and the Lord's Supper. While this in a measure appeared also to be the case in the present instance, still it was mainly from the old established body of Quakers in the district that the young assembly was largely built up. The work at Kendal greatly prospered, and before the passage of many years, the meeting was a large and flourishing one. Many of its members belonged to the leading families in the town, and we find the following names well represented: Wakefield, Crewdson, Wilson and Rhodes. The present hall at Kendal was built by Edward Wakefield, a local banker, who also provided halls for Brethren at Bowness-on-Windermere and Keswick.

Among early brethren sometime resident in Kendal, whose names are remembered because of their labours in the Gospel, and in the ministry of the Word in the upbuilding of the assembly, were the brothers Henry and William Dyer, Henry Groves and James Showell. The latter resided there for a number of years. He was well known as an evangelist and pastor, and exercised his gifts in and about the Kendal meeting. On one occasion during special services in the neighbouring town of Bowness-on-Windermere, the attendance was so great that the floor had to be propped up from below, lest it should give way.

"Both Mr. Groves and Mr. Showell used to visit our home at Bowness in my young days," writes Mr. G. N. Birkett, "and I remember them well. Mr. Groves was of the stern 'valiant for the Truth' type, but mellowed much in his later years. Mr. Showell was a very kindly, gracious man. He spent the closing years of his life with his daughter, who married George Brealey of the Blackdown Hill Mission."

In 1868 Henry Groves came to Kendal with the intention of staying for a few weeks, but here he settled, and though for nearly a quarter of a century he continued to travel across the country in the service of the Lord, the secluded town among the hills of Westmorland became his home until, in the summer of 1891, he passed into the presence of the Lord. The story of the early years of Henry Groves teems with exciting episodes, brimful of heroic moments and unparalleled endurance in face of war, famine and flood, the recounting of which reads not unlike highly coloured fiction from the pen of a novelist. He was the eldest son of Anthony Norris Groves, notable as a pioneer missionary, a record of whose life has already been given in a former chapter. Henry was born at Exeter in 1818. At the age of ten, along with a younger brother, he accompanied his parents in the perilous journey to Baghdad, through St. Petersburg and Moscow and the brigand-infested wilds of Southern Russia. The terrible experience of those torturous years in Persia, and particularly the dreadful months the heroic little band of missionaries passed through during their stay in the plague-stricken city, made a lasting impression. So deeply did the experience fix itself upon the boy's mind that in later years Henry pathetically recalled the fact that after leaving England he could not remember ever having been a boy.

Henry Groves and his brother Frank followed their father to India, and joined in a noble effort to establish a self-supporting mission. For some time the venture prospered, but after years of strenuous labour, the father's health broke down, difficulties arose, and despite privation and personal loss the scheme failed and had to be abandoned. But those difficult and trying years were far from barren, for the Lord was truly laying the foundation of a great building, which to-day has left its mark in many parts of India.

In the year 1857 Henry Groves came to Britain and took the opportunity of visiting many assemblies throughout the country. He afterwards crossed to the United States, and the deep impression created in his mind regarding the work of revival which he witnessed in this country, was accentuated by what he saw in America. He now felt on fire for the Master and longed to go forth at His call. In 1863 the way became clear and the step was taken at Bristol. Five years later we find Henry Groves at Kendal. As a teacher and writer, the name of Henry Groves is notably associated with the activities of Brethren during the second half of last century, and he is still remembered as the editor of *The Golden Lamp*, a monthly which had a considerable circulation amongst Brethren. He was also joint editor with Dr. Maclean of *Echoes* in the early years of that missionary journal.

That the Kendal meeting has ever kept before them the importance of the work in the foreign field is strikingly evinced by their splendid record of service. From this assembly eleven have gone forth to many parts of the world, three of whom belong to the medical profession, while one of the number was married to a daughter of Dr. Livingstone and died in Sierra Leone.

Since its birth a hundred years ago, the assembly at Kendal has maintained a steady and consistent testimony. Brethren, many of whom rank amongst our "chief men," have had happy fellowship in the development and furtherance of the Lord's work in this somewhat isolated corner of England. Among those who have enjoyed a life-long association, the name of Theodore Wilson is lovingly remembered. He was a son of William Wilson, one of the founders of this assembly, and during his long and useful life, the welfare and shepherding of the flock to which he was endeared engaged his wholehearted attention up to the time of his Home-call in 1933.

The original Trust Deed drawn up upon the purchase of the property where the neighbouring assembly of Bowness-on-Windermere now worships, is an interesting document, and is worthy of setting down here. It stipulates that those who meet at Bank Terrace Room—the meeting-place of the assembly—shall be:

"Those who are sound in the Faith, proving it by their works. Holding the True Divinity of Our Lord as well as His perfect Manhood and depending wholly upon His Atonement and Intercession for their Salvation. Holding also the True Godhead of the Holy Ghost as distinct yet one with the Father and the need of His Work for the conversion of the Soul to God for sanctification of believers. Holding also the ruin and utter corruption of man by nature through the fall of Adam and especially for the ministry of the Word at which meetings for worship and fellowship shall be permitted in accordance with directions in the twelfth and fourteenth chapters of the Epistle of Paul to the Corinthians for any Christian who can speak to edification of which the body at large shall be the judge as stated in Chapter 14 verse 29 to exercise his gift at suitable times and in the said place for the purpose of preaching the Gospel of the Grace of God by any person approved by the Church."

This Trust Deed, as is usual with legal documents, is without punctuation; hence some tendency to being involved.

The assembly at Bowness-on-Windermere, in the heart of the English Lake District, appears to have commenced shortly after that of Kendal. There are records of a meeting, and a list of the names of those in fellowship, as far back as the year 1836. The meeting took place in a cottage near what was then known as the Bazaar, opposite St. Martin's, the parish church of Windermere. The place of meeting seems later to have been in a house at Low Side, but later still a Dr. Paisley fitted out a room at a small hydro known as "The Douche," on the site now occupied by the town's gas works. Among those in fellowship at this time was John Pattinson, father of the late Mrs. Herd of the Ambleside Assembly.

George Müller was among visitors who had fellowship with the meeting while at "The Douche." About the year 1851, Edward Wakefield, of Kendal, built the hall at present occupied by the assembly, and it was handed over for their use, rent free. There are records about this time of visits by Robert Chapman, of Barnstaple, and of the then well-known evangelist, William Carter, a converted chimney-sweep, when the hall becoming too small a gallery was erected. Some years later, during structural alterations, the gallery was removed; and in this primitive meeting-place, hallowed by memories of other days, the testimony still continues.

CHAPTER XLIV

CARLISLE AND WILLIAM REID

FAMOUS in Border warfare, and for three centuries the habitation of Roman legions keeping ward and watch along the great wall of Hadrian, the historic city of Carlisle, with its ancient cathedral, its decayed abbey and its memories of the prison-house of George Fox the Quaker, has not been without its days of religious glamour and vicissitudes. But we are living in happier times, and gladly we leave the story of those bygone years as a page of history unread, that we may enter upon an era when the light of the Gospel through the liberty of an open Bible became our lasting heritage.

It was to this city, in the year 1867, that a Scottish Presbyterian minister, in the prime of life, came as pastor to the Warwick Road Church. His name was William Reid. In after years he was to become known as the author of that book of intrinsic worth, *The Blood of Jesus*. It was mainly through the faithful preaching of the new minister and his remarkable exposition of the Scriptures that led to the formation of an assembly of believers in Carlisle. At that time the Church was in a struggling condition. Full of zeal, and with a longing for the salvation of souls, Mr. Reid set to work in an endeavour to bring back life to the decaying community. An able exponent of the Word, his powerful preaching and faithful adherence to the fundamentals of the Scriptures not only brought about a revival in their midst, but very soon attracted numbers from other denominations, and there were many remarkable conversions. While some of the Church elders were slow to follow their new minister in his clearly defined line of apostolic teaching, there were those whose spirituality had been thirsting for "the sincere milk of the Word," and their responsive souls readily drank it in.

Nor were his efforts confined to his own Church, for besides preaching in other places of worship in the neigh-

ALEXANDER BAYNE, M.A.

ALEXANDER MARSHALL.

ROBERT FYFE.

J. R. CALDWELL.

Dr. JAMES WARDROP.

bourhood where an open door presented itself, Mr. Reid on several occasions drew large numbers to hear him in the old Wesleyan Chapel where, a century earlier, John Wesley himself preached.

Of a humble and gracious disposition, William Reid ever sought to honour God by his implicit faith, living in sole dependence upon Him, and receiving no fixed stipend from the synod who appointed him. On one occasion having to make a journey by rail to a distant town, he found himself without the necessary means to take him there. Confident that the Lord would not fail him, Mr. Reid made his way to the station, where a friend, unaware of the pastor's immediate need, handed him the requisite amount of his railway fare. This little incident, related to me by an aged brother who as a youth came under the spiritual influence of William Reid, appears to have been typical of the man.

Towards the close of an eight years' ministry at Carlisle, he seemed to have a premonition from the Lord that "his nets were being disturbed," and realising that he could no longer continue, Mr. Reid severed his connection with the Presbyterian Church and associated himself with brethren whose principles he had in recent years so consistently sought to teach in face of prevailing ecclesiastical opposition.

By this time many of Mr. Reid's congregation, enlightened by his teaching, had already left the Church and were meeting in an upper room in the old Y.M.C.A. building, where later their erstwhile pastor came to break bread with them. Among those who left the Presbyterian Church about this time or soon afterwards, was the Carr family. They, along with others, met in a room in Bank Street. Jonathan D. Carr was the founder of Carr & Co., Ltd., biscuit manufacturers of world-wide reputation. Of Quaker stock, and a gentleman of pronounced Christian principles, Mr. Carr was held in high esteem in the city. He continued with the assembly until his death in 1884, when the Bishop of Carlisle, speaking at a meeting in his diocese, paid a high tribute to the memory of Jonathan D. Carr; "but," added the Bishop, "I could never get him to attend any of my services."

With Mr. Carr were his three sons, Henry, Thomas William and James, all of whom were of influence and ability, and in the early years of the assembly, were indeed towers of strength in the building up of the Church.

The assembly very quickly increased in numbers, which necessitated greater accommodation, and from the upper room in Bank Street they removed to the Albert Hall in Chapel Street. The opening was marked by intensive Gospel meetings under the care of James Carr, which resulted in numbers being brought to the Lord. Others were added to the Church, and in 1876 the commodious and well-adapted County Hall became the assembly meeting-place and the scene of many memorable gatherings of the Lord's people.

Of the Carr family, Henry was perhaps the best known because of his manifold activities in the furtherance of the Lord's work. He was ever alive to the needs of the Gospel, not only in Carlisle but in the villages of Cumberland and the adjacent counties, and there were few efforts launched on sound Scriptural lines that did not receive his sympathetic and practical support. But the interests of Henry Carr were numerous, and by the use of Gospel vans, mission tents, village halls and many other ways, he constantly sought to make known the story of salvation. His active association with work in the foreign field, his collaboration with such men as Hudson Taylor and John G. Paton, as well as his interest in the fruitful work through the channel of *Echoes of Service*, in which he took a very real and practical part, are more than a memory. He was also keenly alert as to the value of carrying the Gospel to the homes of those who could not otherwise be reached. In this way, many millions of Gospel tracts and monthlies were scattered by him during the last twenty-five years of his life.

James N. Carr, his younger brother, at this time in the prime of life, was essentially a Gospel preacher, and despite the many calls of a large and growing business he ever found time to go out with the Gospel. He was a familiar figure, and there were few villages in the Border counties where his voice had not been heard proclaiming the "Good News."

CARLISLE AND WILLIAM REID

But he was at his best in the open-air, and could always command an attentive and respectful hearing. At race meetings, fairs and other such public gatherings wherever an opportunity was afforded, James Carr's stentorian voice could be heard warning the unsaved to "flee from the wrath to come." And on not a few occasions, when he warmed to his work, he has been known to throw off his coat and preach in his shirt sleeves.

It was about this time that the great wave of spiritual revival, consequent upon the Moody and Sankey mission, swept over this country. As Germany was caught in the flood-tide of Luther's hymn-singing three centuries earlier, so Britain in like manner took up the strain that the American evangelists had sent forth on the wings of Gospel song. It had its counterpart in the meetings at the County Hall. William Howitt, the leader of praise, knew the value and power of Gospel singing, and was not slow in using the more tuneful members of the assembly as channels of blessing in the work of soul-winning. People were drawn in great numbers to those services, and there were many responsive hearts to the Gospel appeal. And to this day, the memory of those hallowed times in the County Hall are enshrined in a halo of happy song.

In the spring of 1888, a young man, bearing a letter of commendation from the assembly at Merrion Hall, Dublin, came to reside at Carlisle, and the name of James Dawson was placed upon the assembly roll. Full of zeal for the Lord, he proved a keen worker and an effective speaker; and when the assembly moved to the new City Hall he was appointed superintendent of the Sunday School. Thus, for a time, Carlisle became the early training ground of J. C. M. Dawson, who some years later gave up a promising career as a schoolmaster to go forth in dependence upon God, first as a missionary to China and Singapore, afterwards returning to the home country, where as an able teacher and expositor, he was well-known on conference platforms.

Doubtless because of its position as the gateway to Scotland, Carlisle has always been a privileged halting-place, and brethren whose names are notable amongst us have ministered the Word to edification, almost since the inception of the assembly over sixty years ago.

Among the many returned missionaries whose visits have been an inspiration, the names of Frederick S. Arnot and Dan Crawford stand out prominently. And yet, not only the stirring records of such pioneers, but the simple story of those from the obscure corners of the Lord's vineyard in other lands, which moved us then, are sacred memories still.

To those of the present generation the names of Robert Gall, John Graham, John Laing, William A. Moss and Edwin Page are remembered for their long and faithful devotion in the building up and care of the assembly.

The meeting-place of the assembly, to which they removed from the Gospel Hall in 1920, is situated in one of the main arteries of the city, and though for a time after leaving the County Hall the numbers somewhat decreased, there has in recent years been a steady growth. The Lord has prospered His work, and the Hebron Hall with its many activities shares in one of the largest Gospel testimonies in the city.

. . . . . .

In a former chapter the personal testimony of a Christian lady belonging to a Denominational Church, relating to her first visit to a Morning meeting, is given. From some notes before me I take the following testimony, which is worthy of recounting here as it gives in simple yet forceful language the impressions of a visitor to a Gospel Hall.

"Converted in the Church of England and a communicant and worker for five years, it was indeed a great contrast when I paid my first visit to a Brethren Gospel meeting. I was conducted by a friend into a rather bare-looking hall over some stables and reached by a flight of stairs, with a platform at one end and the area occupied by high-backed forms and plain wooden chairs. As I sat at the back of the hall watching the proceedings, my attention was drawn to an inscription in bold letters on the wall behind the platform, which read:

JESUS DIED TO SAVE,

and I wondered why such beautiful words were not placed prominently in churches instead of the Ten Commandments and the Lord's Prayer. Who the preacher was I cannot remember, but the face of one of the friends on the platform particularly attracted me and I felt that here was a brother who could help me in my spiritual life, for although converted I was ever seeking after some deeper experience. One evening I stayed to what was called an 'After Meeting,' and witnessed the salvation of a man convicted of sin during the evening service. It was a revelation to me to see a number of men and women on their knees wrestling with God in prayer over a lost sinner, patiently reading the Scriptures to him and crying to God that he might be brought into the light. As an interested onlooker I marvelled still more when, after perhaps half an hour, the man suddenly rose from his knees and exclaimed, 'I see it now! I see it now! Bless the Lord, I'm saved!' After this all stood and sang with joy and thanksgiving:

> 'I do believe, I will believe,
> That Jesus died for me,
> That on the Cross He shed His blood,
> From sin to set me free.'

"This incident made me ponder, and I saw that here was a place where work for the Lord was being honoured, and I determined to see more of what was being done through this band of wholehearted followers of the Lord Jesus Christ. Soon afterwards an invitation was given me to attend the Breaking of Bread Meeting, quite a new experience to me after years in the Church of England. To my surprise there were no ministers, no priests, no surplices, etc. All the elders were laymen and dressed just like other people. The method adopted of meeting around the Lord's Table to remember His dying love for His children, and the simple service of worship and praise offered to our blessed Lord won my heart. I began to attend every Lord's Day morning. The teaching given at various meetings began to occupy my thoughts. I then learnt what believers' baptism really meant: a confession of faith in the Lord Jesus Christ as

Saviour and Lord, of being dead to self and alive unto Christ, to walk henceforth in newness of life. Subsequently, I was immersed as a believer and became a member of the gathering."

Such personal testimonies, no doubt typical of what is not infrequently met with amongst our gatherings, is indeed refreshing to recall.

PART II
SCOTLAND AND IRELAND

CHAPTER I

ACROSS THE SCOTTISH BORDER

PROUD of her religious liberty, secured by the life-blood of martyrs, the hardy Scottish race from the stormy days of John Knox, the reformer, down through the "killing" covenanting times, reveals a history which is marked by its deep reverence and loyalty to the Bible. And, before the dawn of the present century, there were few homes north of the Tweed where the family did not gather around the fireside as the day closed, for the reading of the Scriptures. The national bard in his epic poem, *The Cottar's Saturday Night*, calls to mind such a picture, where:

"The cheerfu' supper done, wi' serious face
They round the ingle form a circle wide;
The sire turns o'er, wi' patriarchal grace
The big ha'-bible ance his father's pride;
His bonnet rev'rently is laid aside,
His lyart haffets wearing thin and bare;
Those strains that once did sweet in Zion glide—
He wales a portion with judicious care,
And 'Let us worship God!' he says with solemn air."

With the march of time the customs of bygone years are fast passing into disuse, and the sacred heritage of our fathers is, alas, unappropriated and passed by.

In the town of Hamilton, Lanarkshire, somewhere about the year 1843, the minister of the Congregational Church was the means, in God's hands, of a work of grace in the neighbouring town of Wishaw which, though he little realised it, was destined to have far-reaching results. His were not the stereotyped duties of the order so frequently met with in the churches at that time as well as at the present, for John Kirk had cast aside the formalities required of him when "called" to the ministry, and the staid Scots people who attended those services were conscious of a reality in his preaching that did not permit of any of his congregation dropping off to sleep during the sermon. The religious stir created in the town drew large numbers to hear John preach, not a few coming out of curiosity; but some "who came to scoff remained to pray." Familiar though they were with the Bible, they never before had heard its stories unfolded in such a wonderful way, and before the services closed about sixty people had professed faith in Christ. These afterwards formed themselves into a church at Wishaw in connection with that particular "body."

Full of the joy of salvation, and with a sincere desire for instruction and mutual edification, the new converts set about searching and reading the Word together. Thus they were not long in learning that the Church with which they had connected themselves, did not appear to be following the principles laid down in the New Testament. They made this known to their pastor, who endeavoured to dissuade them from holding such unorthodox views; but finding that no words of his could prevail he resorted to preaching against them from the pulpit, which led to several leaving the church. This took place on the 9th of April 1847, and on the following Lord's Day sixteen of them came together for the breaking of bread in a workshop at Newmains. Thus, without the influence of a Darby or a Bellett, and solely through the guidance of the Holy Spirit, the Wishaw Assembly came into being. The little company continued to meet in Loudon's workshop for a few months, afterwards renting what was known as James Watt's Hall.

In the *Church Record* of April, 1847, we find the following entry:

"In much weakness, but in good earnest, we commenced study of the Word of God for our mutual instruction, and soon learned that the Church, in her primitive state, was 'one body,' with Christ the Head, and was known only by His name. This led us to acknowledge no other name but Christ, and to make our only tests of membership, union with Christ and peace with God by faith in Christ, and wherever we found a saved sinner there did we find a fellow-disciple, and members of one body, and therefore resolved to hold fellowship with all such who would hold it with us; and that nothing in the world would separate us from any individual member but the discovery of a want of Christianity in that individual. We also saw that it was the duty of every gifted brother to teach in the church what he believed God had taught him, though he might differ in opinion in some things. This principle obtaining amongst us, we could never think of differing in affection, and in this did we see the beautiful adaptation of New Testament Church order to restore and keep the Church in its primitive unity and purity."

These principles have been recognised and acted upon by the assembly ever since.

It is not to be wondered at that none of those who had taken the courageous step of severing their connection with the Congregational Church, which, but a few years previously, they had mainly been instrumental in forming, had yet learned the truth of believers' baptism. This knowledge was soon to come. Up to then there was much which to them appeared contrary to New Testament teaching. Reared in the religious atmosphere of the Scottish kirk, where the predominating figure was their ordained minister, they had, without question, accepted this time-honoured rule. But now they had been led to see that the Lord, as it had pleased Him, had given gifts to the members of His body which were to be used for its edification; that the Church should edify itself and that no single person possessed all the gifts needed.

In the study of the Scriptures the subject of believers' baptism soon occupied their attention, and on Lord's Day morning, 25th May 1848, four of their number were publicly baptized in the River Calder. This new sect holding such peculiar religious views, so unlike what the staid Scots folk had been accustomed to pursue, came in for some severe criticism and persecution. But despite the onslaught of their erstwhile religious friends, the little company continued to honour God, and not long after the first public testimony in the river, a large crowd gathered on the banks of the Calder to witness the baptism of twenty others at the same place.

For some years afterwards the assembly continued to go on happily, and with the exception of a brief period, when the enemy of the Church crept in and sought to bring about dissensions, a testimony for the Lord has been consistently maintained. The Victoria Hall, the meeting-place of the Wishaw Assembly, was opened on 29th August 1869, and has been the birthplace of hundreds of souls.

John Wardrop, Joseph F. Hyslop, John Loudon, James Loudon, and later William Paterson, Michael Greenshields and James Weir, were closely associated with the spiritual development of the assembly at Wishaw in the early days. Mr. Wardrop's long and faithful service in the welfare of the Church, until his Home-call in 1892 at the advanced age of eighty-three, is remembered with affection. John McAlpine recalling his Sunday School days at Wishaw when Mr. Wardrop was a familiar figure in the town and a warm friend of the young folks, writes: "The vision of the old man with the long white beard presiding at the annual tea-meeting of the children, giving us kindly words of counsel and encouragement, has been indelibly imprinted upon my mind."

James Weir was received into fellowship of the assembly fifty years ago during the memorable revival meetings conducted by Geddes and Holt, the well-known evangelists, when great numbers in the towns and villages of Lanarkshire were saved. From the time of his conversion, Mr. Weir was indefatigable in the work of the Gospel, and continued to take an active interest in the building up of the Church almost up to the time of his Home-call which took place in 1935 at the advanced age of eighty-five.

Thus over those long years a faithful and unbroken testimony has been maintained, and to-day the assembly, with a membership of about two hundred, continues its many activities in the Gospel, forsaking not the assembly of themselves together on the first day of the week to remember the Lord.

KIRKCOWAN

It was in the autumn of 1892 that a few Christian believers first gathered on Scriptural lines at Kirkcowan in Wigtownshire. During the previous winter, Arthur E. Hodgkinson, just home from Canada, conducted a series of meetings in the village Public Hall, when a number were saved and baptized. There being no one to instruct them further in the truths of the New Testament they continued in the kirk.

Among those with a zeal for the Gospel, William Henry is still remembered. For some years he had been preaching in his native village during the summer months and was frequently to be seen holding forth in the open-air, while in the winter he took his place in crowded cottage meetings. There were others like himself eager to study the Scriptures. He therefore invited all those who had a desire for deeper knowledge of the Word of God to meet in his home. Here they learned from the Scriptures that the early disciples "came together to break bread on the first day of the week." With this happy thought revealed to them, those who loved the Lord decided to meet the next Lord's Day according to New Testament teaching. Mr. Henry had a large room in his house which was used in the course of his business as a dressmaker's workroom, so the little company cleared out the sewing machines and other business equipment every Saturday night, to be in readiness for the remembrance feast on the following morning. Here the assembly continued to meet for a few years until their removal to the Public Hall, where they still gather.

CHAPTER II

IN LANARKSHIRE—LARKHALL

IN the mining village of Larkhall, Lanarkshire, about seventy years ago, nine brethren came together to remember the Lord on the first day of the week. They were men in humble circumstances. Just previous to this they had passed through a time of spiritual revival and their hearts were filled with a joy unspeakable in the happy knowledge of untold riches in their new-found Saviour. The changed lives of those men at once manifested the reality of their conversion, a circumstance which set the village talking. With a desire to honour God they sought guidance from His Word, which became, in a very real way, their food and drink. Meeting together in the homes of one another for the study of the Scriptures, with no one save the Holy Spirit to point the way, they soon became conscious of the true meaning of believers' baptism and the Lord's Supper. As these truths were revealed to them, the religious traditions of their forefathers were cast aside that they might in all simplicity follow what was taught in the Word and practised by the early disciples. Thus those brethren, with a loyalty of purpose and fidelity to the principles and methods of the early Church, inaugurated the assembly now meeting at Hebron Hall.

The meeting-place of the infant assembly was in Walker's Hall, where the little company—which included Samuel Chapman, Robert Miller and Tom Brown—were afterwards joined by other Christians. As numbers increased and their influence began to be felt in the town, those who had identified themselves with this peculiar sect became the target of much persecution. But their zeal and loyalty to the Word was proof against the insidious attention of the enemy and they continued in happy unity, their all-absorbing object being faithful obedience to the will of God and the furtherance of His kingdom. Cottage Gospel meetings were held, and many anxious ones were pointed to the Saviour. Bible readings, where the Scriptures were opened up by brethren of spiritual discernment whom God had prepared to feed and tend the flock, were arranged. Thus the newly-formed Church, many of whom were yet babes in the faith, received instruction.

As the assembly grew, it was more than ever realised that their choice of a meeting-place—that of a publican's hall—had not been a happy one, and it was felt that by remaining there in an atmosphere usually polluted by the decaying fumes of strong drink, the testimony would suffer. Some premises in Raplock Street, consisting of a large room and kitchen, became available, and the property was converted into what proved to be a comfortable hall. It was to this hall that Alexander Marshall, in the early days of his pioneer work, frequently came, seeking to help and encourage in the work.

In his interesting story of the Hebron Hall Assembly, Robert Chapman, of Larkhall—to whom the present writer is indebted for much that is set down here—includes the names of a few worthies, trophies of grace, who in their own humble way witnessed for the Saviour who had so wonderfully transformed their lives.

A notable person who paid frequent visits to the village of Larkhall was James Gilchrist, well known as the Chapeltown baker. When the '59 Revival swept across Scotland, Lanarkshire had an abundant share of the blessing, and James Gilchrist, a licensed grocer and publican, was soundly converted. It is said that the morning after his conversion when he entered his public-house, as he often told, "The whisky barrels stared me in the face, and I stood condemned before them." There could be no half measures with James Gilchrist; the barrels were rolled into the street, and the contents poured into the gutter, while the signboard bearing his emblem as a publican was painted black the same day.

"One Sunday morning," writes Mr. Chapman, "James Gilchrist caused some excitement in the neighbourhood. Clad in a black suit of clothes and mounted on his black horse, he bore a banner aloft, on which were displayed the words, 'Prepare to meet thy God.' As he travelled from Chapeltown to Larkhall on his sombre-looking steed, the people living along the route gazed at him with wondering eyes and in solemn silence, while others declared that the Day of Judgment had surely come. Passing over the Avon Bridge and up through Millheugh, the sight of the black figure with the solemn text proved too realistic for a few who were awakened and made to think of these eternal matters in a way they had not done before."

This valiant for the Truth, who in his day was known throughout the shire and was the means of leading many from the paths of sin to the Saviour, was the father of that devoted missionary, Jeanie Gilchrist, who laid down her life in Central Africa.

These were indeed stirring times, when souls were rescued from the power of darkness to come out boldly for the Saviour. A similar case, vividly illustrating the work of grace going on in that district, is that of Daniel Hamilton. He was a publican who, on taking his stand for Christ, promptly emptied his stock of intoxicating liquor into the street and closed his shop. The last time he preached in Frame's Hall, Larkhall, Daniel was then a frail old man with shaking limbs and trembling voice, but his face beamed with a joy which old age had not bedimmed, as he told out of a full heart, of a Saviour he had known and proved for many years.

The reader who has followed the course of these records will at once observe the contrast between what is set down here, and that of the early days of other assemblies, when men of learning and position were more in evidence. Larkhall is a mining community, and though the doings of brethren who took a prominent part in Church affairs may to those of ultra-fastidious taste appear crude and unorthodox, yet those men were none the less faithful to the tenets of the Word, and their lives manifested in a very practical way, the truths they so consistently sought to uphold. The assembly was largely composed of coal miners. Their working hours were long, often toiling underground from early morning till late at night, and during the winter months when the days were short they rarely saw daylight except on Sundays. And yet many of them seldom missed the evening meetings; and during winter when the kitchen meetings were held, the preacher for the night might have been seen hurrying home from the pithead, in time to take his place in those happy, soul-winning gatherings.

The removal of the assembly, in 1872, to Frame's Hall was an eventful occurrence in its history, for it provided greater accommodation for a healthy Church, and having a hall to themselves—a privilege they had not hitherto enjoyed—the liberty of arranging meetings to suit their convenience was a decided acquisition. The advent of a new hall drew considerable numbers to the Gospel meetings, and many were saved, baptized, and received into fellowship. It is of interest to record that open-air meetings commenced at the Cross by this assembly have been continued for over fifty years.

"For a time," writes Mr. Chapman, "the assembly prospered, but, alas, in the midst of peace and blessing a great trial overtook them. It was thirty years before the Darby trouble reached Larkhall. A few left the assembly and commenced a small meeting in Morrison Hall, Raplock Street, in 1874. It is sad to think that lifelong friends in happy Church fellowship should be cut asunder from each other, in some cases for life, because of diversity of opinion and strife arising between two or three persons some hundred miles away. The progress of the assembly was greatly hindered by those seceding from it. It caused much grief and sorrow, sad hearts and broken ties. However, time is a great healer and the bad effects were gradually overcome. Progress was again made in the work of the Gospel, many being saved and added to the assembly."

Thus they were cast upon the Lord in their helplessness. Most of the original members, still living, continued with the assembly, and it seemed hopeful that their influence and personality, with the all-sufficient help of God, would retrieve much that had been lost, and accomplish greater things for Himself. In a measure this was realised, and from the wreckage brought about by the enemy there came into being a healthy and vigorous assembly. In those days baptism received a prominent place in the ministry of the Church, and many were led to see this important truth. Nor were those desirous of obeying the Lord in this ordinance, deterred because of the lack of facilities in the meeting-place at which they were accustomed to attend, for public baptisms in the River Avon were frequent events in the village.

A visit in 1883 by William Montgomery, evangelist, was long remembered. Quite a revival took place when both saint and sinner received blessing. And not only were young converts seeking to be baptized but a few believers who had come into fellowship unbaptized were stirred up to the realisation of a joy which up to that time had not been theirs. One Sunday afternoon fourteen brethren were baptized in the River Avon at Millheugh, when a vast crowd gathered on the bridge and along the banks of the river to witness this unique spectacle. People came from the neighbouring villages, and it is estimated that about two thousand people were present. From that time considerable development has marked the forward movement of the testimony in this Lanarkshire stronghold, a pleasing feature being a progressive work amongst the young, where the register of the joint Sunday Schools contains the names of nearly one thousand children. To-day the Hebron Hall Assembly, Larkhall, with its many activities in the Gospel, is one of the largest in Scotland.

LESMAHAGOW: IN THE EARLY 'SIXTIES

Had a passer-by stopped outside a certain joiner's workshop in a Lanarkshire village one Saturday night in the early 'sixties, and peered through the half-closed window shutters, the glimmering light of an oil lamp burning within would have revealed a scene reminiscent of what is recorded of the first public meeting of Brethren in Dublin thirty years earlier. Charles Millar, the owner of the little workshop, with his wife, had removed some of the stock-in-trade to one side and swept the place, for in the morning a little company would meet together in that humble apartment to remember the Lord for the first time. Those who sat round the table on that occasion were: James Anderson, draper; Gavin Cooper, weaver; and Charles Millar with his wife. They began breaking bread not knowing of any other meeting of the kind but taking the Word of God as their guide, carrying out what they believed to be the will of the Lord. These Christians in the village of Lesmahagow soon learned, however, that there were others like-minded to themselves meeting together in the same way. The powerful influence of the '59 Revival a few years previously, which brought untold blessing in its train, had not yet run its course. Thoughtful Christians were revealing a genuine desire for knowledge which did not appear to be dispensed from the Kirk pulpits. Thus the Bible became a new book, with an attractiveness which made an appeal they had not hitherto experienced.

The little company was soon joined by others which necessitated removal to larger premises, and after meeting in a weaver's shop for a time, the assembly rented an old schoolroom, where better accommodation was afforded for the Gospel. Nor were their efforts in the Gospel confined to the meeting-room, for, despite carefully planned persecution on the part of some prominent business men in the neighbourhood, aided by a rather officious policeman, the band of Christian workers carried on an intensive open-air work in the public square. When later, the authorities interfered by removing them to a position where it was difficult to obtain a hearing, James Anderson closed his draper's shop an hour earlier on Saturday nights and, with the help of others, preached from the doorstep. This opposition instead of damping their ardour had the reverse effect. Thus we find a letter written by Charles Millar to a friend, under date September, 1868, which, in homely language, tells us: "We have had a precious season here of late. The brethren held a camp meeting on Lord's Day, 5th September. The Gospel Hall was filled to overflowing, there being as many as ninety Christians gathered to remember the

Lord. Afterwards an open-air meeting commenced at three o'clock, when the Gospel was preached by brethren, Robert Paterson, John Wardrop and James Stone. There were never fewer than several hundreds anxiously drinking in the truth, and the power of the Lord was present to heal. The evening meeting was to have been held in the hall at six o'clock, but it was impossible to find accommodation for the great numbers who came and a start was again made outside, where the meeting was continued till dark. The Lord was working in our midst. Many, under deep conviction of sin, refused to go home. Anxious ones were led into the hall and pointed to the Saviour."

A time of revival had begun, and for twelve months two evangelists—Pattinson and Henderson—preached every night on the streets or in the hall, where there were many remarkable cases of conversion. But it is not to be supposed that the enemy remained inactive during those days of blessing. This new form of worship, practised by the seceders from the Establishment, ran counter to the high ideals of the Church, whose minister went out of his way to denounce in scathing terms those "Unlearned, ignorant, yet well-meaning baptists." But, writes one of the brethren —and one can visualise the writer of sixty odd years ago as with the zeal of the true soldier-worker he takes up his pen, that he might pass on the latest piece of news to a fellow-believer in some distant parish—"We have not time just now to engage in discussion. Like Nehemiah we are doing a work for the Lord, and we dare not come down to the plains of Ono in case the work should cease. But we will continue preaching and baptizing believers, both men and women, and we consider every immersion the best exposition of the truth of God that all their weak reasoning cannot gainsay nor resist."

The old schoolroom which had been the meeting-place of the Lesmahagow Assembly for a number of years had now become too small and, through the practical interest and good services of James Anderson, a new hall to accommodate three hundred persons was built in 1876. By this time much of the bitter feeling and prejudice towards Brethren, which in former years existed amongst those of the denominations, was gradually breaking down. A testimony such as had been witnessed in their midst was surely an evidence of the Holy Spirit's operation. The principle of welcoming all God's people, notwithstanding their ecclesiastical connection, was acted on and maintained from the first. Thus godly Christians from other places of worship occasionally found their way to the Lord's Table, where they were kindly welcomed. Quite a number received in this way never returned to their former places of worship.

In the early days, those who desired baptism were taken to the River Nethan, which flowed past the village, and in true apostolic fashion publicly confessed their faith in the risen Lord by immersion.

"An outstanding feature of the work of grace at that time," writes John Anderson, who has been actively associated with Lesmahagow Assembly since 1874, "was the remarkable number converted through the instrumentality of Mary Paterson and Mary Hamilton. The Lord used these two unmarried sisters in a wonderful way in leading many precious souls out of darkness into the marvellous light of salvation.

Others greatly used in the gathering in of lost ones were: Robert Paterson, Colin Campbell, Ebenezer Henderson and Arthur Massie.

In gathering information from various sources with the object of tracing the work of the Holy Spirit in the development of the Lord's work in Lanarkshire, I have been struck by the amazing amount of evidence produced, showing how the Lord used those godly women in pointing men and women to the Saviour.

After the opening of the new hall, the Sunday School grew rapidly, and at one time there were four hundred names on the register with a staff of thirty-six teachers. Nor were the needs of the young believers neglected. During the week a special meeting was held for their instruction in the Scriptures, so that the young might be fitted to take their place in the activities of the assembly. This seemed to manifest itself in a very practical way. About this time

Lesmahagow was a village with a population of one thousand four hundred, adjacent to which were ten other villages forming one extensive parish. Thus, from Lesmahagow workers went out to the villages with the Gospel, which resulted in assemblies being formed at Ponfeigh, Kirkmuirhill and Coalburn. In recent years owing to trade depression and adverse industrial circumstances, numbers have left the district to seek employment elsewhere. In consequence of this compulsory exodus the assembly has suffered considerably in numbers but the testimony continues.

GLENBUCK

It must have been about this time that a party of Brethren from Lesmahagow journeyed over to the village of Glenbuck on Sunday afternoons to preach the Gospel in the open-air. The meetings were continued during the summer months, and although it is not known whether anyone was saved during those weekly excursions, nevertheless this effort to spread the Good News in a district where there was very little Gospel testimony, was the first link in the chain which led up to the formation of the present assembly in that place.

Some years later the Ayrshire tent was pitched in Glenbuck by William Lindsay and William Hamilton, which resulted in considerable numbers being brought into the Kingdom. There was at that time an assembly of believers in the neighbouring village of Muirkirk, and many of the converts joined them and had fellowship there for some time. As the way opened up a hall was built at Glenbuck, and with the assistance and fellowship of the Muirkirk Brethren, an assembly was formed which to-day maintains a faithful testimony for the Lord.

LEADHILLS

From Lesmahagow the Gospel was carried by a few brethren to Leadhills, on the border of Lanarkshire, notable

IN LANARKSHIRE

as being the highest village in Scotland. That was just sixty years ago, when there was at that time very little real Gospel testimony in the neighbourhood. This intrusion upon the sacred precincts of the Establishment by a number of strangers, having what were considered to be very peculiar religious views, was hotly resented by the villagers, at whose hands the visitors received a storm of opposition and were stoned whenever they attempted to preach in the streets. But the seed was sown. A few Christians stood by those who had dared to carry the Gospel into the enemy's camp. One man who found peace confessed the Lord in baptism. Soon afterwards a few others were led into the light of Scriptural truth and began to break bread in the house of a brother. Thus was laid the foundation of an assembly: a testimony for the Lord, whose light, through times of stress and difficulty, has been kept burning for more than half a century in that remote Lanarkshire village.

MOTHERWELL

The origin of the testimony at Motherwell dates back to the beginning of the 'seventies when a few Christians met to break bread in the home of Hope Vere Anderson. A removal to larger premises soon became necessary, and a room —used on weekdays as an infant school—was granted for use on Lord's Days by the proprietor of the collieries. It was actually a two-apartment miner's house with partition removed to make a single room. In the Motherwell Almanac of that period intimation was made that: "The Christian Brethren meet at Number 17 Watsonville Rows, to eat the Lord's Supper, for mutual comfort and edification and for Scriptural exhortation." It was further mentioned that a Sunday School was held every Lord's Day, and parents were invited to send their children.

Mr. Anderson, upon whom mainly fell the responsibility of ministering to the spiritual needs of the company of believers, proved himself to be a faithful pastor. He had in association with him Henry Close, in business in the town as a joiner, and James Muir, a coal miner: men of Christian character and integrity.

There were limitations in the use of the schoolroom, and the worshippers increasing in number it was felt that a better meeting-place was desirable and necessary. The present hall, with accommodation for three hundred and fifty persons, was therefore built and opened in September, 1874. It was indeed a great venture of faith for those early brethren, but it showed remarkable foresight in building a comparatively large hall on the edge of some fields with few dwellings beyond it. It is true that the estate management showed plans of development in buildings and streets, but such development seemed unlikely at the time. However, the plans materialised in course of years, and the Roman Road Hall, as it is called, now stands in the midst of a good working-class population, from which the Sunday School children are mainly drawn. This work has been specially owned of God to the increase and upbuilding of the assembly, many of the present elders having passed through the Sunday School and Bible Class in their young life.

Numbers in the assembly continued to increase, and in 1909 there were three hundred and fifty-six in fellowship. As the town was extending and many of the believers, principally in the south part, were living at a distance from the hall, it was decided that another testimony should be raised. Therefore, in April, 1909, the Shields Road Hall was opened, nearly ninety going from the parent meeting, which had agreed to bear a share towards the cost of the building. This assembly has also prospered and increased. "The blank made by this number leaving for Shields Road," writes Mr. Robert Morton, who was actively associated with the assembly for many years, "was in a good measure made up, rising to upwards of three hundred. During the rush of American emigration, between eighty and ninety left for the United States and elsewhere, but despite this there are at the present time over two hundred and seventy in fellowship."

A few years ago some families left to form the nucleus of an assembly at Carfin—two miles distant—augmented by

Christians from New Stevenston and Newarthill. The work here began with a Sunday School carried on by Roman Road Hall at the mining village of Ravenscraig, two miles away. The village became derelict and the school was transferred to the care of Carfin Assembly. "To meet the need of school and other service," continues Mr. Morton, "a hall was built at Forgewood in 1936. This was done by voluntary labour. Plans were prepared by a young architect in the assembly, work of erecting done by the Christians, helped greatly by others from neighbouring assemblies; while tradesmen friends not associated with us as a community also gave kindly assistance."

A Sunday School of between three and four hundred children is a sure indication of a healthy and prosperous assembly. This is eloquently exemplified in the assembly at Roman Road Hall, Motherwell, and is emphasised by the practical interest taken in the Lord's work in other lands. The assembly is represented by Joseph Adam, Denmark; Robert McCrory, U.S.A. and Canada; John Rankin, West Indies; Mrs. McPhie, Angola; Mrs. Ed. Buchanan, India; and Duncan M. Reid, San Domingo.

The early brethren have long since gone to their reward, yet the Lord has now, as in the past, raised up men to care for and lead the saints in the ways of Christ, and to carry out the order of the Holy Scriptures in the Church.

CHAPTER III

EARLY DAYS IN AYRSHIRE

When the spiritual Movement reached Scotland, and a standard was unfurled in a Lanarkshire village in 1843, its progress across the country does not appear to have been rapid. The staid Scots folk with characteristic caution were slow to set their hand to a new doctrine which, on the surface, did not exactly coincide with their religious principles. To them the kirk, with its dominant ties of religion and tradition, was indeed part of their everyday life. It was not, therefore, till somewhere about the year 1864, that the influence of this spiritual awakening made itself known in the neighbouring shire, where a testimony was commenced in the town of Ayr. In the same year an assembly was formed at Dalry. From that time the power of the Holy Spirit became manifest in a very pronounced way. In less than ten years there were no fewer than twelve assemblies established in Ayrshire,[1] among the earliest being the gatherings at Kilmarnock and Irvine.

At Dalry the testimony commenced in a house in Garnock Street, the home of Samuel Dodds, a North of Ireland man, who had come to Dalry as Free Church Missionary for the district. Possessing a well-equipped knowledge of the Scriptures, Mr. Dodds did not long continue with the Free Church, for he realised that God was pointing him to paths along which He would have him direct his footsteps. A circumstance which first aroused him to a sense that continuing in his present position must be displeasing to God, was the large number of unconverted Church members who were received to the Lord's Table. With a consistence which was characteristic of the man, he visited those who were about to be received as communicants. Knowing them to be unconverted, he took with him the message of salvation,

[1] At the present time there are fifty-seven assemblies in Ayrshire.

EARLY DAYS IN AYRSHIRE

warning them of the judgment passed by God upon those who unworthily partook of the bread and wine. Though blind, he was a man of remarkable energy and influence, and was endowed with gifts which marked him out both as a preacher of the Gospel and an expositor of the Word. He had received a fairly good education and was a fluent and sympathetic reader, which revealed to the listener his sincerity of purpose, as his fingers silently moved over the Braille type of his Bible.

With a view to encouraging his less fortunate brethren in the study of the Scriptures, he held Bible readings in his own home, which led up to the formation of an assembly. It was about this time that another North of Ireland young man came to Dalry as district missionary and found lodging at the house of Mr. Dodds. His name was William Thomson. The two being of like mind, and having a heart for the work, which they felt had been planned by the Lord, it was not long before the new arrival threw in his lot with Mr. Dodds. They laboured together in happy fellowship seeking to build up the newly-formed Church and to carry the Gospel to the outlying districts. Mr. Thomson afterwards went out evangelising, and for many years his name as a faithful soul-winner was well-known throughout the South of Scotland.

The missionary duties of Samuel Dodds, when he was associated with the Free Church, were to visit and preach in the surrounding villages and farmhouses. This he continued to do almost up to the time of his Home-call, which came in 1931, at the advanced age of ninety-six. His natural infirmity of blindness was no deterrent when it came to visiting the sick in the homes of the poor, for Samuel could make his pastoral calls at almost any time and under conditions which might otherwise have been embarrassing, without the least fear of perturbing the good housewife, who might at the time of his visitation be in the midst of her domestic duties.

Among visiting brethren who gave help in the early days of Dalry Assembly, and whose names are familiar as pioneers and exponents of the Word, are: Jeremiah Meneely, John

G. McVicar and William Lindsay. The latter witnessed throughout the West of Scotland and far beyond for over fifty years without a break. He eventually made his home at the Ayrshire town of Prestwick. The assembly for the most part consisted of brethren of the mining class, whose energies in the Gospel were not confined to regularly appointed services, but where opportunity was afforded, many of them were to be found holding kitchen meetings or proclaiming the Gospel in the neighbouring villages.

"In those days," writes Mr. George Campbell, who has been actively associated with the assembly for over fifty years, "it was more a time of sowing than reaping, although there were quite a number of outstanding conversions; and thus the assembly was built up. When I arrived at Dalry in 1880—not out of my teens—the assembly was meeting in a room in Vennell Street known as the Pique Shop." The meeting afterwards removed to various parts of the town as the work among the young increased, until in 1911, the present hall, with a seating capacity of about three hundred, was built.

TROON AND PETER HYND

At Troon the assembly had its inception through the visit of two Glasgow business men. William Caldwell (father of J. R. Caldwell) and Thomas Cochrane were in the habit of spending their summer holidays at this Ayrshire seaside town. There being no assembly of believers, the two brethren met each Lord's Day morning in the house of Miss Pearson, a Christian lady, for the purpose of breaking bread. And as the three sat round the table and passed the sacred emblems to one another, they realised, as never before, the sweetness of His promise: "Where two or three are gathered together in My name, there am I in the midst of them." From this obscure beginning an assembly came into being which steadily increased in numbers until about the year 1872, a small cottage in Academy Street was acquired and altered to serve the purpose of a meeting-room. In

EARLY DAYS IN AYRSHIRE

that place the testimony was continued for a number of years.

Bethany Hall, the place where the assembly now meet, was at one time a church, and subsequently a public hall, but through the interposition of God, at a time when the assembly's need for greater accommodation was pressing, the property passed into their hands. At that time other arrangements were in progress, and indeed plans had been prepared for a new building. But difficulties arose, and in the end it was clearly seen that the Lord's hand was in this, as the public hall came into the market and it was found possible to procure it at a very reasonable figure. The central position of the hall in one of the main streets of the town, affords every facility for the furtherance of the Lord's work in a healthy assembly, which had its beginning in circumstances so far removed from the activities which now happily exist.

It was at the town of Troon that John Ritchie, founder and editor of *The Believer's Magazine*, spent the closing years of a long and devoted life, the greater part of which was spent strenuously upholding the principles of Truth, both by pen and speech, while building up the publishing business at Kilmarnock which still bears his name. He was laid to rest there on 22nd March 1930, by the side of his wife, who predeceased him. His eldest son, John, spent about twenty years at Troon and gave much help in the assembly.

One is apt, in the recording of an assembly's activities, to unwittingly pass by those who avoid the public glare, but are, nevertheless, as truly "chief men" as those whose names are written large in the annals of Church history. There are in every assembly many of such: faithful men and women whose names and works are known only to the local assembly to which they belong, and to the One they lovingly serve. Harry Adams, one of the oldest members in Troon Assembly, first broke bread over sixty years ago. Keenly interested in the young, he was for over forty years actively associated with the Sunday School.

The brother most prominently identified with the Movement from the early days at Troon was Peter Hynd, one whose name was known throughout Ayrshire and over a much wider area. An able and gifted teacher, he was happiest when ministering to the Lord's people, whether on a conference platform or to believers meeting around the Lord's Table in some out-of-the-way assembly. He was a tower of strength in the Troon Assembly, whom he tended with the sympathetic care and watchful eye of the shepherd; and though located there, yet his energies sought a more extensive field. In the difficult days of the 'seventies, when small and struggling assemblies were to be revived and strengthened, and when new meetings were springing up in various parts of the shire, it was then that his wise counsel was sought and the voice of the true shepherd heard among those primitive gatherings.

Of his power as a minister of the Word a close friend of Mr. Hynd gives in a few well-chosen words a true pen-picture, which recalls to our mind the once familiar voice: "Peter Hynd had a quiet style of ministry; but as he had always 'something to say,' he commanded attention. His matter was always interesting, and it was always given out in an orderly way that unfolded itself much in the same way as a panorama passes before the eye. He proceeded on the principle of 'line upon line, precept upon precept.' A wonderful amount of instruction was conveyed, even in a single address. His subjects took a wide range, according to the known need of the place he was visiting, or the burden of some particular line of truth upon his own spirit." Mr. Hynd stood out boldly for the Truth, and when, during a critical period, the enemy of the Church sought to bring about dissension, his firm yet tactful handling of a difficult position effectively succeeded in thwarting the evil designs of the aggressor. He was a strong advocate for the great principle that all children of God are "one in Christ Jesus," and that we should recognise a believer, not because he belongs to a particular assembly or church body but because he belongs to Christ.

The passing of Peter Hynd of Troon to his heavenly rest, in January, 1904, removed an outstanding personality amongst Brethren—a man of wide sympathies and great toleration for those with whom he might differ on minor points.

A few Christians met in Loan Hall, Stevenston, Ayrshire, for Bible readings, about the year 1870. Soon afterwards, an assembly was formed, among those who first came together being: Thomas Hynd, father of Peter Hynd of Troon; Alex. Park and Henry Hynd, who later went out to serve the Lord in Africa.

KILMARNOCK AND JOHN RITCHIE

The testimony at Kilmarnock commenced about seventy years ago. John Stewart, a prominent business gentleman in the town, began breaking bread with a few others in a small hall erected and maintained by him in Nelson Street. To this meeting the saintly John Dickie, of Irvine, who lived in the town from 1858 to 1878, often resorted, and here he ministered to the young assembly, exercising with power and unction the spiritual gifts with which God had so richly endowed him.

The outstanding personality of Mr. Stewart as a Christian, together with the tender and gracious disposition of Mr. Dickie — surely a beautiful combination — largely contributed to the blessing which attended the early years of those gatherings. Ever kind and ready to help the poor and needy, Mr. Stewart had many interests towards their welfare both in soul and body. Thus his association with the noble work of the Ashley Down Orphanage brought him in close touch with George Müller who, on several occasions, along with his wife, broke bread at those little gatherings.

The meeting begun and continued in the hall in Nelson Street, though full of spiritual enthusiasm for the Master, did not exactly observe what we now know to be the true Scriptural principles. Still, those were times when there were fewer privileges of sitting under sound doctrinal teaching such as we enjoy to-day; besides, those believers were faithful to the Truth in so far as they had received light through the Scriptures. They realised their rightful place at the Lord's Table outside the denominations, believing that God would guide them into paths well pleasing and honouring to Him. It was given to Hugh Lauder to shepherd the young assembly at a time when the flock was seeking spiritual nourishment in unfenced pastures. Indeed, it was mainly through his wise counsel and discernment that the assembly life in Kilmarnock began to take shape.

From what can be gathered, the history of Kilmarnock does not appear to claim distinction because of outstanding events in the building up of this Ayrshire stronghold of Brethren, but rather on account of its associations with not a few stalwarts of the Faith, who in their day and generation added their quota to the spiritual structure and passed on. Thus we find that among the first places visited by Alexander Marshall, soon after being commended to the Lord for the work in the Gospel, was Kilmarnock. This was in the year 1876, when the future pioneer-evangelist, whose name among Brethren is a household word, was just twenty-nine years of age. His untiring zeal in the Lord's work and his deep concern for the souls of the perishing, which characterised Mr. Marshall to the closing days of his long and useful life, had its early manifestation at that time. Large numbers were drawn to hear the Gospel, and many were added to the Church.

Three years later — in 1879 — there came to the town another young man whose name, because of his manifold works, will always be linked with the place of his adoption and the scene of his life labours. His arrival followed a time of spiritual blessing, when a great ingathering of souls had taken place under the preaching of Rice T. Hopkins and Alexander Marshall. Thus John Ritchie came at a time when his youthful zeal and gift received an impetus for the work of the Lord which the passage of years did not impair.

As the names of John Ritchie and Kilmarnock have almost become a synonymous term, it is fitting that a brief sketch of his life work be given here. Born in the village of Meldrum, Aberdeenshire, in 1853, he was reared in a typically Scots

DONALD MUNRO.

DONALD ROSS.

WILLIAM MACKENZIE.

ALEXANDER STEWART.

religious atmosphere. The Free Church of Scotland, which John attended as a lad, had for its minister a sincere believer in the "new birth"; thus he had the inestimable advantage of hearing the Gospel story from his earliest years. This made a lasting impression. When he was eighteen his employment took him to Inverurie. Donald Munro was conducting Gospel meetings in the town at that time, and though there was tremendous opposition, crowds flocked to hear the preacher. There was evident manifestation of the Holy Spirit working mightily, and in one week about twenty young men and women confessed faith in Christ—among them was John Ritchie.

At the close of the mission and the departure of the evangelist, the young converts returned to the ministrations of the pulpit, but feeling the dearth of Christian fellowship and the utter absence of spiritual food they resolved to come together for mutual edification in the study of the Scriptures. It was not long before there was revealed to them the teaching and practices of the early believers, showing the path God would have them follow. In the neighbouring village of Old Rayne, Donald Ross was meeting with a few others to remember the Lord. Hearing of this, several of the young converts walked over on a Lord's Day morning and joined the little company around the Lord's Table. And so it came about that soon afterwards they publicly obeyed the Lord in baptism, and commenced breaking bread in the simple manner which had just been revealed to them. This marked the starting point in a life henceforth devoted to the work of the Lord. Beginning in a quiet way to witness for his Master at kitchen meetings and in barns, it soon became evident that the young grocer's assistant was endowed with the gift of the evangelist. Thus John Ritchie "increased the more in strength," until through his powerful and fruit-bearing preaching he was called to wider spheres of labour.

"In the years of young manhood," writes a brother who lived in close touch with Mr. Ritchie, "the preaching of the Gospel was his forte, and there were few who excelled him in holding the attention of an audience by his incisive presentation of the foundation truths of the Faith, illuminated as his addresses were by striking phrase, illustrated by telling incidents, interspersed by frequent flashes of homely humour and yet always thrusting for the consciences of the hearers. ... His avidity for the Word of God, his wonderfully retentive memory, his fluent and flaming appeals to the consciences of his hearers, his indomitable zeal in the service of his Master, combined to mark him out as a 'vessel unto honour.'" As he launched further into the work, he began to realise that material duties which were now hampering the claims of spiritual activity would have to be relinquished, and receiving the wholehearted fellowship of his brethren, John Ritchie gave himself entirely to the service of the Lord.

His arrival in Kilmarnock opened out an altogether new sphere of labour, for it was revealed that he had the pen of a ready writer; and from small beginnings in the little home, where the editor acted as his own clerk and packer, there went forth the first copy of the *Young Watchman*, to be followed at a later period by *The Sunday School Workers' Magazine*, *The Little Ones' Treasury* and *The Believer's Magazine*, the latter being edited by Mr. Ritchie for the long period of thirty-seven years. He was a prolific writer, and besides successfully conducting his various monthlies, his fertile mind produced over two hundred volumes and booklets in addition to hundreds of tracts. His more ambitious writings, such as *The Tabernacle*, *Egypt to Canaan* and *Foundation Truths*, have run into many editions, and have been translated into various Continental languages.

In the midst of the rapidly increasing work of writing and publishing, he still found opportunity to give freely of his time in ministering to the people of God, not only in his home assembly at Kilmarnock, but in many parts of the country where he was a familiar platform speaker at conferences.

Mr. Ritchie was succeeded as editor of *The Believer's Magazine* by J. Charlton Steen, at whose Home-call, after a comparatively brief term of office, the reins were taken up by William Hoste, B.A., of London.

A Biblical expositor of rare ability, William Hoste takes a prominent place amongst Brethren. He was the son of General D. E. Hoste, C.B., whose residence during the boyhood of William was Dover Castle, an ancient stronghold dating back to Saxon times. Educated at Clifton College, Mr. Hoste proceeded to Cambridge University, where, under the direction of Dr. Handley Moule, he took a theological course with the intention of entering the ministry of the Church of England. When, however, the time drew near for his ordination, the young student found himself unable on conscientious grounds to subscribe to the doctrinal formulas.

"From his studies in the Holy Scriptures," writes A. W. Phillips in *A Brief Life Sketch of William Hoste, B.A.*, "he was convinced that the Church of England was in grievous error on such matters as baptismal regeneration, episcopacy, apostolic succession, and the whole conception of the 'clergy' as a class among God's people distinct from the less privileged 'laity.'"

He had arrived at the crisis of his career; but his mind was made up, and at the sacrifice of earthly prospects, valued friendships and present gain, he determined to abandon all thoughts of ordination. Thus he left Cambridge to enter on a pathway of service, depending on the never-failing guidance of the Lord. Soon after leaving the Church of England, it was his joy and privilege to be baptized by immersion and to identify himself with assemblies gathered only to the name of the Lord Jesus Christ.

Eager to serve the Master in the Gospel, the thoughts of Mr. Hoste were directed across the Channel, where he would be able to utilise his excellent knowledge of European languages; and he spent several years in evangelical work in France, Italy and other Roman Catholic countries. Mr. Hoste's interest in missionary work led him to undertake extensive tours in India and other countries for the encouragement of workers. He also made two journeys to Central Africa in days when travel in that dark continent was attended by dangers and discomforts almost unknown to-day. It was, however, as a teacher and expositor of the Holy

Scriptures that William Hoste excelled; and as editor of *The Believer's Magazine*—a position he ably filled for several years—he found abundant scope for his prolific pen in the exercise of his singular gifts. Mr. Hoste was called Home in the Spring of 1938.

With this digression we return to Kilmarnock. This Ayrshire town was also the home of William J. Grant, M.A., whose name is still remembered and revered amongst Brethren throughout the British Isles. He was a Baptist pastor in the town, but owing to his loyalty to the principles of Scripture his position became untenable, and eventually led him to give up his ministerial calling that he might be identified with the local assembly of believers. Of a gentle and kindly disposition, he was also a man of devout character and an able preacher and expositor of the Word.

In the early days, after a period in the Temperance Halls, the assembly gathered in various meeting-places, the most outstanding being the Wellington Hall, where there were over four hundred believers in fellowship. In recent years as the work developed, the Elim Hall and later the Central Hall were built, where the testimony continues.

IRVINE AND JOHN DICKIE

In a former chapter it is stated that Dalry Assembly was thought to be the first to be formed in Ayrshire. It has since been discovered that previous to that time, five believers were breaking bread at Irvine, in the sitting-room of a dwelling-house situated a few yards from the site of the present assembly hall. This was about the year 1860. Those present were James Holmes and his brother Alexander, with their wives, and James Watson. When it became known that meetings to celebrate the Lord's Supper, without the presence of an ordained minister, were being held in a private house during the hour of Church service, there was much opposition, and those who attended became the objects of bitter persecution. Notwithstanding such provocative attentions the little company continued, happy in the thought of a Father's smile upon His obedient children. As the object of their coming together became known others were added, among them David Gibson, a man endowed with the boldness of Peter and the tenderness of John. He, along with James Holmes, became intensely concerned about the souls of the unconverted, and the two made regular excursions to the neighbouring parishes, preaching in the open-air and visiting the cottagers in their homes. David was a noted character and rarely missed an opportunity of testifying for the Master, frequently accosting passers-by with a searching enquiry as to their eternal welfare.

The first hall occupied by the young assembly at Irvine, not unlike many of such before and since that time, was to be found through the proverbial close and up a stair in High Street. "I can remember as a small boy," writes Alexander Wilson, who is still in fellowship at Irvine, "being taken by my mother, who was in fellowship, to a small hall rented by the Brethren, known as Boyd's Hall. That would be about the year 1871. The company by that time had increased, there being among them men whom God had raised up and whose power and influence in the Gospel was a living reality, not only in the town of Irvine but in the outlying districts of the shire, where they went preaching the Word."

About this time there came into the district a young man who entered wholeheartedly into the work of the Lord. His name was Robert Campbell. He had been associated with a little company of believers in Glengyron, and had also been instrumental in forming an assembly which first met in his home at Auchinleck. His coming gave an impetus to the growing assembly, who at that time were featuring aggressively in Gospel work. Boyd's Hall had now become too small to accommodate the numbers who were drawn to those services, and the Templars' Hall was hired.

The Lord's hand was manifestly with them, so that by

the year 1894 the believers set out on a big scheme of faith—to build a hall of their own. The assembly at that time consisted mainly of working-class people, but in a comparatively short time the present substantial building, known as Waterside Hall, was completed, and has since been the birthplace of hundreds of souls. The opening of the new hall marked the beginning of a steady development of spiritual activity, the work among the young receiving particular attention. Kitchen meetings and open-air services were notable features; and there are still those who retain happy memories of the days when John Houston, at the head of the popular marches through the streets, led the singing of the old-time Sankey hymns. God honoured the faithful testimony of those days, the fruits of which still remain. Nor has the spiritual interest of the assembly diminished, for during the past few years the number in fellowship has been considerably over two hundred, and the Lord has graciously raised up a number of gifted brethren whose ministry has been blessed not only in the local assembly but elsewhere.

The name of John Dickie, of Irvine, is so well known that it seems fitting that a brief record of this saintly man should be given here. Of a sensitive and retiring temperament, accentuated by a delicate constitution, his early years, spent at this invigorating seaport town on the Firth of Clyde, seemed to share little of the brightness known to youth; and the leisure hours which might have been spent in healthful bodily exercise, found him poring over his books in laborious study. In this pursuit he made rapid progress, and in the year 1841, when just eighteen, the lad entered Glasgow University. Soon after entering upon his scholastic career, he became deeply disturbed and concerned about the hopelessness of his spiritual condition before God. This led him to the only Source of peace and lasting happiness, and the great crisis in the life of John Dickie had its consummation in a complete surrender of soul and body to the Lord.

His desires were set upon becoming a minister of the Gospel, and with this in view he entered the Divinity Hall; but before completing his theological course, the young

EARLY DAYS IN AYRSHIRE

student had a serious breakdown in health, which gave rise to grave fears of a premature close to a promising life. Dispirited and depressed, and yet not without a ray of hope that the Lord would yet use this frail form, he returned to the more friendly air of his native Irvine.

Instead of being revived in body he slowly became worse, and for a long period his voice, consequent upon the harassing chest trouble, completely failed, so that he was unable to converse with his friends except by means of the dumb alphabet. A visit to London to consult a distinguished specialist gave no hope of his recovery. "Turning his back on the capital," says the writer of a brief record of John Dickie, "he said to himself: 'If it is God's will, notwithstanding this verdict, I shall survive; if not, His will be done.' Studying his own constitution, he adopted a system of dietetics which he believed suitable, and lived a life of extreme abstemiousness. This treatment was doubtless the means of prolonging a singularly useful life for a period of over forty years. His health improved considerably, and for several years he found a sphere of much usefulness as a missionary in his native town."

As has already been stated, John Dickie removed to Kilmarnock, where he resided for about twenty years, during which trying period he was rarely free from physical weakness and disability. And yet, despite his infirmity, he was seldom idle, going about ministering to the sick and needy in their homes, as well as carrying the Gospel to the haunts of the ungodly, where his labours were honoured in the conversion, among others, of a notorious drunkard named Philip Sharkey, whose subsequent life and testimony in the town was a remarkable triumph of the Gospel. It was at Kilmarnock that most of his hymns and poems were written; a particular ministry which has proved a channel of blessing and a means of comfort to many.

In the year 1878 Mr. Dickie returned to his native town of Irvine, where he resided until his Home-call in 1891. For a few brief years, though in great physical weakness he sought in a quiet way to serve the Lord as his failing health permitted, his habit being to rise at four o'clock in the morning that he might commence the day with prayer and meditation on the Scriptures. Four years later, the little strength left in the frail body gave way, and the brain which had outrun an overtaxed constitution, was threatened with a severe form of nervous irritation. This mental distress necessitated the invalid remaining in the loneliness of his room, and seeing only those who ministered to him in his affliction. It was during this "shut in" period that the greater number of his letters were written, which afterwards appeared in two volumes under the title, *Words of Faith, Hope and Love*.

VILLAGES IN AYRSHIRE

In the gathering together of notes relative not only to the early days of the Movement, but to more recent times, it is intensely interesting and invigorating to the soul to glance back over the years, and all unconsciously breathe again the spiritual atmosphere of those days. In our search for material in an endeavour to place on record a faithful, unvarnished story of the humble beginnings of many of our assemblies, not infrequently there comes by mail, conveyed in a letter from some unknown correspondent, just that homely touch which is ever pregnant with a multitude of hallowed memories. From Maryfield, in far-away Saskatchewan, Canada, where there are seventeen in the little meeting, and distant by two hundred miles from the city of Regina, the nearest assembly, comes this homely note: "Just after our family reading this morning," says the writer, "I picked up one of our monthlies sent from the homeland, and noticed the few lines concerning the assembly at Catrine in Ayrshire. Immediately my mind was flooded with memories of long ago, for I spent my boyhood days in the old village. My parents moved there from Auchinleck when I was quite young. That would be about the year 1886, and I believe it was then that the assembly at Catrine was started. My father, the late John Hogg, along with a dear brother of the name of James Young, and an old lady whom we knew as Granny Clark, were the three who first came together to remember the Lord. The meeting was held in a side room of the Wilson Hall and afterwards in a hall in Wood Street, or rather behind the street, as we had to go through a close to get there. Though I was a very small boy I well remember going regularly with my parents, my father taking my hand all the way there and back." The writer mentions several names of those who afterwards joined the little company; tells in homely language how the Lord blessed the humble testimony; of the help and encouragement received from the assemblies in Ballochmyle, Auchinleck and Old Cumnock; and wonders whether after all those years there are any of the same name—related to those he mentions—in the assembly to-day. The writer informs us, too, with a touch of tender affection and unconcealed pride, how that his mother was used through the Spirit of God in leading a neighbour of the name of Mrs. Campbell to the Saviour. He is reminded of this event by a brief note in the same paper recording the Home-call of the sister referred to. Our correspondent also recalls a visit of Dan Crawford to Catrine, and later James Anton—the latter having a connection with the village—previous to their going forth as missionaries to Central Africa. And so from a Scottish emigrant in an isolated settlement in Canada, I learned how and when an assembly in Ayrshire was formed half a century ago.

As has already been stated, there are at the present time fifty-seven assemblies of the Lord's people known as Open Brethren in Ayrshire, the following being a list given in chronological order of those commenced over fifty years ago. In a few cases, where no records have been preserved, the dates are approximate:

Irvine	commenced about	1860
Ayr	,,	1864
Dalry	,,	1870
Kilmarnock	,,	1870 or earlier.
Galston	,,	about 1872
Auchinleck	,,	about 1872 or soon after.

Prestwick	commenced	1877
Kilwinning	,,	about 1875
Hurlford	,,	1877
Newmilns	,,	1878
Darvel	,,	1880
Plann	,,	1880

Each assembly has its own particular story to tell; its times of sowing and reaping; its trials and triumphs; its seasons of spiritual blessing; its joys and sorrows. It is not, however, the purpose of this book to give a record of every assembly: the exigencies of time and limitations of space at our disposal at once preclude such indulgence, interesting and edifying though it may prove to be. We will, therefore, proceed on our journey to other Scottish shires after a short visit to the Ayrshire villages of Kilbirnie and Annbank.

Of the latter assembly there is little of special note to record, other than what one may expect to find in the upbuilding of the average Church, which dates its birth from small and insignificant beginnings in far-off and almost forgotten times. And it is not improbable that Annbank, a village lying between Ayr and Mauchline, would have been passed by with but a casual reference, but for a tiny photograph I received, which to me had a peculiar appeal. It is the picture of a humble whitewashed cottage with the appended words: "This is the house where the meeting started fifty years ago." A somewhat commonplace picture bearing a seemingly commonplace phrase, which might otherwise have called for no special remark; and yet that dwelling had once been a royal abode, for was it not the very house of God? Nor is this an isolated picture, for in our survey it must have been observed by the reader that from such obscure beginnings, there came into being many of our present-day thriving assemblies.

When the village of Annbank was remodelled, modern houses were built behind the two long rows of but-and-bens. When, with the march of time, those humble dwellings were demolished and a wide street and square formed, the Gospel Hall, occupying a prominent central position, was allowed

EARLY DAYS IN AYRSHIRE

by the authorities to continue the testimony begun in the whitewashed cottage seen in the picture.

Although the date of the first meeting for the breaking of bread in the mining village of Kilbirnie is given as 1889, the circumstances leading up to the commencement go back about seven years earlier, when what was then known as the Blue Ribbon Gospel Army—which had its headquarters in London—came to the village. Gospel meetings were begun in the Good Templars' Hall which was hired for the occasion. This new departure in religious services received a rather mixed reception, and from the start was met with opposition. Nevertheless, large numbers gathered to hear the itinerant preachers. On the night previous to the opening meeting there had been a theatrical performance in the hall, and the scenery was still in position on the Sunday night. Thus amid these surroundings the Gospel was preached to a crowded audience and a remarkable work was begun. Almost from the opening meeting the power of the Holy Spirit became manifest, and many who came to those services indifferent as to spiritual matters, but curious to know what was going on, had their consciences awakened and were led to put their trust in the Saviour.

At the close of the mission the young converts came together with the object, not only of continuing the Gospel testimony but for the study of the Scriptures. This spiritual exercise of soul led a number of them to the truth of believers' baptism and the remembrance of the Lord's Supper. Not all of those who up to that time had been united in the work of the Gospel, could see their way to sever a connection with the denominations to which they were still attached. This meant a separation which was keenly felt on either side. The first company that came together to remember the Lord numbered fifteen. Since then the testimony has been wonderfully honoured of God, and at the present time there are over two hundred and seventy in fellowship, with a Sunday School of about four hundred scholars.

It may have been observed in following the course of assembly life in Scotland, that a notable feature of Gospel activity has been the conducting of kitchen meetings during the winter months. And many a Gospel preacher whose name is familiar amongst us to-day, received his early training at those homely gatherings, where anxious souls were won for the Master, and where it was indeed a rare occasion that the Holy Spirit's power could not be felt in a very real way. In the early days aggressive Gospel work, mainly in the kitchens of the working-class people, was an outstanding characteristic of Kilbirnie, and the remarkable development of the assembly and Sunday School is due in no small measure to this particular activity.

From Kilbirnie there went forth to serve the Lord in the foreign field: James Clifford, Argentine; Matthew Brown, India; Dr. Robert Kennedy, West Indies; and Miss Maggie Barclay, Central Africa.

Kilbirnie was the birthplace of James Clifford, whose Home-call, at the close of forty years' service for the Lord in South America, removed a prominent figure from the great harvest field. The little but-and-ben in which he was reared, stood on the ground now occupied by the Kilbirnie Assembly Gospel Hall. Jamie was saved in the old Free Kirk during a special mission by the Ayrshire Christian Union. He was then in his early teens. Soon afterwards he became identified with the assembly, which at that time had amongst its leaders such men as John Barclay and John Peebles. Very early in his Christian experience Jamie manifested a keen desire to serve the Lord, and entered wholeheartedly into the many activities of the assembly. Of a genial and kind disposition, his life was characterised by a sincerity of purpose which marked him out as a chosen vessel, eminently suited for the great work to which in later years he was called.

The life work of James Clifford, across the measureless tracts of the Argentine, which constituted his vast parish, is so well known that it is necessary only to make a passing reference here. From a fellow-labourer comes this testimony: "He was known and beloved from the Bolivian border in the north, right to Montevideo, one hundred miles beyond Buenos Aires up the River Plate: over a thousand miles! He had a knowledge of the Scriptures that enabled him always to minister and refresh and build up the saints, with such ministry as was invaluable." James Clifford lived to see the fruitful results of his labours in a great ingathering of souls, and in the establishment of assemblies of Christian believers throughout that dark priest-ridden country.

CHAPTER IV

EARLY DAYS IN GLASGOW: THE MARBLE HALL

Not till a coming day will the full story of the '59 Revival be told. Nor shall the hand of time efface its Divinely marked-out course, or remove its hallowed landmarks. Taking in its wake both city and hamlet, that God-sent wave of spiritual revival swept across the country unhindered, invading the hall of the rich as well as the kitchen of the poor. Smouldering embers of pent-up fires were fanned to a living flame, bursting forth at the clarion call of the Gospel into an endless chain of beacon lights. Begun in the North of Ireland, where scenes of unparalleled religious fervour were witnessed, it quickly spread to Scotland, and Glasgow was caught in its irresistible tide. Churches in many parts of the city were thrown open to laymen preachers of the Gospel, and from the plush-lined pulpits of the orthodox ecclesiastics, as well as from the austere rostrum of the Calvinist persuasion, the old Gospel was faithfully proclaimed to congregations thirsting for the living Word.

Public buildings and other places were brought into service. A large canvas tent at the foot of Saltmarket Street, used during the Glasgow Fair week as a circus for performing horses, was hired by Gordon Forlong—a Christian gentleman gifted as an evangelist, whose name is notably associated with revival times—and became the spiritual birthplace of many souls. On the removal of the tent, some of the converts met for a time in a hall close by, and later moved into Qontine Reading Room, which was situated at the foot of High Street, near Glasgow Cross, where an assembly was formed. "This reading room," writes Robert Barnett, "opened from a covered piazza where, on week days, recruiting officers marched to and fro, seeking to enlist young men for the army. Here on Sunday evenings Gospel meetings were held and much blessing was granted."

EARLY DAYS IN GLASGOW

In other parts of the city Brownlow North, Gordon Forlong, and other stalwarts, besides many lesser lights whose names are long since forgotten, were drawing large crowds, and many remarkable conversions took place. Those were times when the city seemed laden with a religious atmosphere, which all unconsciously arrested the careless and ungodly, and sent thoughtful Christians to their Bibles.

It was through the ministry of Gordon Forlong that two men (in later years so powerfully used in the Lord's service) were led to a knowledge of the Truth. They were John R. Caldwell, teacher and expositor, and for many years editor of *The Witness*, and Alexander Marshall, evangelist and author of *God's Way of Salvation* and nearly a thousand other tracts. Other notable men whose powerful preaching moved the City of Glasgow in those memorable days of evangelistic fervour, were Harry Moorhouse, Russell Hurditch, John Vine and Harrison Ord.

It was about this particular time that the Movement which has engaged our attention began to make itself manifest in the city. A number of brethren rented what was then known as the Marble Hall, 85 Dumbarton Road (now 927 Argyle Street) for Sunday School and Gospel work. The hall derived its rather ambiguous appellation from the fact that the premises had originally been used as a marble workshop and showroom. While this work was being carried on, the brethren engaged in it came together to remember the Lord on the first day of the week in a small hall in West Campbell Street. This is said to be the first meeting for the breaking of bread, as we know it, in Glasgow.

Thus the year 1860 marks the laying of the foundation of a spiritual structure, which, during the seventy odd years that have passed, has increased so that to-day there are thirty-six assemblies of Christians in the various districts, which constitute this vast metropolis of the Clyde. A study of the history of assembly life in Glasgow, at once presents a formidable task to one who sets out to disintegrate and place in chronological order the assemblies which followed the little gathering in West Campbell Street. If, therefore, the thread is taken up and it is found expedient to divert into other channels in our search of sequence, we crave the patient indulgence of the reader.

With this necessary digression we return to the company of believers which formed the first assembly. As most of those who had been saved and brought into fellowship as the result of this Gospel effort resided in Dumbarton Road neighbourhood, it was decided, after much prayer and exercise of heart, that the meeting-place for worship and the breaking of bread should be at the Marble Hall. Among the brethren who gathered around the Lord's Table at the Marble Hall on this memorable occasion, which was destined to be the forerunner of many happy gatherings in years to come, were: William Caldwell and his son John R. Caldwell, Thomas Cochrane and George Young. This meeting was the outcome of Bible readings held in the home of William Caldwell, where the Scriptures were carefully examined and various doctrines discussed, with the result that J. R. Caldwell, then a young man of twenty-one, along with his friend and future business partner George Young, followed the Lord through the waters of believers' baptism.

From this humble gathering, composed of believers who were at that time feeling the bondage and spiritual dearth in sectarianism, there sprang up in many parts of the city similar companies. Nor were their activities in the fulfilment of His will, according to the new revelation, confined to the hour spent around the Lord's Table on the first day of the week, for their zeal found ready expression in channels which were opened to the call of the Gospel.

The visit of D. L. Moody and Ira D. Sankey to Glasgow in 1874, brought in its train a wave of blessing reminiscent of the revival times fourteen years previously. Followed by a series of united prayer meetings, the great mission started with a meeting for Sunday School teachers, held at nine o'clock in the morning in the City Hall, which was attended by about three thousand people. The evening evangelistic service was advertised for half-past six, but more than an hour before that time the City Hall was crowded, and the waiting multitude outside repaired to the three nearest

W. H. McLAUGHLIN.

WILLIAM McLEAN.

Dr. JOHN
SINGLETON DARLING

ARCHIBALD BELL.

churches, which were soon filled. The city was stirred to its foundations. Thousands flocked to hear the Gospel, and large numbers were brought into the Kingdom. Dr. Andrew Bonar thus referred to the meetings not long after they started: "Men are coming from great distances to ask the way of life, awakened to this concern by no directly human means but evidently by the Holy Spirit, Who is breathing over the land. It is such a time as we have never had in Scotland before. The same old Gospel as of aforetime is preached to all men: Christ who was made sin for us, Christ the substitute, Christ's blood, Christ's righteousness, Christ crucified; the power of God and the wisdom of God unto salvation."

At the close of the campaign the converts were taken into the circle of the various places of worship. Under such shepherding care not a few, in the flood-tide of their first love, having a zeal for the Master, sought spiritual sustenance and guidance in an intensive study of the Scriptures. This led many to the truth of believers' baptism, and men and women were brought into contact with those Christians who were gathering in New Testament simplicity. Thus the great mission by the American evangelists gave new life and an impetus to the young assemblies gathering in different parts of the city, and their numbers and spiritual influence in and around Glasgow increased perceptibly.

About forty years after the opening of what was regarded as the premier assembly in Glasgow, a meeting was convened in the Marble Hall, to which the original members, who were then alive, were invited. "The purpose of this meeting," writes George Milne, "was, as Israel of old (Deut. viii, 2), to remember all the way the Lord had led them during these forty years, and to return thanks and praise to the Lord as they caused to pass in review all His faithfulness, goodness and grace. At this meeting George Young recalled the fact that shortly after the opening of the hall, they found the words, 'A band of hope who have no pope meet here on Sundays,' chalked on the outside wall of the building." The numbers increased, and steady aggressive work continued until the year 1907, when, owing to the building falling into an unhealthy condition, it was decided to remove to what was thought to be a more suitable hall. The valedictory address was given by Duncan McNab, who faithfully laboured for thirty-four years with the Caledonian Bible Carriage, and the assembly removed to Albany Hall, 534 Sauchiehall Street. Situated in a fashionable part of the town, the rent was high and became a drain on the assembly funds, preventing them from having the practical fellowship to the extent they desired with the Lord's servants labouring at home and abroad. Negotiations were opened with the believers meeting in Union Hall, Graham Street, which ultimately resulted in an amalgamation of the two assemblies. William Kyle, a brother of revered memory, was connected with the Marble Hall in the early days, and continued with the assembly throughout all its wanderings, being at the helm of its affairs for many years previous to his Home-call in June, 1923. Among other well-known brethren formerly associated with the Marble Hall were Alexander Marshall and Henry Pickering.

Among the first assemblies to be established in Glasgow after the formation of the West Campbell Street meeting, was the one which met at Buchanan Court Hall. This was about sixty years ago. Since the inception of the parent assembly there was a manifestation of the Holy Spirit's power amongst His people, but it would appear that it was not till about this particular time that there were any evident signs of marked development along these lines. Crosshill was then a rising suburb, and believers living on the south side of the river, realising the need of a Gospel testimony in that district came together in Buchanan Court Hall, where the Lord's Table was eventually set up. Dr. James Wardrop and Thomas McLaren, with other brethren who had the gift of ministry as well as a keen desire for the souls of the unsaved, are remembered for their faithful and consistent labours, not only in the early days of the assembly, but in later years when difficulties and times of trial confronted the growing Church. For many years it ran well, with times of happy fruit-bearing, and from its increase in numbers there was formed the Elim Hall Assembly.

But a time of testing came when the subtle attentions of the enemy of the Church brought about discord among the believers, which threatened the peace of the assembly. It was evident that to continue in this unhappy state the testimony was in danger of an unfortunate breach taking place. But God intervened by opening another door at Eglinton Hall, where an assembly was formed. The remnant remaining at Buchanan Court Hall continued for a time, but ultimately the hall was closed down. God manifested His approval of the work at Eglinton Hall in a marked degree. Many well-known names appear on the roll. Amongst them we mention particularly: William Inglis (one of the founders of Pickering and Inglis), James Anton, father of James Anton of Central Africa, Robert Gunn, Alexander Harris, R. F. Beveridge of Gospel song fame, and C. H. Judd of the China Inland Mission.

When the Eglinton Hall Assembly first came together in 1892, there were sixty at the breaking of bread. Fourteen years later, when, owing to lack of sufficient accommodation, the assembly moved to Wellcroft Halls, the number in fellowship had increased to one hundred and sixty. These halls, which formerly constituted the premises of an Independent Church, were purchased by Mr. R. G. McInnes, who had the interior of the building remodelled and suitably furnished.

At the opening conference in 1906, at which Dr. McKilliam and David Steel were the speakers, the hall was crowded. "And thus," writes one of the brethren present on that occasion, "there was inaugurated that which for a number of years was one of the happiest meetings in the city of Glasgow. Not only was the work in the Gospel carried on in the hall, but kitchen meetings and open-air services were held in the neighbourhood, while the inmates of Greendyke Street Lodging House were visited regularly with the Gospel, the blessing of the Lord being clearly visible in these activities."

The wise and sanctified leadership of Dr. Wardrop and Mr. McInnes was manifested not only in the growth of numbers but in the spiritual atmosphere which pervaded the assembly gatherings. Although Dr. Wardrop was not what might be termed a front rank man in the sense of being a preacher, there were few who so continuously and diligently spread the Gospel by personal effort as he did for well over sixty years. A consistent believer in the influence of the printed message, it was rarely the good doctor went on his rounds without a supply of attractive Gospel tracts, which found their way, accompanied by a kindly smile and a word of cheer, into the homes of the poor and the well-to-do. In public as in private, the good seed was sown in this way, for as a tract distributor he excelled, mingling with the theatre crowd and with the idlers around the public-house door.

James Wardrop was born in Glasgow, and early in life, while groping about in the twilight of uncertainty, he found peace and satisfaction for his troubled soul by an implicit trust in the Saviour. As a young man, while pursuing his daily calling, he spent much of his spare time serving the Lord among the canal workers and their families in the northern part of the city, where he was encouraged in this service by many tokens of blessing. In later years, in the midst of the arduous toil of his profession, while ministering to the body and its ills, this devoted worker sought also to bring spiritual life and health to the soul. In this, the Christian physician has an opportunity of service entrusted to few others to administer the healing balm of the Gospel to the weary sin-sick soul of the sufferer. "His ready help," wrote John Ritchie at the time of Dr. Wardrop's Home-call, "was ever at the call of the poor and needy, in whose homes he appeared as a ministering angel. To recognise God and kneel by the bedside of his patient was no uncommon experience with him, nor did he fail to bring the message of salvation to the soul while seeking to relieve the pains of the body. In his hospitable home, in which servants of Christ of many lands found a welcome, the old-time habit of singing the Psalms of David, reading the daily chapter of the Word and kneeling in prayer, continued throughout the doctor's long life, and many who shared it will recall the godly savour of that hour of worship."

A man of unremitting energy and spiritual zeal in the

EARLY DAYS IN GLASGOW

service of his Master, he continued to take part in active Christian work when beyond his four-score years. It was while attending a baptismal service at the close of the weekly prayer meeting in Wellcroft, and while engaged in leading in prayer, that the stroke of paralysis came, which was the messenger to call him Home, in his eighty-seventh year. The doctor will live in the memory of those who were associated with him as a gracious personality of the old school and a brother beloved.

In the early 'eighties a number of brethren in fellowship at Buchanan Court Assembly became exercised about the spiritual need of the people living in Oatlands district of Glasgow, and after much prayer for guidance they commenced open-air meetings. They afterwards rented what was known as the Cooking Depot in Sandyfaulds Street for the Gospel on Sunday evenings, following up this effort with kitchen meetings in the homes of some of the brethren. God gave His blessing, many were drawn to the Saviour through the Gospel and the meetings increased in numbers so that it was found necessary to remove to other premises. A large shop at the corner of Polmadie Road and Wolseley Street was rented and converted into a Gospel Hall. Thus the foundation was laid for an assembly of the Lord's people, and on 26th February 1882, eight believers—among them John Faulds, David Hill and Sandy Burns—came together in fulfilment of our Lord's loving injunction: "For as often as ye eat this bread, and drink this cup, ye do shew the Lord's death till He come" (1 Cor. xi, 26).

The young assembly gave early indication of its spiritual life and vitality, and with the willing help of such brethren as Robert Duncan and Thomas McLaren, from the Buchanan Court Hall, the Church made considerable increase, so that after twelve years a hall large enough to accommodate three hundred persons was built in Rutherglen Road. For a number of years notable progress, especially amongst the young, continued with encouraging results, and as the Sunday School became overcrowded it was decided to build on the present site a hall capable of seating five hundred persons. Here, in the midst of a needy working-class population, many of them indifferent to the claims of God, the Wolseley Hall testimony continues.

The Springburn Assembly in the north-east of Glasgow was formed in the spring of the year 1881, when a number of brethren, who up to that time had been actively associated with assemblies already mentioned, and who resided in the district, came together in a shop which had become vacant in Millerbank Street. This they rented and had it converted into a Gospel Hall. From the first the little company was active in the spread of the Gospel, there being a manifestation of the Holy Spirit's power and presence, and many conversions took place.

In the summer of 1884, W. J. Meneely, a North of Ireland evangelist, arrived in the Springburn district with a Gospel tent. He was then in his prime. Meetings were large and fruitful in real conversions, and greatly heartened and helped the young assembly. The corner shop with the double window, which proclaimed to passers-by that the Gospel was preached here, now became too small, and the meeting was removed to a larger hall in Cowlairs Road, where the assembly remained for a number of years.

As the work of the Gospel developed and the Church of God continued to grow, it was decided to build a new hall. A piece of ground in Hillkirk Road was secured and the present spacious hall was erected. Here the assembly, which is one of the most active and aggressive in the city, continues. Springburn Assembly, with a membership of between two hundred and fifty and three hundred on the roll, ranks among the largest on the Clyde-side. Among the last living links of the early days is William Renfrew, who, as a boy of fourteen, came with his mother on the second Sunday after the assembly was formed, having previous to this associated with believers gathering at Union Hall.

Six years after the commencement of the Springburn Assembly, two Christian men became deeply concerned regarding the spiritual needs and the apparent dearth of any real Gospel testimony in the neighbouring district of Garngad. They bore the same name—James Wilson—and for some years previously had been fellow-labourers in the

Gospel, itinerating Glasgow, holding kitchen meetings and preaching in the open-air. Their first connection with Garngad district was in the autumn of 1888, through a visit paid to a man who had recently been saved in the old Bridgegate Mission. But we will let our brother—the James Wilson who is still actively associated with the assembly—tell the story in his own words: "Garngad was a new district to me. On my first visit, having some time to spare, I took a walk up and down several of the streets and was greatly impressed by the lack of any evidence of Gospel work among the people. This so gripped me that during the ensuing winter months, along with two other brethren, we met weekly in my home for long periods of prayer. Assuredly gathering that God was calling us to make an effort to reach the people of Garngad with the Gospel, we rented a small shop at the top of Cobden Street. After purchasing some timber, I, along with another brother, on Saturday afternoons, made twenty seats and a platform. The whole furnishings cost the sum of £5, which at that time represented practically our all."

The meeting-room was opened on the first Saturday of May, 1889, with a tea meeting. A start had been made, and although for some time the gatherings were small it was felt that the Lord's smile was upon them. Usually the open-air meetings consisted of two brethren, their wives and five small children. Their task was made no easier by the fact that the only Christian person known to them in the district, an Irish Presbyterian, spread it abroad that those who were carrying on the work in the Cobden Street meeting-room were "dippers"; being thus uncharitably dubbed because they were at that time associated with the Baptist Church. "Our sole aim," says Mr. Wilson, "was to preach Christ; so we hammered away at Ruin by the Fall, Redemption by the Blood and Regeneration by the Holy Spirit, counting upon God by the power of the Spirit to do His own work."

At first the meetings were not so encouraging, the few who attended being mostly women, the wives of the working men of the district, who came wearing shawls and without hats. Afterwards a few men came. The first convert was a woman whose profligate habits had earned for her considerable notoriety in the locality. She was a real trophy of grace, and for upwards of twenty years bore a bright and faithful testimony to the manifold grace and keeping power of God. During the first two years a goodly number of men with their wives, who had no connection with any religious place of worship, were brought to the Saviour. As numbers increased, the workers were faced with the problem of what to do with those who had been brought into the Kingdom, as up to that time their chief concern had been the salvation of the lost. The young converts were now seeking spiritual nourishment for their souls, and they looked for guidance to those who had led them into the fold. Thus they met together to consult the Scriptures, and from the only true source of Divine guidance, those who had come to be taught, as well as those who sought to teach, learned for the first time the truth of gathering to His name in the simple and unostentatious way so clearly defined in the Scriptures.

Singular though it may seem, the little company of Christians knew nothing of the people known as Brethren, and had been coming together to remember the Lord for some time, before they were aware that there were similar gatherings of the Lord's people in Glasgow, who were meeting in like manner. Their first association with assemblies was in 1892, when a tent was pitched in the district for five weeks. James McAlonan, an evangelist, was the preacher, and at the close of the mission many who had been saved in the tent were added to the Church. Two years later the assembly removed to larger premises in Turner Street. It was about this time that John Ferguson arrived for a fortnight's Gospel meetings, but so evident was the manifestation of the Spirit's power in their midst that the meetings were continued for six weeks. It was a time of remarkable spiritual revival. Over fifty professed faith in Christ, the greater number of whom were baptized and received into fellowship.

A notable feature among assembly activities in Glasgow, which has had such wonderful results, is the work of distributing tracts in hospitals and other institutions in the city. How the work began is an interesting story. A remarkable conversion which took place in connection with the Garngad Assembly was that of Allan McKenzie, a seafaring man. His two children attended the Sunday School, where they heard the sweet story of Jesus. The elder girl fell sick and was dying. As the grief-stricken father sat by the bedside of his child, the little girl sang so sweetly the hymns she had learned at Sunday School, that the hardened heart of the seaman, which cyclone, storm and shipwreck could not move, was touched by the tender appeal of the hymn; and God, through the words of the child, led him to see his exceeding sinfulness. The following Sunday McKenzie came to the hall and was saved. Shortly after his conversion, his wife became ill and was removed to the Royal Infirmary. During his visits to the institution, Mr. McKenzie took the opportunity of distributing tracts to the patients. After his wife's recovery he approached Dr. Thomas, the Superintendent of the Infirmary, and received the doctor's permission to visit the institution and to continue the distribution of tracts. From this small beginning the mission of spreading abroad the Good News by means of the printed message, and of holding Gospel services in the various hospitals in the city, continues to the present time.

During the last fifty years the district has undergone a considerable change, more than half the population now being Roman Catholic. Though this circumstance has increased the difficulties in reaching the people, nevertheless a living testimony is still maintained. At the Garngad Fortieth Annual Conference, W. J. Grant, when told that God had sustained the assembly all those years in a district where the Salvation Army had twice tried and failed, glorified God for His faithfulness to His Word.

Elim Hall

Allusion has already been made to a testimony for the Lord in the Crosshill district of Glasgow, begun in the late 'seventies. Towards the end of the year 1882, between twenty and thirty Christians, the fruit of this earlier gathering in the neighbourhood, met together in a small room at 22 Allison Street, Crosshill, to remember the Lord in the breaking of bread. From this meeting a letter went forth to the neighbouring assemblies requesting their fellowship and prayers in this new effort to spread the Gospel, and in the carrying out of Church principles according to Scriptural teaching.

The little company was happy in having among them one whom God raised up as a leader of the flock in the person of Robert Duncan. A man of commanding appearance and gracious manner, he was ably fitted for the task of directing the new assembly in its various activities. "As the work continued," writes a brother who has made a careful record of the assembly's life-story, "the numbers increased until the meeting-room became too small, and in order to carry on the Gospel work more effectively it became necessary to look for larger premises. About this time, in the year 1889, the way was opened up for the assembly to remove to the building at 5 Prince Edward Street, vacated by the Baptist Church. To-day on this site has been raised the new Elim Hall, a handsome and commodious building capable of seating seven hundred people. On the morning of the first day of each week nearly two hundred and fifty believers gather together around the Lord's table, and in the evening the large hall is filled with eager listeners to the glad Message of the Gospel.

Besides Robert Duncan, other brethren prominently associated with the assembly in the early days were: James Morton, Fred A. Leith, John McDermid, Matthew Garrey, and a little later Robert Fyfe, remembered as a leader of praise of true musical ability. He was eminently a sweet singer whose soul was attuned to the One he ever sought to magnify in spiritual song. Born at the Ayrshire village of Kilbirnie, Mr. Fyfe came to Glasgow in his youth. Having received a godly upbringing, he associated himself with religious work in connection with Cunninghame Free Church, where he became choir leader. It was not, however, till some time later that the religious young man passed through the experience of the New Birth. This all-important

EARLY DAYS IN GLASGOW

event, as he was wont to relate, took place under a street lamp at the top of Renfield Street in the city of his adoption.

Full of life and vigour and with a new song in his mouth, Robert thereafter flung himself wholeheartedly into the work of the Master. His connection with the Elim Hall Assembly began shortly after it moved to Prince Edward Street. Mr. Fyfe acted as precentor, and under his able leadership Elim Hall held a high reputation for the excellent quality of its singing. As leader of praise at Glasgow half-yearly conferences, which are attended by Christians from many parts of the United Kingdom, he was a prominent figure. Mr. Fyfe was indeed a master in the leading of praise, and the remarkable freedom and ease with which he led the singing of those vast audiences, unaided by organ or choir, gave evidence of the gift of this particular ministry with which he was endowed.

The testimony at Elim Hall now began to reach out beyond its borders, and in the year 1900, with the fellowship and help of the assembly, F. A. Leith and John Fyfe with a few other brethren commenced Gospel meetings in Cathcart Road, Govanhill. The building in which the work began was called Bethany Hall, but owing to its being confused with a hall of the same name in the east end of the city, it was later changed to Hermon Hall. Much blessing attended the labours of these brethren, which resulted, a year or two later, in a worship meeting being started for the celebration of the Lord's Supper. In 1907 they were joined by Archie Fraser. For many years a successful work was carried on, and from this testimony came the nucleus of the assembly which now meets in the Victoria Hall, Langside Road, in the Govanhill district. This assembly, meeting in one of the finest Brethren halls in Glasgow, is noted for its vigorous Gospel activities. Particularly is this so amongst the young folk, and as an evidence of the interest taken in their welfare, it may be remarked that at the Annual Sunday School soirée, the largest public hall in the district, accommodating over twelve hundred people, is insufficient to seat all who wish to be present.

But to return to Elim Hall. "Few assemblies have prospered and increased in the work of the Lord in the same measure, and this to a large extent can be attributed to the able leaders who have been given to this Church since its inception. They have been men of God," continues our brother, "men of ability, men of intelligence and men of grace. A marked and outstanding feature of the assembly has always been, and still is, their willingness to welcome to the Lord's Table all Christians who are sound in the faith, and who in their daily walk are consistent with their profession."

About forty years ago Henry Pickering came to reside in the district, and the growing activities and welfare of the Elim Hall at once engaged his constant thought and care. A prominent figure among Brethren, his presence in the assembly was immediately felt. A man of outstanding ability, cheerful in disposition and renowned as a Gospel preacher as well as a voluminous writer, he proved to be a valuable asset to the assembly. During the years of his residence in the district the meeting grew rapidly, was a centre of much blessing and exercised considerable influence upon meetings far and near.

On the departure of Mr. Pickering to London, in 1922, the leadership fell on Alexander Bayne, M.A., a brother of considerable erudition yet withal of a very meek and gracious disposition; one who shrank from publicity, who coveted not the place of honour, and yet the place of honour was literally thrust upon him. The gift of ministry was his in a very special way; his words of comfort and exhortation were an inspiration, not only in Elim Hall but to the Lord's people in many parts of the country. His services were in constant demand at home and away; but God's ways are not our ways, and in 1928, in the midst of his labours at the comparatively early age of fifty-six years he passed into the presence of the Lord.

The assembly was again fortunate in having one among them, in the person of William Dalrymple, suitably gifted to undertake the responsibility of leading so large a gathering. On Christmas Day, 1935, Mr. Dalrymple was called Home very suddenly, after giving faithful service to the assembly for twenty-six years.

The call to labour in the foreign field had its ready response, and from Elim Hall five of its members passed out to service in Central Africa: Dr. Barton, Miss Euphemia Dunbar, Charles E. Stokes, M.A., and Mrs. Stokes, while Miss Janet Wilson sailed for China.

The Albert Hall Assembly, Shawlands, is an off-shoot of Elim Hall, and had its origin about thirty years ago in a weekly Gospel meeting held in the kitchen of the home of John Sinclair and his wife in Baker Street, Shawlands. This homely gathering, begun by a few Elim Hall brethren, attracted the people of the neighbourhood, and some who came seeking an hour's rest after their daily toil found a peace of soul that passeth all understanding. There were many tokens of God's gracious approval, and as the kitchen of the worthy Christian couple soon became taxed to its utmost capacity, it was felt that the work should be extended. Most of the brethren who had taken a practical interest in these kitchen meetings resided in the neighbourhood, and they accordingly met to consider the formation of an assembly in the district.

The way being opened up, it was decided to go forward looking to the Lord for counsel and guidance in the step they were about to take. A hall in Skirving Street, Shawlands, suitable for its central position and excellent accommodation was found to be available, and with the hearty goodwill of the parent assembly, as well as the full fellowship of the neighbouring Pollokshaws meeting, the Albert Hall Assembly came into being. On the first Sunday in June, 1909, thirty brethren and sisters joined in breaking bread in remembrance of the Lord.

Among the early leaders of this assembly were George Young (partner of John R. Caldwell), John Steel and William Dykes.

The origin of the Porch Hall Assembly, Glasgow, may be traced to a Gospel mission begun by John McLachlan in a disused shop in Gateside Street situated at the corner of Duke Street. The premises were acquired and suitably altered for the purpose of holding meetings, and became known locally as McLachlan's Hall. This was in the early 'eighties. Gifted not only as a convincing preacher of the Gospel but as an able exponent of the Scriptures, Mr. McLachlan drew the people of the neighbourhood to hear him, and many happy cases of conversion were placed on record. As the work of grace developed there was a manifestation of spiritual interest amongst Christians who had joined in the activities, and it became evident that fresh responsibilities had fallen upon the shoulders of those who had the care of the little mission.

By this time Mr. McLachlan was joined in the invigorating exercise of soul-winning by a few helpers, among them being John Paton, Andrew Hamilton and Thomas McAulay. Thus they began to study the Scriptures, infused with a desire to learn the Father's will towards His children. And so they were led to the truths of believers' baptism and the Lord's Supper. This caused those who were loyal to the Word to dissociate themselves from the various places of worship they had up to that time attended as Church members, and they began to meet in His name, counting on the guidance of the Holy Spirit, as in simple faith they gathered to remember the Lord in loving obedience to His will.

In the summer of 1887 a Gospel tent was pitched on a vacant piece of land at the corner of Duke Street. The preacher was William Montgomery, well known as an evangelist. He was then in the prime of life, full of vigour and "mighty in the Scriptures." A memorable time of revival took place which was felt throughout the district, the canvas walls of the tent being witness of the new birth of many who attended the services. To the believer in happy communion with God, the telling again of the "Old, old story," and the soul-stirring spectacle of lost ones seeking the Saviour, is indeed a tonic far above the mysteries of the apothecary's art. Thus it was that the mission of the Gospel to the district, proved to be a source of strength and a real spiritual stimulus to the little company of Christians gathering in the meeting-room near by.

EARLY DAYS IN GLASGOW 255

About this time a small church built in the days of the Disruption in Scotland, and latterly used as a place of worship by the E.U. Church, became vacant. It was in the immediate vicinity of Gateside Street, and, as the assembly had considerably increased in numbers, the brethren rented the building. It became known as the Porch Hall, the name being derived from the not altogether unusual architectural feature of a porch entrance. It was John McLachlan who casually remarked when a name was being considered: "Believers were together in Solomon's Porch; why not call it Porch Hall?" Thus it was named, and has since been a place of rest and blessing to all who sought sanctuary within its sacred walls. It was from Porch Hall that James Anton went forth in 1902 to Central Africa.

Through the help of Mr. E. Tainsh, who for long years has been actively associated with believers in Glasgow, we are able to sketch a brief summary of dates and other details from the formation of the Round Toll Hall Assembly, until their reunion with Christians gathering in Union Hall, West Graham Street — covering a period from 1889 till 1926. Confident of the guidance of God, a number of believers in happy fellowship went out from Union Hall, and after a journey covering thirty-seven years round the northern district of Glasgow, came back as one man—although numbering about one hundred and fifty—to Union Hall, the place where their tent was pitched in the beginning. Here is the story. Close on half a century ago a few Christian people with a heart for the perishing around them, were privileged to hold forth the Word of Life in and around what was known as the Black Quarry District, Round Toll. At that time there was little or no Gospel evidence in the district, and meetings for the preaching of the Gospel were convened during the summer and winter, both in a large tent pitched in the neighbourhood and in a music hall hired for the purpose when it was available. The campaign proved to be a time of intensive sowing and reaping, and was carried through with the generous and stimulating help of such preachers as John Ritchie, W. J. Meneely and Henry Downie. It was a time productive of much fruit, and souls were gathered into the Kingdom. Many of the converts found their way into Union Hall.

At the close of the meetings it was decided to continue a Gospel testimony in the district, and to do this after a godly fashion it was thought expedient that an assembly should be established who would be responsible to the Lord for the continuance of the testimony. Among those called to share in the undertaking and who thus formed the nucleus of the Church were: James Kelly, William Taylor, Henry Davidson, Robert Kerr, Tom Dryden and Dan Turner, still remembered as "Happy Dan." Later, the ranks were augmented by Robert Leggat and others, during which time numbers were saved and added to the assembly.

For over four years the testimony was maintained before removing to Camperdown Hall, where the assembly remained for ten years. Many were the miracles of grace during those years; notably a drunken mason who persistently disturbed the open-air meetings, yet God wondrously saved the profligate and he lived for many years to proclaim from platform and street corner his unbounded faith in the Gospel he once sought to defame. Then another call came for the assembly to remove to Garscube Hall, the place once occupied by what is now The Tabernacle, St. George's Cross, and latterly by the Union Hall, as a Gospel testimony. Such stalwarts of the Faith as Alex. Marshall and David Rea, with others, unfurled the banner of the cross with lasting results. After ten years the assembly returned to Round Toll Hall, still under the able leadership of James Kelly and Robert Leggat, where, following a testimony of eighteen years, circumstances came in which made another removal necessary. This time back to Union Hall, where twenty of their number, with others, had started the testimony in Round Toll at the beginning. It was in this assembly that Alexander Stewart so ably ministered for many years. He was the author of "O Lamb of God we lift our eyes," and "Lord Jesus Christ we seek Thy face," hymns sung by assemblies of believers the world over.

An aged brother, who for over half a century has been actively associated with assemblies in Glasgow, gives this testimony: "We are commanded to remember our guides," he writes. "Looking back, the writer sees three outstanding men whose personality and ministry were most markedly used of God in supplying spiritual food for edifying babes in Christ, as well as those of more mature experience. These were: John R. Caldwell, Alexander Stewart and Thomas Cochrane. The ministry of these brethren was most edifying and uplifting. But there was a something about their demeanour and movements which impressed one even more than their addresses—a fact which indicates that the man is more than his message; and is explained by the Great Woman of Shunem's words to her husband concerning the prophet Elisha: 'Behold now, I perceive that this is an holy man of God, which passeth by us continually' (2 Kings iv, 9). Elisha's character was perceptible in his personal demeanour. So it was with these elder brethren, whom we will do well to remember and seek to imitate as they followed Christ."

It must be obvious to the reader that the purpose of these records has not been to chronicle the birth, progress and spiritual life of the thirty-six assemblies in Glasgow. To attempt such a formidable task would run far beyond the limits of space at the disposal of the writer; nor would we presume upon the patience of the reader in pursuing a course which in a variety of instances must of necessity lead along parallel avenues. Since the early days when the fire was first kindled in Campbell Street, remarkable development in the upbuilding of the Church of God and the furtherance of His Kingdom has taken place; so that to-day, probably no other body of Christians wield so powerful an influence in the spread of the Gospel in the city than the various assemblies of believers known as Brethren.

DUMBARTON

The assembly at Dumbarton was commenced about seventy years ago, the first meeting for the breaking of bread being held in the home of a sister by name Mrs. Miller. Their path at the beginning appears to have been rather a

R

chequered one, but despite the inroads of the enemy to sow discord, a testimony was established which God has since been pleased to sustain.

KILMACOLM

Fifty-three years ago, the only Gospel testimony in the village of Kilmacolm, Renfrewshire, was under the care of Mrs. Brown of Old Hall, a Christian lady whose love for the souls of the perishing was ever her constant thought. In the work of soul-winning she had the fellowship and able assistance of Mr. Martin, Town Clerk of Paisley, who resided in the village. Gospel meetings, held twice a week, were well attended, and God honoured the work in many conversions taking place. About this time, David Wight and his wife took up residence in Kilmacolm and at once cast in their lot with the few Christians.

There was no Sunday School, although there always seemed a plentiful number of children playing about the streets who might be willing enough, if invited, to come to hear Bible stories on Sunday afternoons; so Mrs. Wight gathered some of them together. Before many weeks had passed, the numbers had increased to nearly a hundred. Thus began a fruitful work which developed in a remarkable way. As time went on, many of the young people were led to trust the Saviour and became helpers together in the Gospel mission. There now came a desire amongst the believers to celebrate the Lord's Supper in the apostolic simplicity of the Scriptures. This was carried out, but only once a month, until the arrival in Kilmacolm of William Farquharson (brother-in-law of Alexander Stewart, of Glasgow), and family, when they began to come together to remember the Lord on the first day of every week; and the testimony has since continued active in the work of the Gospel and faithful to the principles of gathering in His Name.

BRIDGE OF WEIR

Bridge of Weir, in the same shire, whose name will always be associated with Quarrier's Homes for Children, has an assembly which was begun just over forty years ago, following a Gospel mission in the village. David Wight had recently come from Kilmacolm to reside in the district, and with the help of his wife together with a few Christian friends, was the means of building a hall in the centre of the village for the preaching of the Gospel. It was opened with a conference, when William Quarrier and Alexander Stewart ministered words of encouragement to those who had put their hands to the plough. This was followed by a two weeks' mission conducted by Alexander Brown. Among those who were saved was a blacksmith, well known in the village for his intemperate habits. He immediately went and paid all his debts for drink and began to testify, showing by his changed life his newly-found joy. Soon afterwards his wife and only son were converted. Thus began a work of grace. People were attracted to the meetings in such numbers, that one of the ministers in the village was heard to complain of the members of his congregation forsaking his Church for the meetings in the hall.

As the interest increased, those who had found the new life began to read their Bibles. In this, the seekers after spiritual food received refreshment by the visit of J. A. Garriock, who ministered the truth of believers' baptism and the Lord's Supper, the outcome being that a good number obeyed the Word. Thus a company of believers began to break bread on the first day of the week.

CHAPTER V

IN THE SCOTTISH CAPITAL

In the recording of the work of the Holy Spirit relative to the formation of assemblies of Christian believers during a particular period of last century, one cannot fail to observe, in a considerable number of instances, the lack of documentary evidence as to when and where the first stone of a present-day thriving Church was laid. To the historian whose sensitive mind has been trained along lines of authenticity and exactitude in the fixing of day and date, the absence of such records may present a difficulty. But Brethren in earlier years, so it would seem, were more concerned about fundamental truths in the building up of a spiritual structure, than of recording upon stone or parchment what to them appeared to be a non-essential.

Thus in Edinburgh comparatively little is known of the early days of Brethren, and although the original meeting-place is said to have been in Bank Street, only a few fragmentary facts can be gathered as to the actual founding of the Movement in the Scottish Capital. As in other parts of Scotland about the time of which we write, the Holy Spirit had been preparing many hearts to receive a fresh enlightenment of the Scriptures. Pioneers had fearlessly proclaimed the Truth, and the ground was being broken up for the time of sowing. Reports of what was taking place farther south had reached Edinburgh, and were gladly received by a few with a prayerful desire for a fulfilment of the Scriptural mode of assembling themselves together in the Name of the Lord. Thus when the saintly Robert Mitchell came to Edinburgh, sometime in the late 'sixties, he found quite a number of earnest Christians of like mind to himself, whose spiritual outlook had recently undergone a great change.

Among the early leaders—and these included such stal-

IN THE SCOTTISH CAPITAL

warts as Donald Ross, Albert Boswell, Henry Groves and Colin Campbell—Robert Mitchell was, in many ways, outstanding. An Ayrshire man, he had spent some years in England, where he was on terms of happy fellowship with Lord Congleton and other "chief men among the Brethren." He came to Edinburgh in order that he might study languages and otherwise prepare himself for missionary work in the foreign field. The Lord willed it otherwise. A severe illness supervened, and the lifework of Robert Mitchell was mainly in the shepherding and building up of the Lord's people in the homeland. "He was an old man as I remember him," writes Mr. Robert G. Mowat, who has kindly furnished the present writer with much of the information relating to the Edinburgh Assemblies, "and the years had mellowed his winsome character so that we young folks loved him for himself, while we revered him for his knowledge. He was, in the truest and best sense of the word, a saint—simple yet profound, full of gracious dignity, with a charming personality which Divine love had rendered truly beautiful. Of him it could rightly be said that the radiance of the sanctuary glowed on his countenance and hallowed his speech, so that we who listened were hushed with the sense of the Sacred Presence: for he dwelt much in the secret place of the Most High."

Robert Mitchell was a Biblical scholar of considerable standing, and collaborated with Robert Young in the preparation of his monumental work, *Young's Analytical Concordance*. During his residence in England he formed one of that circle which included Dr. Maclean, Henry Groves, Lord Congleton and others who came together by arrangement, to read and study missionary news and letters. As the circle grew and interest in the Lord's work in the foreign field increased, so there became a real need for a periodical containing reports from overseas, which might reach a wider community. And as we have already seen in a former chapter, in the year 1872 the *Missionary Echo*, forerunner of our missionary monthly *Echoes of Service*, was first published.

The little company at Bank Street went on happily for some time. But it is not to be supposed that the arch-enemy of the Church would remain inactive in the presence of such a spiritual renaissance in Edinburgh, without casting about in a subtle endeavour to break up the harmony of the young assembly, and it was not long before serious doctrinal trouble arose, and the meeting was divided. This naturally led to a corresponding loss of power and blessing over a considerable period, though we are thankful to be able to add that unity has now for some years been re-established. Soon after this a small hall at 16 Picardy Place was acquired, and another at Lochrin Place, thus suiting the convenience of believers who had previously met at Jamaica Street, Melbourne Place and Greenside Place. "From that time," writes Mr. Mowat, "the work began to prosper. The meeting-room at Picardy Place became a truly hallowed spot to many a soul who was won for the Lord there. With steady increase of numbers the hall was enlarged, and such was the spiritual vigour of believers that it seemed as though nothing could stay their enthusiasm as the work developed. There was a happy family feeling of fellowship, and all, both young and old, were on fire for souls. Thus the good work spread."

At the seaport of Leith, a mile or two from the city, an assembly was established about this time. Henry Mowat and Ernest Gerrie began the work in the Blackburn Hall there. Mr. Mowat remained for several years to give pastoral care until the infant assembly was built up, after which he returned to take his place in the Picardy Place meeting. Ernest Gerrie was afterwards called to devote the whole of his time to the Lord's work, and became well-known in many parts of the country as an evangelist. The activities of the various companies of believers in Edinburgh continued to bear fruit. The blessing spread to the near-by village of Davidson's Mains, and later to Portobello where, under the guidance of James Straiton, an assembly was formed.

A feature of the Picardy Place Assembly, which was attended with much blessing, was the going forth of singing parties to carry the Gospel in song and story to hospitals and other institutions. A zealous band, led by Henry Mowat, also engaged in a constant war of aggressive evangelism, not only in open-air services, but at various times small halls were engaged in needy districts of Edinburgh and Leith, where some wonderful cases of conversion were recorded. The assembly at Picardy Place had already removed to a larger hall but even this became inadequate, and at the outbreak of the Great War when the German Chapel in Rodney Street became vacant, this handsome and commodious building was acquired and was given the name of Bellevue Chapel.

At Lochrin Place there was also steady progress, and the assembly increased in numbers until its removal to the present hall in Lauriston Place, where the testimony continues. Since those almost forgotten days when the Lord so wonderfully came in, dispelling the cloud which had for so long overshadowed the path of His people, there has ever been present in the various assemblies that atmosphere of happy fellowship, which has in no small measure contributed to the remarkable development of the testimony in and around the historic Scottish Capital.

LOANHEAD, NEAR EDINBURGH

When Donald Ross visited Edinburgh in 1876, he carried his pioneer work to the districts lying within easy distance of the city. At the mining village of Rosewell, where his tent had been pitched, he was joined by John Scott, of Shrewsbury, and a remarkable work of grace followed. Here the evangelists were met with bitter opposition, the chief instigator being the local clergyman. On the first night of the meetings, the ropes were cut and the tent brought to the ground. This necessitated a watch being kept, and the evangelists were obliged to take turn about each night. Nevertheless, the Lord honoured the faithfulness of His servants and when the tent was removed, those who had found the Saviour met together under the care of Donald Ross to break bread. As all the suitable places in the village were in the hands of the enemy, the meeting was held in the workshop of a joiner, who, along with his wife and some members of his family, had been saved at the tent meetings. Thus they continued in happy fellowship for some time. Subsequently a number of the Christians removed to Bonnyrigg and Penicuik, these places being a few miles from Rosewell in opposite directions; the result being that the meeting at Rosewell became extinct, while testimonies were raised in each of the two towns named.

In the spring of 1889 the assembly at Bonnyrigg decided to remove their meeting-place to Loanhead, about two miles distant, as nearly all those forming the assembly lived in that locality; and here they have continued to gather in His name. During recent years there has been a fresh testimony at Bonnyrigg, where a few believers gather to remember the Lord on the first day of the week.

CHAPTER VI

CHIRNSIDE

At the village of Chirnside, Berwickshire, in the early 'seventies, a few young men—some of them recently saved—commenced a diligent study of the Scriptures. It was not long before there was revealed to them the truth of believers' baptism and of gathering to the Lord's Name alone. Thus they began to break bread, although they knew of no other similar meeting. Shortly afterwards Colonel Molesworth came to Chirnside, and through him they heard that there were other such gatherings and they became identified with them in fellowship.

CHAPTER VII

IN THE HIGHLANDS OF SCOTLAND

THE assembly of Aberlour in Banffshire was mainly the result of a visit paid to that district by Donald Ross. This was in the beginning of the year 1869. He was then Superintendent of the North-east Coast Mission, an organisation whose sphere of service extended from Ferryden in the south to Thurso in the far north, a distance, following the coastline, of probably five hundred miles. In this vast field Mr. Ross laboured continuously for some years before freeing himself from what he felt was an organisation which fettered his Spiritual activities.

At that time Donald Ross knew nothing of gathering in the name of Jesus; indeed had not even heard of it. "We heard of 'Brethren,'" he wrote, "but only as bad, bad people, and we resolved to have nothing to do with them. Our information, however, came from the parsons." Associated with him in the mission were many devoted men, among them Donald Munro and John Smith, who in the years that followed, became powerful in publishing the Gospel at home and abroad.

The unpretentious presentation of the old Gospel by these itinerating preachers, captured the ear of the country folk who came in numbers to the meetings. But this aroused the jealousy of some of the clergy, who denounced in scathing terms the unorthodox doctrine and methods of those who had invaded the territory of the Established Church. Ever fearless and outspoken, Donald Ross met the onslaughts from the pulpits with a tract which he wrote and published as a challenge "suggesting to the ministers to go on strike for a year or more and allow nine pairs of evangelists to be let loose on Scotland, pledging our word that more conversions would be seen through the eighteen than through all the ministers put together in the same time."

It was about this time or soon after that Mr. Ross took a definite step for the Truth revealed to him in the Scriptures.

He had preached one evening at a place near Aberlour, on the text, "Come out from among them, and be ye separate" (2 Cor. vi, 17). At the close of the meeting a brother, an elder in the Parish Church, laid his hand on the preacher's shoulder and said: "All true, dear brother Ross; but where are we to go?" "That is just what is troubling me," came the unexpected reply. And that was really the case.

A LORD'S DAY AT OLD RAYNE

A living pen-picture by John Ritchie, eloquently descriptive of a primitive gathering around the Lord's Table in a Highland village about the time of which we now write, is worthy of recounting here. "It was on a summer Lord's Day morning," he writes, "that four of us started on foot to Old Rayne, where we had heard that a company of believers had begun to gather, outside of all denominations, to worship God and to shew forth the Lord's death in the breaking of bread. We had seen this to be our privilege in the Word and were anxious to see it in practice. After a delightful eight-mile walk, a rest by a spring of clear water, a Psalm from the Word, and a little season in prayer, we started on the last stage of our journey and arrived at the village a quarter of an hour before the hour of the meeting. We were told the gathering was in a workshop which was easily found. A few brethren were standing at the door, who gave us a hearty welcome. A brother who had been in Inverurie during the week, and had gone to reside in that district, introduced us to the elder brethren, and we were received as 'young believers from Inverurie, where as yet there is no gathering.' We got a royal welcome.

"It was a wonderful gathering—the first of its kind we had ever seen. The place was a country joiner's shop, with whitewashed walls, plank seats supported by cut logs of wood, a plain deal table covered with a white cloth on which the bread and wine stood near the centre; there was no platform, no chair, no chairman. We had often gone to hear the Lord's servants and to seek His blessing on the Word spoken by them; here we had come to meet the Lord Himself, to hear His voice, to see no man save Jesus only. The seats filled up, mostly by middle-aged country people all plainly clad; there were no flowers or feathers, no gold ornaments or sparkling jewels there. When all had assembled, the door was shut and we felt that we were shut in with God.

"There was true worship there that day, such as has to be shared to be understood: it cannot be explained. Never before had we heard such singing—possibly never shall we hear it again till we go to Heaven—not the music, but the heart that was in it—true melody, produced by the Spirit operating in the hearts of the worshippers. It is not to be expected that everything was done 'after the due order,' for these believers were groping their way out of the mazes of worldly Christianity and following light as it dawned upon them from the Word. A critic would have seen plenty to find fault with. But there was heart and soul in all that was said and done; the prayers led you right into the presence of the Lord, the praise was like a fountain springing up, and whatever words of ministry were given, were fresh as the manna freshly gathered from the dew and newly fallen from Heaven. The bread and wine passed round—it was the first time we had handled the sacred symbols. We stood as we partook of them, like Israel in Egypt—some of the old farmers literally staff in hand—and when the hymn was raised and sung, still standing—

> 'Come, Lord, we wait for Thee,
>   We listen still for Thy returning;
> Thy loveliness we long to see,
>   For Thee the lamp of hope is burning;
>   Come, Lord, come!'

it actually seemed as if we were on the move upwards; we certainly were waiting for the call."

Towards the end of 1870 there was a remarkable work of grace in Dufftown and Aberlour, which resulted in a number of believers publicly confessing Christ by being baptized in the River Spey. It was not, however, till the first Lord's Day in 1872 that an assembly was formed in the parish of Aberlour. For a time the meeting-place for the breaking of bread was in a farmhouse, but as a number of believers came over from Dufftown and Boham to join the little company, as well as others who left the Parish Church, a hall was taken in the village of Aberlour, where a testimony has since been maintained.

INVERNESS

Just over fifty years ago, four men, members of the Free High Church, Inverness, then under the godly ministry of Dr. John Black, were much perplexed and exercised in heart regarding their position as believers at the Lord's Table, partaking of the sacred emblems with unconverted people; so they left the Church. Three of these brethren rented a room in Church Street, and the Lord's Day following, being Communion Sunday at the Churches, they spread the table in apostolic simplicity, in preparation of remembering the Lord's death. As in the case of many other Christians at that time, they knew nothing of the Brethren Movement but were solely guided by the Holy Spirit through a diligent study of the New Testament.

On this particular Sunday, Frank Edgar, who had come out with the others, not knowing where to go and unaware of the intentions of his friends, left home after asking God to lead him where He would have him go. Whilst walking along Church Street he seemed to hear a voice telling him to stand still. He stood where he was and noticed that the time on the steeple clock was five minutes to eleven. "I'll stay here for five minutes," he said to himself; "then I'll go over to the Wesleyan Church." Looking over the street he saw Alexander Mackenzie, one of his Free Church friends, standing with his Bible under his arm.

"Is that you, Frank? And where are you going?" he said.

"I don't know," was the young man's reply.

"I'm going to a room in Church Street to remember the Lord in the breaking of bread with Murdo Campbell and James Grant," said his friend. "Will you come?"

"Yes, I'll come," was the ready response. Those were the beginning of eventful days in Inverness.

But these faithful believers, loyal to the Word and true to the dictates of their conscience, very soon became the target of the enemy. The following Sunday, and for some time after, most of the pulpits in the Highland Capital were preaching against this new sect, who, in the eyes of the Establishment, had committed gross sacrilege by presuming to participate in the Holy Sacrament outside the sacred precincts of the Church, without the presence of an ordained minister.

Days of persecution followed. Alexander Mackenzie, whose master was a prominent elder in Dr. Black's church, received a fortnight's notice to terminate his employment. The others were slighted by former friends and threatened in many ways. This bitter persecution against those who dared to come out boldly for the Truth continued for a considerable time, until the assembly increased to a membership of fifty. The storm from without had long since abated, and a real manifestation of spiritual activity had become evident in the growing assembly, when, almost without warning, came the rumbling sound of strife from within. Inspired by the subtle and assiduous authority of Brethren hundreds of miles distant, who probably had never heard of this little assembly in the North of Scotland, the enemy of the Church came in. The flickering light which had braved the tempests of early years, and through times of difficulty and opposition had become a bright illuminant, was almost quenched. Barren years followed, until the arrival in the city, of William Mackenzie of New Zealand, when the remnant of a once healthy Church gathered together in the house of one of the brethren, who in the early days had " come out " in defence of the Truth.

This was the beginning of happier times, and through the weary cloud which for long lost days had cast an ominous shadow, there came once again the sunshine of a Father's smile. To-day there is a large and active assembly in premises of their own, where the fruits of their labour may be observed in an aggressive Gospel testimony, and a happy and hopeful work amongst the young in the two Sunday Schools which are maintained by the Ebenezer Hall Assembly.

BRECHIN

Breaking away from the tradition of the systems where it was felt that the liberty of the Holy Spirit was being hindered, a few Christian men, about the year 1887, commenced what was called the "Brechin Christian Union," in the village from which the Gospel Mission took its name. They had as their object the preaching of the Gospel and the study of the Scriptures, which they resolved to accept as their guide. Unfettered by ecclesiastical rule, they soon learned the true meaning of being gathered in His Name. James Soutter had some time previous to this been baptized in the river and, along with three others, he sought the fellowship of the Montrose Assembly in the spreading of a table to the Lord's Name in Brechin. This was realised in the spring of 1891, when these four, with three sisters, broke bread. George R. Masson, of Aberdeen, hearing of this, came along and spent three weeks ministering the Word, which greatly cheered and encouraged the little company of believers. Before he left, four were added to the assembly, and seven publicly confessed the Lord in baptism.

The meetings for the Gospel and ministry were held in what was known as the Masons' Hall, while the gathering to remember the Lord's death took place in the home of one of the brethren. In 1904 the old Town Hall became vacant, and, as numbers increased, it was rented for sixteen years, the name being changed to Gospel Hall. The assembly next moved to the Congregational Kirk, an iron building which was offered for sale and purchased by the Brethren. Believers were added from time to time, yet the numbers have never reached a high figure, many of the younger people in fellowship having to move farther afield in quest of employment.

From the little assembly there have gone forth to serve the Lord in other lands: A. Whitelaw, who went out to China; W. G. Smith, whose itinerating work in the United States of America resulted in the founding of a few assemblies; and Dr. W. R. Soutter, who sailed for Manchuria to join J. H. Brewster in the Lord's work there. Since the founding of the assembly at Brechin, the burden of the work and of the ministry rested principally on the shoulders of James Soutter. Loyal to the principles of Scripture, he proved to be a tower of strength amongst those who have ever been faithful to the testimony of the Gospel.

NAIRN

Towards the end of the year 1894 Mr. and Mrs. Meiklejohn opened their house to receive Brethren to the Lord's Table, and were later joined by others. This attempt to establish a permanent testimony failed owing to the ill-health of Mr. Meiklejohn and other causes. In the spring of 1899 William Ness, of St. Andrews, arrived in Nairn, and a few months later, the Lord's Table was spread in a room in the Public Hall Buildings. Since then there has been steady and consistent progress.

BALLATER

In the burgh of Ballater, not far from the royal residence of Balmoral Castle, three maiden sisters, relatives of a distinguished British soldier, with a few other Christians came together to remember the Lord on the first day of the week over fifty years ago. They were on a visit to the Highlands, but so charmed were they with the beautiful scenery and the peaceful valley of the Dee, that they eventually took up residence there. Some years later the brothers Logg pitched a tent in the neighbourhood, and this invasion aroused considerable interest in the Gospel. Before the evangelists left, the Misses Haig became exercised as to continuing a Gospel testimony, and decided to convert the stable belonging to the mansion into a meeting-room with suitable accommodation for a baptistry. The sisters visited throughout the parish from door to door, and with a kindly word invited the people to come. So remarkable was the response that the "meeting-room" had to be enlarged by taking in the coach-house and the laundry.

It was evident that the Lord was with those who sought to uphold the Truth, there being a number of men and women,

F. C. BLAND.

DAVID REA.

WILLIAM TALBOT CROSBIE.

RICHARD J. MAHONY

IN THE HIGHLANDS OF SCOTLAND

who, following the divine order, were baptized and added to the assembly. Bible readings were arranged and help in the exposition of the Scriptures by brethren from Aberdeen, was the means of stimulating the assembly. A Sunday School was commenced, and some who were long past day-school age attended. Thus the good work continued for many years, until one after the other of the aged sisters were called Home, leaving those whom the Lord had raised up to follow in the path marked out by Him.

In later years, through various circumstances, numbers were reduced, but the testimony begun by those saintly women, is still kept alive in the village where their name will long remain a fragrant memory.

DINGWALL

In the summer of 1907 Francis and Matthew Logg pitched their Gospel tent in the corner of a field in Dingwall, and before the season closed, several believers broke bread under the canvas roof which has been a silent witness of the blessing that accompanied the labours of God's servants.

On the removal of the tent the friends took a small room in the district of the town where the work had been carried on. In the following year William Robertson, with his wife and family, took up residence in Dingwall and proved to be a stimulus to the struggling assembly, who continued in different meeting-rooms until 1926, when a new hall was built. Here a testimony has since been maintained.

PETERHEAD AND THE '59 REVIVAL

Delving into the past in an endeavour to trace the source of what is now a living stream of spiritual life, one cannot but be forcibly impressed by the tremendous religious influence of what is still affectionately referred to as the '59 Revival. What that immeasurable wave of blessing brought in its course as it swept across the country, can never be estimated, nor shall we know its full story till some future day. Thus we find that here an assembly and there an assembly, separated it may be by hundreds of miles, had each its own individual existence, and spent the early days in an atmosphere pregnant with the Holy Spirit's power.

In the north-east corner of Aberdeenshire, about this particular period, there was great spiritual activity. James Turner, a man full of zeal for the Master, became a prominent figure. He gathered together a band of faithful workers, who went out preaching the Word in public and from house to house.

To him may be attributed the founding of a sound and vigorous Gospel testimony in Peterhead, in which the need of the Holy Spirit's power and guidance was emphasised. The effects of this were later seen, as light on Scriptural principles was given.

It is said that anyone who heard James Turner pray must have been convinced that he was on intimate terms with the living God. Largely attended meetings for prayer were held in Peterhead and Boddam, which were composed mainly of fishermen. And *such* prayer meetings: "No cold, formal recitations of theology or doctrine, but men laying hold on God, demanding that He would fulfil His promises, pleading for the salvation of sinners, and the awakening of whole towns and parishes for hours upon end, while tears flowed down their cheeks in torrents." As may well be supposed, those faithful souls, on fire for the Gospel, were branded as religious fanatics. James Turner became marked as a dangerous leader, and was turned out of the Kirk in Peterhead for no greater offence than publicly praying that God would awaken all the unconverted ministers and elders in the town. But the ardour of the praying band was in no way damped because of such treatment at the hands of their fellow townsmen. With the kirk door shut against him, James Turner gathered with his faithful followers in his fish-curing yard, where they could preach and pray to their hearts' content.

Gospel meetings were convened in a large fish-curing shed, dimly lighted with two crude oil-lamps, and having rough planks of timber for seats. It was in this place that

IN THE HIGHLANDS OF SCOTLAND

Gordon Forlong preached on more than one occasion, his pulpit being formed by an inverted herring barrel overhung by a small and smoking oil-lamp. Those were marvellous times. The power of the Spirit of God became manifest among the people, strong men were broken down in tears of repentance, and many in anguish of soul found peace and eternal repose in the cleft Rock of Ages. A great awakening had begun. Work almost came to a standstill, and for days at a time fishermen did not put out to sea. Such was the beginning of revival days in Peterhead.

Among younger workers was William McLean, afterwards well known as an evangelist in the North of Ireland. He was a Scotch Baptist, and was led to sever his connection with that denomination through a seemingly casual remark of a Christian lady visiting Peterhead. William had told this lady that he was a Baptist, and she remarked: "Do you not think that the names given us in the Word of God should be sufficient for a believer?" Further conversation led to exercise of heart, and he became enthusiastic over the oneness of all believers in Christ Jesus. He realised that no denominational walls should divide what God had joined together in eternal union. The sufficiency of the Word and Spirit of God as Teacher and Guide, to provide for all the spiritual needs of any company of Christians, became increasingly impressed on his mind and heart, and this led to action.

So it came about that in 1868 an advertisement appeared in the local newspaper announcing that the Church of Christ in Peterhead would meet in a room at No. 1 Rose Street. On the day appointed, over a dozen believers were seated in the best room of Mr. McLean's own house, over his place of business, when two ladies entered. Mr. McLean rose to welcome them. The younger of the two, one of the first Mildmay deaconesses and a warm friend of Mr. and Mrs. Pennefather, as also of Mr. Denham Smith, whispered to Mr. McLean: "We saw your advertisement." Then her keen eye ran over the room as if taking in its dimensions, and she said: "Was it not rather a big claim to make—'the Church of Christ in Peterhead,' to meet in this room?

But," she continued, "I believe you really meant, 'Where two or three are gathered together in My Name, there am I in the midst of them.'" "Yes, yes," was Mr. McLean's ready reply, "that is exactly what we meant." This lady afterwards gave Mr. McLean many helpful suggestions from the Scriptures and the assembly was launched.

"That room," writes Mr. Robert Stephen, who has for over fifty years been associated with the activities of Peterhead Assembly, "was often as the very gate of Heaven to the little company. Often a statement something like this was made in the early years: 'We can lay claim to nothing great, for we are but a fragment of the great Church on earth. We seek to carry out primitive order while acknowledging all who are the Lord's, who do not meet with us; and welcome all whose walk and doctrine would not exclude them. So we cannot be a sect unless we claim what does not belong to us: a position which disowns all others.'"

Believers' baptism was taught and practised, and Mr. McLean had a baptistry placed in his drawing-room. Here, many recently saved, as well as a few Christians from other places of worship, passed through the waters in obedience to the teaching of Scripture, which, through the faithful exposition of Mr. McLean, was revealed to them. In 1869 the assembly was moved to a hall in Maiden Street, where it continued, with the exception of one brief interval, till the present convenient and commodious hall in Prince Street was occupied in the mid-'eighties, in which there are now over two hundred in Church fellowship.

When William McLean moved to the North of Ireland, James Napier, one who was at the first meeting of Brethren in Peterhead, greatly helped the assembly for many years. Those pioneers were men of God who closely studied the Scriptures and applied their teachings to the daily life. Such gatherings were despised for the "peculiar" way of meeting, but those identified with the assembly were highly respected by the people of the town. They bore that best of all testimonies—godly and consistent lives.

DONALD ROSS AND ABERDEEN

The name of Donald Ross, which shall always remain indelibly imprinted across the record of pioneer evangelists among Brethren, first came to be known about the time of which we now write. And as we shall see, it was mainly through the labours of this giant for the Truth that a work which was to reach far beyond the boundaries of his native land was begun. In a great measure the history of the early days of assembly life in Aberdeen is bound up with the story of his life and labours. A man of pronounced native talent, a good judge of character, strict and rigid in doctrine, blunt and fearless in expression, yet deeply spiritual withal, he was known throughout Scotland, and his quaint and pithy sayings were the frequent subject of common remark. When the spirit of revival reached Aberdeen in its passage northward, Donald had just recently been appointed to the position of Superintendent of the North-east Coast Mission, Aberdeen. The city at that time was being stirred by the preaching of such men as Reginald Radcliffe and Brownlow North, and Donald Ross at once threw himself heart and soul into the invigorating and healthful exercise of soul-winning. With his soul on fire for the perishing around him, he felt that his present position greatly restricted his usefulness to his fellow-men. After a time he found himself out of sympathy with the churches, and becoming convinced of the necessity of being free from everything in the shape of human organisation, he resigned his position that he might devote himself to evangelistic work in what was known as the Gallowgate Chapel.

And now we approach the inception of the first assembly of "Open Brethren" in Aberdeen. Up to this time there had been no recognised meeting for the breaking of bread as we now know it. The revival had given a spiritual warmth and vigorous incentive to believers in the city, which created a desire for a deeper and more practical knowledge of the Bible; and following some informal meetings where an intensive study of the Scriptures was a prominent feature, a meeting was formed in the old Record Hall (or Dispensary) in Castle Street about the year 1870. The company consisted of a few men and women, without any brethren of outstanding ability to minister. A number of them attended Donald Ross's meetings in Gallowgate, and Donald Ross in turn joined the Castle Street company in the breaking of bread on Lord's Day. After fraternising in this way for some time, John Ritchie, the leader of Castle Street meeting, suggested that the two meetings should come together, to which Donald Ross readily agreed. So the two companies became one, with the Gallowgate Chapel as headquarters.

The Gallowgate Chapel—which was destroyed in 1904 through a fire which originated in some adjoining property—became the scene of a great revival movement, when people from all over the city were drawn to hear the Gospel.

Donald Ross continued to take a leading part in evangelistic work, and was untiring in his energies in building upon the foundation he had been mainly instrumental in laying. In 1879 he removed to America, settling for some time in Chicago. Later on he travelled across country to San Francisco, afterwards pioneering the thousands of miles from west to east, and finally returning to Chicago, where he made his home until called to higher service in 1903, at the advanced age of seventy-nine.

So rapidly did the work in Aberdeenshire prosper that in course of time the Gallowgate Chapel was found to be too small for the company, and another meeting-place had to be sought. The hall in St. Paul Street with seating accommodation for two hundred people was secured, and would also have proved inadequate long ago had there not been a frequent "hiving-off" to the various districts in the city. The work in Aberdeen, which is characterised by vigour and activity, continues to grow, so that there are now assemblies at Footdee, Holburn Hall, Torry and Woodside, all of which are offshoots from the parent assembly in St. Paul Street Hall, and still in fellowship with the company of believers there.

CHAPTER VIII

EARLY DAYS IN IRELAND

WHEN John Nelson Darby crossed from Dublin to Plymouth in 1830, carrying with him the glowing embers of a spiritual fire destined to light its way to many lands, he left behind an infant assembly as yet nameless. That assembly had already become an historic landmark. And yet, while subsequent years revealed a remarkable development in the work of the Holy Spirit in England, there appears to have been little, if any, marked progress in the region which claimed to be the birthplace of the Movement. Nor can we find any tangible trace of similar assemblies having been established in the neighbourhood of the Irish Capital consequent upon the historic meeting in Aungier Street. It is true that Darby made frequent excursions across Ireland to Limerick for the purpose of holding Bible Readings—or what was then known as Reading Meetings—but no evidence can be found of an assembly having been formed in that place at that particular time.

The present testimony at Limerick is unable to trace its origin to those visits, although it is not at all improbable that some connection must have been maintained. It is known that a small assembly existed in the city somewhere about eighty years ago, for it is on record that a rather famous preacher amongst Christians known as Friends—Evans by name—went over to the Brethren. This fresh infusion of life into the struggling assembly greatly increased their influence in the city. About this time many of the leading business men in the district appear to have been associated with the assembly which, between fifty and sixty years ago, met in the present hall in Mallow Street. Both Darby and C. H. Mackintosh are known to have ministered here on several occasions.

The fact that Dublin figured so conspicuously in the early

days of the Brethren Movement must surely have been the outcome of a series of circumstances, brought about by the divine will of God, at a particular period, consequent upon a world-wide state of religious unrest. As has already been hinted, spiritual activity and development in Dublin following the epoch-making meeting alluded to, did not rise to the degree attained in more distant parts of the kingdom, and it was not until about the time of the '59 Revival that there was a definite manifestation of the working of the Holy Spirit throughout Ireland in general and Ulster in particular.

We must, therefore, look beyond to Northern Ireland, and in our search we find in a country cottage, some four miles from the village of Banbridge in County Down, what is supposed to be the earliest Brethren meeting in Ulster. It came to be known as the Clare Meeting, and here the Lord's death was remembered from the year 1840—eighteen years before the '59 Revival. Recalling the early days of which we now write, Dr. W. J. Matthews, who for over half a century did much arduous pioneer work, preaching the Gospel, establishing and building up assemblies throughout Ulster, told the writer that during a visit in 1882, he became acquainted with the Cairns family, who were among the last survivors of the little assembly. At that time there were three aged members of the family, one of whom was blind, and she told Dr. Matthews that the Lord's death had been celebrated in the breaking of bread in that little room for forty-two years. There were then only two of these sisters there, also a niece, and one old brother to keep the feeble light burning. Soon afterwards the aged sisters died, and what remained became absorbed in another assembly which was established, following a season's Gospel meetings, in a parish near by. "The meeting referred to in Miss Cairns' house," says Dr. Matthews, "was the first in Northern Ireland so far as I know, and must have been composed of only a very few members, including old Mr. Plunkett, a customs officer, Mr. Patrick McKee, a bank manager in Banbridge, an old man named Kenaran, and the father of the old Cairns sisters. These would be about all;

and after their decease, visitors from Lisburn in later years, and from Banbridge, kept alive the testimony till we arrived in the district in 1882, and formed the assembly near by, which picked up the remnant that was left. Mr. Plunkett was a very frail old man when I first knew him about 1880; probably he was the first to lead the Cairns family into the Truth."

That notable work of grace in the year 1859 began near Kells, County Antrim, through the exercise of several young brethren, amongst them being Jeremiah Meneely. The Movement spread far and wide, one of the first districts to be reached being near the town of Randalstown, County Antrim, where many were saved through the ministry of the renowned C. H. Mackintosh and a brother called Moore. Some time soon afterwards, perhaps about 1860, a meeting was formed at a place called Groggan, two miles from Randalstown, in a little two-roomed house heated by a peat or turf fire.

The principal brethren connected with the assembly were Boyd McDowell, Robert Vance, Joseph French, and a very well-known character, Rodger Luke, who is the subject of a tract written by W. H. McLaughlin. Rodger was a very wild character in his unsaved days, well known to the police, but when "subdued by Sovereign Grace," he preached to all and sundry, including Roman Catholic priests. Gospel work was carried on constantly in his home.

After some time at Groggan, the assembly was moved to a district, more central for believers, called Clonkeen, where a wooden hall was built in which the assembly met for over fifty years, only recently moving into a splendid new hall near by.

Shortly after 1859 a few Christian men and women, whose hearts had been stirred by the wonders God had wrought in their midst during the great spiritual revival, which had invaded both Church and home, met together in a private house in Belfast to read the Scriptures and celebrate the Lord's Supper. Among them were Martin Shaw and his wife, Francis Moore and John Marshall. The little company were later joined by C. H. Mackintosh, who arrived in the city from Westport. He intended remaining in Belfast, but finding that these brethren would not go with him in his exclusive circle, he removed to Coleraine and took up residence there. Later on these few met in what was known as Abercorn Rooms, where they continued until about 1874. In that year a new departure took place. James Campbell and James Smith, two pioneer evangelists, commenced Gospel meetings in the city, and by means of tent and schoolrooms, people were drawn to hear the preachers. The outcome of this fruitful effort was the ingathering of many souls; and those who had been reached by the gospel were taught the truth of believers' baptism and gathering unto the Lord. By this time the Abercorn Rooms meeting had grown considerably, and it was found needful to acquire larger premises. Victoria Hall was secured, and here for a time the assembly met. W. H. McLaughlin, saved shortly before this time, cast in his lot with them and became a lively helper. Other leading brethren who ministered to the spiritual needs of the Church, were Charles Lepper and Samuel Spence.

The advent of the Moody and Sankey mission, when there prevailed an atmosphere of spiritual revival, reminiscent of the stirring times in Northern Ireland, was the means of bringing many into the fold. From that time there was a steady increase, and as the work among old and young developed on every hand, it became essential that another place large enough adequately to accommodate a thriving assembly should be sought out. This was done, and a building in May Street, known as the Music Hall, was purchased and suitably adapted. The name was changed to Victoria Memorial Hall. At the close of the Great War there were just under two hundred in fellowship. At the present time there are twice that number on the assembly roll. It is of interest to mention that Mr. A. Hamilton, who is still in fellowship, has been actively associated with this assembly since 1878, when the little company of believers met in the Victoria Street Hall. In the early days, he gathered together the children of the district into old King Street Hall, and formed the first Sunday School amongst Brethren in Belfast.

EARLY DAYS IN IRELAND

About the time of which we write, another assembly commenced in Queen Street, Belfast. Relative to this meeting there is rather an interesting case respecting R. M. Henry, M.A., a well-known clergyman belonging to the strict orthodox Church of the Covenanters. He was then Moderator of the Covenanters. The year he resigned his Church, he called the clergy and elders together, and told them he had been reading his Bible in Hebrew and Greek for years, but failed to find anything in Scripture to warrant the baptizing of infants. This unexpected declaration of Scripture truth was like a bomb dropped in their midst. There was a long silence. The first to jump up was John G. McVicker of Cullybackey, a fellow-clergyman. "What nonsense, Henry," he cried; "doesn't Jesus say, 'Suffer little children to come unto Me'?" "Yes, Mr. McVicker," was the reply; "but if you substitute baptism for the Lord, you can make anything you like out of the Scriptures. A thousand commands to bring children to Christ is not one to baptize them." He was then asked when he would preach his farewell sermon to his church. Nor must he mention baptism in doing so. "It is not likely I will mention baptism," was Mr. Henry's quiet reply, "but if I have to enter the pulpit muzzled, I will give no undertaking." The result was, he never got preaching his farewell sermon.

Mr. Henry then joined the Baptist communion, but a few years later associated himself with the assembly of believers who were then meeting in King Street Hall, where he continued, ministering to the spiritual needs of the little flock for many years. The assembly now meets in a more commodious hall in Apsley Street.

AFTER THE '59 REVIVAL

As we have already seen, the Brethren Movement in Ulster had its beginning, to a large extent, in the Revival of 1859, when there was peculiar evidence of a visitation of the Lord, attended by a remarkable ingathering of souls. The land had lain in spiritual darkness for centuries, when, all unheralded, the light of a new era pierced the gloom and spread over the country, apparently with little human instrumentality. Very little clear Gospel truth was known save to a few who received the new birth about this time, or a little before.

Side by side with real work for the Lord, another element crept in. It was what came to be known as "being stricken," and rather took the form of an epidemic. For instance, during the course of a meeting, people in different parts of the building would suddenly fall down with screams and shoutings, and have to be carried out, many of them crying to God for mercy.

Throughout the counties of Antrim and Derry, the work gave striking evidence of the prevailing power and presence of the Holy Spirit. Districts where Satan held sway, and over which indifference and cold religious formality had cast its mantle, gave ear to the clarion call of the Gospel. "It is well worthy of notice," says a writer of that time, "that in many cases, the work of conviction was carried on without reference to any special agency in the shape of ministry. In the field, by the wayside, in the home, souls were stricken in a moment, and led to cry, in excessive anguish, for mercy. Convicted souls were led to see the fulness, the extent, the efficacy, the infinite preciousness of the sacrifice of the Cross."

Another notable feature of this remarkable Revival may be observed. In almost every locality the Lord seemed to lay hold of some notorious character as if He would have a signal monument of grace to hold up to the view of the enemy. Some person who had been the pest of the neighbourhood was stricken down by the convicting power of the Spirit of God, and brought to sit at the feet of the Saviour, "clothed and in his right mind," and then sent forth among his old associates to tell what great things the Lord had done for him. So mightily was the power of God felt at that time, that a public-house keeper in Coleraine was heard to lament that on Saturday, the first weekly market day after the Revival commenced, there had not been a *measure wet* in his house the whole day. Thus in such an atmosphere of spiritual effulgence, not a few New Testament churches came into being; for many of those who were saved through a diligent reading of the Scriptures, having learned the truth of gathering simply in the name of the Lord, to remember His death, formed themselves into little assemblies.

Such was the case in Ballymena district, where a testimony —which is still maintained—was established. This would be about the same time as the beginning in the city of Belfast, but the testimony here never took shape aggressively in definite Gospel work (to be followed by the gathering of believers into assembly life) until 1872-73, when William McLean came from Peterhead in Scotland. He was the first evangelist to live with the people in their homes, going out daily to visit and minister to them by their firesides. This homely form of pioneer work was continued as the warm-hearted Scotsman, with soul on fire, journeyed from place to place, preaching and scattering the good seed in cottage, or hall, or by the wayside, wherever opportunity came his way.

Still the district of Ballymena had not altogether been neglected, for, in a measure, the long grass had been trodden down by such men as Jeremiah Meneely and John G. McVicker. The latter, whom we recently found in warm debate with his friend Mr. Henry, over the vexed question of infant baptism, had continued his ministerial duties in the Church of the Covenanters at Cullybackey, until his conversion, which came about in a remarkable way. He was preaching from the pulpit of his Church one day, when suddenly the light of the Gospel broke in upon him. The congregation saw the change at once and thought their minister had taken leave of his senses. "It was a mercy I did not wreck the pulpit," he afterwards said. But John was saved and the countryside soon realised it.

He gave up his Church and moved into Ballymena, where he joined the few already gathered there; and went round the countryside preaching. A large hall was built, and Mr. McVicker took his place amongst a goodly number of Christians who gathered there to remember the Lord. The ministry of John McVicker was of an order that was appreciated all over the country. After many years in Ballymena he moved to London to a wider field of usefulness; and it was there that we first introduced him to the reader in an earlier chapter.

As the assembly at Ballymena grew, little companies branched off to meet in like manner in different places. Thus we still find a testimony at the village of Kells, four miles distant, and another at Ahoghill.

NEWTONARDS AND THE ARDS PENINSULA

In the year 1860, James Patton, a Newtonards watchmaker, while on a visit to Dublin accompanied by his sister, attended a meeting for the breaking of bread. As the service proceeded, the presence of the Lord became blessedly real, and the young woman, visibly impressed by what was taking place, was heard to whisper to her brother, "James, this is just what we have been looking for." On their return home a meeting was commenced in a private house.

Isaac Finlay, then a young man in business, had only recently been converted, and on reading his Bible made the startling discovery that believers in the Lord Jesus Christ should be baptized by immersion and meet together to remember the Lord on the first day of the week. He found that, contrary to the traditions of the Church in which he had been reared, this was possible without the presence of a clergyman; in fact, Isaac saw that Paul had no notion of such an ecclesiastical dignitary in the New Testament. Thus shortly after his conversion Isaac, along with one or two others, joined the few who were meeting in the private house referred to.

The little company afterwards moved to a hall in Mill Street, and later (about the year 1890) a grain store was rented and reconstructed for use as a hall. During those years an aggressive Gospel testimony was maintained and a Sunday School was commenced. This fresh development eventually necessitated a new hall being built, which was opened in 1921. At the present time there is a thriving assembly with about two hundred in fellowship, and a Sunday School of upwards of five hundred.

In the early 'eighties Mr. Patton, when on a trip to Stranraer, made the acquaintance of a young man named John Walbran. When the latter crossed over to Ireland at the invitation of Mr. Patton, he was taken by his friend to a hill overlooking the Ards Peninsula. As the two men stood gazing across the fertile stretch of country, Mr. Patton, with a touch of pathos in his voice, remarked to the young man: "There, before you, is a district of eighteen miles in length without spiritual light." John Walbran took up the challenge and did pioneer work there for many years. Butterlump Assembly—afterwards moved to Portavogie—was commenced, and the Gospel was preached throughout the peninsula. Besides Portavogie there are now assemblies at Cardy, Ballywalter, Ballyhay, Scrabo and Comber. James Patton was taken home in 1888; Isaac Finlay lived to be ninety and passed away in 1916.

Ten or twelve miles east of Belfast, on the County Down coast, lies the town of Bangor. Early in the 'seventies, W. H. McLaughlin and John C. Graham, who usually spent the summer months of each year in Ballyholme, started a little meeting there. They were joined later by R. McClay and G. Lowden. These two brethren were greatly used in Bangor and district and through the Ards Peninsula, where at cross roads, in barns and halls the voice of these pioneers was heard proclaiming the Gospel. With many Christians coming from Belfast, they deemed it expedient to move to Bangor, where more accommodation was found in Holborn Hall. Here these brethren continued with H. B. Thompson, J. Anderson and the Watt brothers. This fresh impetus to the little assembly created a lively spiritual interest, and with the increase in numbers it became necessary almost to rebuild the hall. There are at present three assemblies in Bangor: Holborn, Central and Ebenezer.

About this time a meeting was commenced by Robert Sparks in the little town of Holywood, on the main road to Bangor and about four miles from Belfast. He was then solicitor to the Ulster Bank Head Office, Belfast, which position he later relinquished to share in the world-wide missionary responsibilities of *Echoes of Service* at Bath.

Previous to the commencement of the assemblies in the neighbourhood of Belfast just referred to, a few brethren were meeting to remember the Lord's death in the house of Mr. Hermon in Young Street, Lisburn, a town about ten miles from the city. After a time they moved to a hall in Conns Yard. About the year 1874, Robert and James Stewart, mill owners and thread manufacturers, purchased the Methodist Hall in Market Street, where a testimony was maintained for some years. Following the death of Robert Stewart, the property passed into other hands, and the brethren subsequently built the present hall in Wallace Avenue, where there is still a progressive Gospel testimony.

In the autumn of 1873, following a visit to America, James Campbell arrived in County Down. He was accompanied by John Boal, a Presbyterian elder, who had been saved through the preaching of Mr. Campbell in America. Energised with the zeal of a first love, the young convert, on the return to his native country, became deeply concerned as to the salvation of his relatives in Ballymaconaghy, near Belfast. This he made known to Mr. Campbell, who about that time was joined by Mr. James Smith, of Aberdeen. An intensive Gospel campaign followed, and large numbers were brought to the Saviour. Among them were the relatives of the young convert. This season of general awakening, when old and young were roused from a spiritual lethargy which seemed to have become part of their daily lives, became a starting-point from which radiated Gospel activity, that continued all over the North of Ireland. But Campbell and Smith were men of much prayer, full of the Holy Ghost and very active Gospellers. And through their labours for the Master may be attributed, not only the laying of many foundations, but the building of not a few Churches which to-day are a living testimony. Thus from the circumstance of the fervent prayer of a young convert, accompanied by a remarkable work of grace, an assembly was formed in the

HENRY BEWLEY.

WILLIAM FRY.

J. G. McVICKER.

district of Ballymaconaghy, the meeting-room being in the house of the relatives of John Boal, who were among the first to be saved.

The two evangelists now moved to Belfast, and having obtained the use of a schoolroom from a Christian clergyman who also gave assistance in the work, they carried the Gospel into the homes of the people. This was followed by a summer campaign, when a tent was pitched on Donegal Pass. Then in the autumn of the same year came the Moody and Sankey visit to Belfast, when the city was stirred as never before and hundreds of souls were brought into the Kingdom. An important feature of the work of grace during that memorable year, was the large number of young men saved and afterwards gathered into the assemblies of Christians, of which there were four or five in Belfast at that time.

PIONEER WORK IN ULSTER

From the city of Belfast the activities of Campbell and Smith extended to Dromore, Crossgar and other districts of County Down. As a result of their visit to the neighbourhood of Crossgar, an assembly was formed, the first meeting for the breaking of bread being held in the house of Mrs. McCleery at Ballywoollen, near Crossgar, in June, 1874. Shortly afterwards, the meeting was moved to a loft behind the house, when twenty members gathered around the Lord's Table. On the first Lord's Day it was held there, the roof had not been completed, so that the remembrance feast was celebrated under the open sky. Here they continued for two and a half years, after which the assembly moved into the present hall at Crossgar.

The converts were baptized in the stream that runs beside the house at Ballywoollen. Where the river crosses the road, it was dammed at the bridge, and the volume of water allowed to increase till of a sufficient depth to suit the purpose of baptism. When the neighbours saw the stream being dammed up they knew what was about to happen, and people gathered in large numbers to witness the ceremony.

T

At one particular baptismal service, a large crowd, mostly Roman Catholics, gathered and threw stones and sticks at the converts. Mr. Campbell, who was baptizing the believers, was cut in the face, while several others received injury from missiles thrown during the ceremony. The house was then attacked and most of the windows were broken. Despite this persecution, which was urged on by the priests, twelve converts were baptized that evening. Nor did the little company of Christians suffer depression of spirits because of the cruel treatment received at the hands of the enemy. On the contrary, such wanton acts of violence seemed only to give them fresh impetus. On one occasion when Campbell and Smith had been preaching at Ballywoollen, the audience continued singing hymns outside till late into the night, and it is said that the singing was heard two or three miles away. As the meeting continued, one after another confessed faith in Christ, to occasion a fresh outburst of praise.

The Crossgar Assembly in its hey-day numbered about seventy to eighty, but it gradually diminished as one family after another migrated to the colonies. Many of the young men who went out preaching on the Lord's Day, gathered on Saturday night at the house of a brother in Belfast. A prayer meeting would take place, after which it was decided where they should go preaching the following day, going out in apostolic fashion, two by two, to the small country assemblies.

James Smith was called Home in 1878. His fellow-labourer in the Gospel continued full of work for nearly thirty years after. We come now to another remarkable development of the work in which, undoubtedly, James Campbell was the chief promoter and pioneer. For the first three years since his coming to Ireland he preached almost every night. Burdened with the great need, so evident on every hand, Campbell constantly prayed the Lord to raise up more labourers. Young men whom he considered well fitted for service, he encouraged to give themselves to the work. This in time bore fruit. One after another was raised up of the Lord to go forth on the same lines, pioneering all the time; for there were few assemblies to go to for help in those days.

About this time Dr. W. J. Matthews felt the call of the Gospel, and became greatly exercised in soul at the overwhelming need of men ready to go forth with the message of salvation to the outlying districts yet unreached. He had just graduated in medicine at the Royal University of Ireland, and, after long inward constraint, decided to give up his newly acquired profession, to go preaching without salary or means. This he continued to do uninterruptedly for upwards of half a century. From the first, God seemed to bless the work, and not only was he used in the conversion of a vast number of souls, but in later years was an outstanding figure in assembly life in Northern Ireland, having been the means of the founding and the building up of Churches in many parts of Ulster. Dr. Matthews was joined by Thomas Lough, a draper, who took a fortnight's holiday to lend a hand in the Gospel, and continued for twenty-four years, till the Lord called him Home. Others went out about the same time, and all continued for years. Possibly the last survivor is John Knox McEwen, who went forth about fifty-seven years ago, and though now advanced in years is still preaching.

Almost all were unmarried young men who had no family responsibilities, and were thus able to go on year after year. There were times when the pioneer labourers were faced with almost insuperable difficulties, not a few occasions arising when it was with difficulty money was found for the week's lodging. But the Lord never failed to supply their every need. The work went on and considerable numbers were brought to a knowledge of the Truth. Assemblies were formed throughout the province, and this development continued with the passage of years, till at the present time there are about one hundred and fifty assemblies in Ulster alone, out of perhaps a million and a quarter population.

The next district to be opened up about this time was County Armagh, through the labours of William McLean and David Rea. The latter had for some years been associated with the Irish Evangelisation Society, which he left that he might obey the whole Word of God. In doing so he gave up a salary, to trust in God alone for support, and be free to follow the Lord in believers' baptism and in the breaking of bread. He was joined by Mr. McLean in 1878. From that year onwards; the two pioneers carried the Gospel to those who lived in religious darkness, and made known the unpreached truths of the New Testament throughout the scattered districts of Portadown, Armagh and Keady, with lasting results. Assemblies gathered in various places, and the Ahorey annual believers' meeting, which was commenced about that time, continues to the present day, with a company of about six hundred attending for fellowship and the ministry of the Word.

During the summer of 1882 John Halyburton, a Scottish evangelist, accompanied by Alexander Scott, the son of an Irish farmer and gifted as a Gospel preacher, arrived in the neighbourhood of Dunadry and pitched a Gospel tent on some farm land there. Their reception, although not exactly hostile, was far from cordial, for these itinerant preachers had landed amongst a people of the staunch Presbyterian type, who, though devout enough in their form of worship, thought it sheer presumption that anyone could be sure of being saved. It is not to be wondered, therefore, that when these men preached after the manner of the Puritans, keeping the three R's—Ruin, Redemption and Regeneration—prominently to the fore, there was no small stir in the countryside. But the hand of the Lord was with His servants, and men and women were convicted by the Holy Spirit, and soon afterwards brought to Christ. Then as these preachers, faithful to the text of the commission, sought to teach the converts to observe all things, those who sought to follow the Lord began to know something of bearing His reproach, and suffering shame for His name.

A number were baptized in what was then known as the Old Lodge Hall, Belfast, and in the following year they gathered in the capacity of an assembly in the home of Mrs. Boyd, a widow, who herself had been saved some time prior to the coming of the tent to Dunadry. Here they continued for some years, until the present modest hall was built.

David Rea's steps were directed to the village of Killeen, through a letter received from his friend William McLean, who had recently been there. He had preached in the Orange Hall, and could only remain one night, but he assured his friend that he would find the hall filled with people, "sitting like little birds in a nest, waiting and hungering for the Gospel." David Rea responded to the call. Night after night the building was packed, many being unable to gain admission. Soon afterwards he was joined by Mr. McLean and the meetings were continued for six months, during which time the Spirit of the Lord moved mightily upon the people, and large numbers were truly converted to God.

The evangelists now gathered together those who had been saved and instructed them in the doctrine of baptism by immersion, and the breaking of bread on the first day of the week. To some who had been brought up in the Church and reared on its ecclesiastical creeds, this was quite new teaching and caused much bitterness. The first to be baptized was a man named James Henderson. Mr. Rea had been told that this brother wanted a conversation with him on the subject. He called upon him and enquired if he wished to speak on the question of baptism. "Not now," was the ready reply, "I have been to the Word, and I now want to get to the water." He was baptized soon afterwards in a river near by. Thus the foundation of a new Church was laid at Killeen.

On another occasion, during a mission at Karvagh, a baptism took place in the river, when six converts, among them being the daughter of a clergyman, passed through the waters. "A man threatened to shoot me if I dared to immerse anyone in this locality," says David Rea, in his interesting biography; "and while the baptism was taking place, he came armed with a gun and concealed himself adjacent to the river bank; but the Lord prevented him from carrying his threat into execution."

IN THE VILLAGES OF ULSTER

In the early 'eighties Gospel concentration was made upon the central district of County Down. The responsibility fell to the lot of Dr. Matthews and a brother named Oliver, who for several years laboured together all through those parts, where at that time there was no testimony at all. God signally owned the labours of these men, toiling upon virgin soil, in the raising up of true believers and the formation of several healthy assemblies. A pleasing feature was the attendant circumstance that many saved during this time were raised up to carry the Gospel to other parts of the world. Through lack of employment in the old country, considerable numbers from time to time emigrated to the colonies, and there are assemblies in Canada and New Zealand, as well as in the United States of America, who can trace their origin to those pioneering days in Northern Ireland.

About this time, the Omagh district in County Tyrone was visited by James Campbell and William Matthews and an aggressive campaign was carried on, attended with much blessing, meetings being held in tents and barns through lack of more suitable housing accommodation. In the process of such work at this period, it should be remembered that these labourers in the Gospel, going out in true apostolic fashion, did not enjoy the comforts and comparative luxury that fall to the lot of some of the present-day evangelists; and their means being scanty, it frequently happened that it was with difficulty they were able to make ends meet. One feature, however, prevailed then which, possibly because of changed conditions, does not appear so much in evidence to-day, and that to the extent of assisting each other during a difficult and trying period. Thus, when one labourer had more than necessary to meet his present financial requirements, he would share with others. Especially was this the case towards those who were labouring in isolated parts, breaking up new ground. In this way a close fellowship and brotherly love in the truest sense existed amongst the little band of pioneer workers, which linked them together and in a powerful measure contributed largely to the success which attended their labours in the laying of a foundation upon which succeeding generations have built a spiritual structure.

During the summer of 1879, Campbell and Matthews pitched a tent a mile out of Cookstown on the Moneymore road. Almost from the first night of their arrival there was a continuous work of grace, productive of blessing in the conversion of souls. After two months the tent was moved to Agulas, about a mile and a half on the other side of the town. Here the Gospel meetings were followed by Bible readings, where the Scriptures were opened up and New Testament truths revealed to those who had recently experienced the new birth, and were now thirsting for a fuller knowledge of the divine will of God. Soon afterwards a few believers gathered to remember the Lord Jesus in the breaking of bread. Through the summer large numbers were brought to the Saviour, and by the month of October the number gathering around the Lord's table had increased to about seventy. Mr. Campbell rented the upper room of a store in the town, but this apartment in course of time became too small and a hall was built in Cookstown.

"Campbell and Matthews had meetings in Guilley," writes an aged sister, "but it was Dr. Matthews who started the morning meeting. He stayed at our home, and I went with him across the country as he did not know the way. Someone always accompanied him at night; one who knew the district led the way, Dr. Matthews next, and about ten or twelve followed behind. We went through fields and over by-roads, which would have puzzled a stranger. However, God blessed the Word and many people were saved." Recalling the memorable visit of Campbell and Matthews, my aged correspondent writes with the zeal of youth in her vivid description of those stirring times, when many of the country folk walked six or eight miles to the meetings, arriving back home about midnight, or soon after. This happy exercise of soul and body was continued three nights a week for six weeks.

Campbell and Matthews laboured in season and out of season, in busy city, country town, lonely hamlet, and rural district throughout the unreached parts of the North of Ireland. "Fairs and markets were visited," says another writer, "open-air meetings held, thousands of pointed messages distributed, and numbers dealt with personally about their eternal welfare. Souls were saved and churches planted in very many parts, the crowning time in soul-winning being in Cookstown district in 1879-80, hundreds being led to Christ. As a father in the faith and a true shepherd of souls, no name is more cherished in these parts than that of beloved James Campbell."

In the summer of 1893 County Donegal, which is largely Roman Catholic, was visited by James Megaw and George Watt. The evangelists pitched a Gospel tent at Ramelton, a village not far from Letterkenny. Later they were joined by Dr. Matthews. From the start they were faced with tremendous opposition, and the fortresses of Rome appeared almost impregnable. The pioneers, therefore, reluctantly confined their attention to isolated Protestant districts where, amid difficulties and discouragement, the two brethren laboured assiduously for two years. At Letterkenny their efforts in the Gospel were rewarded in seeing a number of men and women brought to the Saviour. An assembly was formed, and after much difficulty, fostered by local prejudice, a suitable hall was secured, where there is still a living testimony, surrounded by the forces of Roman Catholicism. Afterwards some useful pioneering was carried into the enemy's camp by Hugh Crichton and others, but it was chiefly upon the shoulders of Dr. Matthews and James Megaw that the burden of pioneering in Donegal was borne.

Later a survey was made of County Derry, Coleraine and Limavady, and it was decided to launch a Gospel effort, chefly in the outlying districts. In Coleraine, two brethren with a few women began to remember the Lord. For a time the assembly was cared for by visiting brethren. As the testimony grew, God raised others locally who have since kept the light burning.

Limavady is a district lying between Derry and Coleraine,

and had not yet been reached by the Gospel, until in 1901, when Dr. Matthews, accompaned by a young man named R. McCracken, pitched a tent in the neighbourhood. While the work was in progress the doctor's health gave way, due to the prolonged strain, and the reins were taken up by his brother, Abram Matthews, who continued the work in the tent with fruitful results. Here again, the New Testament truths of believers' baptism and the Lord's Supper were taught to those who had recently confessed faith in Christ, and an assembly of believers was formed. From such beginnings a prosperous assembly now gathers in a splendid hall, once the old Court House of the town.

Somewhere in the early 'seventies a few Christians met in a private house in the town of Lurgan. About this time Lord Carrick, from the South of Ireland, came along with Charles Inglis, of London, and a brother from Dublin known as Fiddler Joss. The Mechanics' Institute was hired for Gospel meetings and a remarkable work of grace followed, many being converted to God. Soon afterwards a company of believers commenced to remember the Lord's death.

Some years after this, a young Christian named Dr. Darling came to reside at Lurgan, and rapidly established an extensive medical practice. His coming proved a great help to the young meeting. Dr. Darling had the inestimable blessing of a godly upbringing, and at the early age of ten—as recorded in his diary—he was brought to a saving knowledge of his Lord and Saviour. To the little meeting he became a tower of strength, and was much used of the Lord in ministering to the growing Church. For many years David Rea and Archibald Bell laboured in this district, and greatly encouraged and strengthened the believers in and around Lurgan and Portadown.

The assembly at Kilmore, in County Armagh, about three miles from Lurgan, had its origin in a barn, which had been hired for the purpose of Gospel meetings, by the two evangelists, about the year 1888. At the opening meeting, although it was a bleak winter night with snow lying thickly on the ground, about forty people gathered in the cold barn to hear the Gospel. The Lord gave much liberty, and a fruitful time of sowing and reaping followed. Recalling that eventful night, which was the beginning of a remarkable work of grace in the district, David Rea relates that after the first meeting, he and his fellow-workers were leaving the barn when a young woman came running out of a house near by, and in an excited manner shouted to them to stop and come into the house. They went in, and there on the floor knelt three women and a young girl with arms upraised imploring God to save them. The two brethren knelt down beside them and asked God to reveal Christ to their anxious souls. In a few minutes one of the women rose to her feet and went out praising God for having saved her. By this time a number of people had gathered outside the door, and when the brethren left, they joined those in the house and remained until after midnight.

On their return to the meeting in the barn the following evening, the evangelists were met by seven women and a young man. They had trusted the Saviour in the house into which the two brethren had been called the previous night. This was the beginning of a time of revival in that district. Those who had been gathered into the Kingdom met together on the first day of the week to remember the Lord. A Sunday School was commenced, and the Lord manifested His power in the salvation of many of the young folk.

At Bessbrook, County Armagh, a village with a population of about three thousand four hundred inhabitants, the foundation of an assembly was laid amid stormy scenes and violent opposition. This was about sixty years ago. Though known as "the model village of Ireland," because of the fact that it possessed neither public-house, pawnshop nor police barracks, the reception given by the inhabitants to the messengers of the Gospel of peace, did not exactly accord with the rather dubious appellation assigned to that particular Irish village. David Rea and Francis Logg arrived in the district with a Gospel tent, and for two months toiled under disheartening conditions. At times the evangelists were obliged to obtain the assistance of the police from a neighbouring town for protection. Several attempts were made

EARLY DAYS IN IRELAND

by the mob to pull down the tent while the meetings were going on. Stones and other missiles were thrown upon it, and on one occasion the canvas was set on fire. And yet, despite the furious onslaught of the enemy, the Lord manifested His power and grace in a number of remarkable conversions.

The baptism of ten believers in the river near by was the occasion of a hostile demonstration by an unruly crowd, who gathered to witness the ceremony. Then in the evening, as if to give vent to their derision, a bonfire was kindled, when there was a further display of the hatred and contempt with which the evangelists were assailed. With a prelude, accompanied by such violent scenes, when the preachers were constantly beset with danger and difficulty, it would seem almost beyond belief, but for the wonder-working power of God, that at the close of what proved to be one of the most trying Gospel campaigns, David Rea was able to write in his diary: "We gathered together the converts on the first day of the week to remember the Lord in the breaking of bread. It was our privilege to have the assistance and fellowship of James Stewart, who was very helpful in ministering the Word to the young believers and establishing them in the truth." Surely a striking instance of the triumph of the Gospel in the armed camp of an unsleeping enemy.

IN SOUTHERN IRELAND

The history of the Movement in Southern Ireland forms reading less soul-exhilarating than that of its neighbour, the thriving northern province of Ulster. The circumstance of the first public meeting of Brethren having been held in the Irish capital does not appear to have inspired the countrymen of Darby and Bellett with the same spiritual zeal which lent courage and conviction in the carrying out of the dictates of conscience by the breaking down of ecclesiastical barriers, reared by the traditions of their fathers. It is true that isolated companies of Christian believers were meeting on Scriptural grounds, but few got beyond the embryonic stage; and the process of time gave evidence of meagre growth. The spiritual decadence of the Movement, due principally to political and religious conditions, has been singularly marked during the difficult times through which the unhappy country has passed.

The existence of a company of believers breaking bread in an improvised meeting-room in Aungier Street, Dublin, where the lamp was first lit (which was destined to cast its unbroken beams across the world), was of comparative brief duration, and almost a quarter of a century had to pass before the broken link was taken up by another generation. We will, therefore, leave the Irish Capital for the present, to return again in the course of events.

For some years, interest was focused mainly upon the southern counties of England, radiating from an axis ranged upon the old-time seaport which gave its name to that stretch of water known as Plymouth Sound. To the reader who has unweariedly sojourned with the writer the names of the early brethren and the days to which we now allude are familiar history. Thus, as we observe a notable development in the progress of the divine plan in England, we will turn aside to follow the operation of the Holy Spirit in a distant corner of the Emerald Isle.

While John G. Bellett is universally recognised as one of the earliest Irish exponents of the revived truths for which the Brethren Movement stands, the name of his brother, George Bellett, a clergyman of the Episcopal Church, is not so well known. The latter was curate in the parish of Bandon, County Cork, between the years of 1830 and 1840. He was a man of sterling character and high Christian principles. A sister, now in her ninety-sixth year, who is still in fellowship in Bandon Assembly, states that on frequent occasions she heard her father say that the clear expositions of the Truth propounded from the pulpit by George Bellett, marked the beginning of a work in the consciences of many to whom he ministered; and although Mr. Bellett himself maintained his connection with the denomination to the end of his life, several whom he led into the light and liberty of Scriptural Truth were unable to remain with him. Thus, it would be towards the end of his curacy, or soon afterwards, that the Bandon Assembly was formed. An old assembly pass-book is still in existence, which recounts the expenses for rent, coal and other commodities, its first entry falling under date 1843.

In the years of the Kerry revival, three-quarters of a century ago, the preachers from that county visited Bandon regularly. By this time very few of the first generation of believers were left in the little meeting. The visit of the preachers resulted, under the blessing of God, in a further accretion to the assembly, there being about thirty saved and added to the Church. Possibly the only notable visitor spoken of in connection with the very early days was Dr. Tregelles the distinguished Biblical scholar. Later in the 'seventies, several well-known men were numbered among those who gave spiritual sustenance and exerted a vast influence for good in spite of the dominant power of Romanism. These included F. C. Bland of Derryquin Castle, Richard Mahony of Dromore Castle, Sir Robert Anderson (at that time a student), George Trench of Ardfert, and later, the Earl of Carrick and Lieutenant Mandeville of the Royal Navy. Periodical visits by such gifted brethren not only built up and stimulated the little assembly but, as meetings were frequently held in the Town Hall, a much wider circle was reached and the work was productive of lasting blessing.

While the Protestant population of Southern Ireland is now less than that of the early days, still the meeting has continued, although in recent years numbers have been seldom over thirty. During the period of the civil war in Ireland, emigration from the country took away a considerable number of men and women, with their children, and only by God's watchful care was the assembly kept alive.

About forty-seven years ago, through the generosity of the late Gordon Oswald, a building since known as Bridge Place Hall was provided as a place of worship. The new hall was opened with an evangelistic campaign conducted by Alexander Marshall, who was then in the vigour of youth. Previous to this time the meetings for believers had been held in a private room, while the Sunday School was conducted in the ballroom of an hotel.

Among the assembly's activities, the welfare of the young has been the constant thought and care of those who watched for souls; and for over sixty years, often amidst much opposition and discouragement, a Sunday School has been carried on with a membership fluctuating between fifty and ninety. During the years of the Great War, the hall was made available as a home for soldiers, and there was a real work of grace during that period of Gospel opportunity. In this particular work the sisters did valiant service, and with the assistance of other local Christians, gave of their time and substance in caring for the men and seeking to lead them to the Saviour.

A distinguishing feature of the Irish revival, which in due course reached the Southern provinces, was that it changed the whole aspect of many aristocratic Protestant families. In County Kerry many of the leading gentry, to whom we have already alluded, became obedient to the teaching of the Word, and in a remarkable manner were the means, in God's hands, in the conversion of considerable numbers, and to the establishing of small assemblies of Christians.

From an Irish emigrant in South Africa, there has come to me a letter relative to the Movement in Kenmare. It has just that homely touch reminiscent of bygone occurrences which in a peculiar way remain fixed on the mind, to be unconsciously flashed on the screen of remembrance, at an unexpected moment, upon the recurrence of some particular circumstance. "The influence of the Revival," writes my correspondent, "first began to be felt in the far South in the 'sixties. In 1861 my father was in County Kerry. He had made up his mind to have a really good time in Galway, where he could attend places of amusement all through the winter months and enjoy himself to his heart's content. God ordered that he should go to Kerry. At Kenmare he was asked by a gentleman to tell Mr. Mahony of Dromore Castle that they were having times of much blessing and that God was bringing souls into the Kingdom. As might be expected, my father, being unsaved at the time, was not at all keen on taking such a message, but he managed somehow. At the time he gave the message, Mr. F. C. Bland of Derryquin Castle was present. Mr. Mahony remarked that he did not see why they should not have something of the kind there, in Sneem, whereupon Mr. Bland promptly suggested that the school where my grandfather was master should be engaged. The meetings began, and I believe C. H. Mackintosh was one of the first speakers. It was on this occasion that Mr. Bland and his wife were converted. Another convert was George C. Needham, afterwards well known as an evangelist in America. He was then a young fellow of about eighteen. One night when my father was at the meeting, this lad stood up and testified that he was saved, and was as sure as he stood there that if God called him away he would go to Heaven. 'What presumption,' thought my father, who had always been taught to believe that no one could have this assurance till afterwards; 'it's a wonder God does not strike him dead.' That very night, however, my father was gloriously saved."

At Kenmare, Ardfert and many other places, little assemblies sprang up. Alas, since then how many candlesticks have been removed! For those who were faithful to the Word had ever to contend against the forces of Romanism; and Protestants of all denominations were compelled to find sanctuary in other lands.

In the town of Kenmare, a few believers, among them Joseph Mansfield, John Milne, Townsend Trench and John Brennan, met for the breaking of bread and for ministry. John Milne had come to Ireland from Aboyne, Aberdeenshire, to fill a situation under Lord Lansdowne, who had extensive estates in County Kerry. Saved before leaving home, John was a bright Christian, and full of enthusiasm for the spread of the Gospel. The opportunity afforded by the fellowship of brethren with a heart for the perishing, presented an outlet for his pent-up energies, and so an effort to win souls for the Master was successful in bringing some into the Kingdom. A few believers were meeting for about six months in Mr. Milne's home at Kenmare before they heard of Christians known as Brethren, and it was a great joy to them when they learnt that many others had been led to carry out the simple principles of the early Church, as they themselves had learned from the Scriptures. Townsend Trench, who was an outstanding personality, associated himself with the little company at Kenmare, and entered heartily into the work of the Lord. The truth of the Second Coming of the Lord so gripped his heart, that he travelled far and near proclaiming the great event.

Mr. Mahony of Dromore Castle, six miles from Kenmare, built a meeting-room on his estate for an assembly, which was composed mainly of his household and tenants. Another assembly was formed at Ardfert, and William Talbot Crosbie and George Trench became a power for God in that district. F. C. Bland of Derryquin, a country gentleman of culture, grace and gift, preached the Gospel and ministered with great acceptance among these young assemblies.

Recalling the work of the Lord in the early days in Kerry, a brother who visited Townsend Trench in London shortly before his Home-call, told the writer that Mr. Trench, with tears streaming down his handsome face, exclaimed, "There was much sunshine in those wonderful years!" A recollection of happier times, tinged by a note of sadness. Alas, all those assemblies have ceased to exist, and darkness has again settled down where the light and peace and joy of the Gospel of grace once held sway. "The last time the meeting-room at Dromore Castle was used for a Gospel meeting," writes Mr. Robert Milne, of Aberdeen, "Mr. Archie Bell, of Lurgan, and I preached in it. The castle was empty, and the agent allowed us the use of the building. Kenmare, the last assembly in Kerry, went out of existence only a few years ago, through the death of Mr. A. Mansfield, whose revered father saw the commencement of the testimony in that place."

There was much spiritual darkness and but few saved people in the village of Greystones, in County Dublin, when, in the month of January, 1888, a man gifted as a preacher of the Gospel arrived and rented a small room in the centre of the village. He commenced Gospel services which, for a time, were continued on alternate Sunday evenings. There was little encouragement and much persecution; but the Lord blessed the efforts of His servant and gave him the joy of seeing many turn from sin's bondage unto God. As the work prospered, the enemy stirred up opposition. For a time the position became almost untenable, and some were hindered from attending the meetings. But God was with the faithful soldiers of the Cross and their forces increased, until a year or two after the start, a little company gathered each Lord's Day morning to remember His death.

As the infant assembly gained strength a special Gospel mission was undertaken, when even the most prejudiced people were brought in—some coming two or three miles from the country districts. The meeting-room became filled to overflowing, and the presence and power of God were manifestly experienced in many conversions taking place. Soon afterwards the call came to gather in the children and a service was held on Sunday afternoons, where willing helpers sought to lead the little ones to know and love the Saviour. This initial effort amongst the young folks, largely due to the untiring labours of Miss F. Buckley, who tended the lambs with unceasing care, was productive of much real and lasting spiritual fruit. "Many of the children who were converted here," says one writer, "are grown up, and to-day are scattered far and wide throughout the earth, bright witnesses for the Master. One has been a missionary in Burma for the past five years, while another is to-day in training for work in the foreign field."

From Greystones the Gospel was carried to outlying districts; but as the activities of the little assembly increased so did their difficulties, and it soon became evident that amongst a people hostile to the Word of Truth, there were few halls available for the purpose of preaching the Gospel of grace. This difficulty, however, has been overcome by the provision, in answer to prayer, of a portable wooden hall which could conveniently be taken from one district to another. Thus many of the isolated parts, hitherto untouched by the Gospel, had the message of Salvation brought within hearing of their dwellings, as well as having it told by their own firesides; for the visitor to the homes of those humble Irish country folk invariably met with a kindly welcome.

The building of a new hall to meet the needs of a growing assembly, was by this time engaging the attention of the little company of Christians, although they had not as yet definite guidance as to the structural erection, nor had they in hand the necessary funds. Night after night for several months, the believers crowded into the small meeting-room, with hearts burdened in prayer for what at that time seemed a thing almost impossible to perform. It was indeed a time of patient waiting upon God, as His never-failing purposes were slowly but surely being unfolded. A site was chosen, and on an appointed day soon afterwards, possession of the ground was taken. On the following morning a letter arrived from Switzerland containing £10 for the Lord's work. It was the first sum of money sent in. Other sums followed just as the need arose for the purchase of the building materials. Stones and sand were freely given, while horses and carts were lent for conveying the materials. "Night and day," we are told, "the workers laboured; those who could not work with their hands, labouring in prayer. The walls rose rapidly, for, as it was in the days of Nehemiah, the people had a mind to work. The passers-by looked on, and while one or two questioned, what do these poor men? and thought it presumption to attempt such a building, yet others perceived that 'this work was wrought of God.'" Five busy months passed, and God granted the workers the long-cherished desire of their hearts. The hall, a substantial building, capable of seating three hundred people, was completed. And they sang:

> "We believe God answers prayer,
> We are sure God answers prayer,
> We have proved God answers prayer!
> Glory to His name!"

Throughout the years that have passed, the hand of God has been upon the work carried on in Ebenezer Hall, a testimony to the power and grace of a never-failing Lord and Saviour, whose remembrance feast on the first day of the week is indeed a sweet and refreshing oasis in a desert land. And so the witness at Greystones goes on, sowing and reaping until the Lord of the harvest comes, when sower and reaper shall rejoice together in His presence, as they cast their sheaves at the feet of Him Who has called and chosen them for His service.

DUBLIN AND MERRION HALL

Of Southern Ireland comparatively little remains to be set down here. In thought we take a last look back to the momentous years which immediately followed the first quarter of last century. Strange though it may seem, the candle that was destined to give light to the world, became pale beside its more illustrious luminaries on the other side of the Irish Sea and, gradually weakening, it flickered for a time and went out. On the other hand, before a decade had passed by, Plymouth, Bristol and London, to whom it had transmitted the first germ of spiritual life, in turn loomed largely on the horizon of this new and irresistible spiritual influence. Thus Dublin, the birthplace of the Movement, for a period of time lay dormant; and while there would doubtless be those away from the public gaze, who chose to carry out God's will in humble obscurity, still it was not till the early 'sixties that the mists of uncertainty were dispelled by the penetrating beams of the Gospel light, bringing in its train a joyful return to the carrying out of New Testament teaching.

The re-birth of the testimony in Dublin may be traced to the days of the great revival. Mention has frequently been made regarding the power of the Holy Spirit in those stirring times. As in Ulster, so this spiritual visitation was experienced in and around Dublin in a very marked degree, consequent upon which multitudes of souls in the bondage of sin, were brought into the conscious enjoyment of the peace of God, while many of His own people were awakened to a fuller knowledge of their spiritual blessings in the Risen Christ.

J. Denham Smith—whose revered name will ever be associated with the '59 Revival—was at that time pastor of a Congregational Church in Kingstown. When this remarkable outburst of spiritual blessing swept across the land, it very soon made itself felt in the Kingstown church. Impelled by a loving desire and a yearning for souls, Denham Smith responded to the call of the Lord and left his church for Dublin, where the old Metropolitan Hall, Lower Abbey Street (on the site of which the Christian Union Buildings now stand), was engaged by William Fry, a well-known and highly esteemed Dublin solicitor. Here, with the help of friends of like mind, Denham Smith commenced evangelistic services such as had never before been known in the Irish Capital. It is said that "thousands flocked together in the morning and remained hour after hour—many without refreshments—until ten and eleven at night. Careless ones were awakened, anxious ones led into peace, and persons of all classes rejoiced in a newly-found Saviour."

A brochure published in 1913, at the close of fifty years, gives a brief history of the assembly, and is a fitting tribute to the memory of the early pioneers of the Gospel. The inception of the now famous Merrion Hall came about through frequent consultations between Henry Bewley, William Fry and J. Denham Smith, as to the best means to adopt whereby the great masses òf the unsaved might be reached with the Gospel. The first proposition was to secure the Metropolitan Hall, and remodel it so as to render it suitable as an evangelistic centre. This was subsequently found to be impracticable, and finally it was determined to erect an entirely new building. The suggestion, as expressed in the prospectus issued at the time, was the erection on a suitable site, of a building to be an Evangelising Centre for the whole country. In 1862 a most eligible site was secured in Lower Merrion Street, adjoining Merrion Square, considered to be one of the best positions for the purpose, in the City of Dublin. It was decided forthwith to erect a hall which would accommodate two thousand five hundred persons, and this was accordingly done, at a total cost for building and furnishing of over £16,000. The opening

EARLY DAYS IN IRELAND

took place on the 26th of August 1863, and thus Merrion Hall started on its career of blessing. Before proceeding further, it should be mentioned that in the year 1878 the hall became the property of the assembly, and was vested in trustees on their behalf.

It has already been stated that Merrion Hall was primarily built to be a centre of evangelistic effort, and this original intention has never been departed from. During all these years the preaching of the glorious Gospel of God's salvation for sinful men has been kept well in the forefront. In early days the Gospel was heralded from its platform by such stalwarts as Denham Smith, Richard Weaver, Grattan Guinness, Shuldham Henry, Harry Moorhouse, George Müller, F. C. Bland, Dr. Barnardo, besides others whose names are as household words. Nor has there ever lacked a supply of gifted preachers to proclaim the message of salvation in Merrion Hall. It is computed that the congregation gathered each Sunday evening under the sound of the Word, has for many years been one of the largest to be found in any Protestant place of worship in Dublin; and eternity alone will reveal the numbers of whom it may truly be said that "this and that man was born there." From this assembly many have gone forth to various parts of the world, serving God as evangelists and missionaries who owe their salvation to the Word they heard preached in Merrion Hall.

Although the preaching of the Gospel and the ingathering of souls has from the start, over seventy years ago, occupied a foremost place, it by no means exhausts the record of the work of the assembly. This is revealed by its various activities, notably amongst the young life which constitutes a large Sunday School. It is worthy of note that the workers in these services for the Lord, are for the most part themselves fruit of the work.

The assembly at Merrion Hall has ever maintained a clear testimony for the truth of God and the authority of His Word. "Thus," says the writer of the brochure referred to, "through His grace the unity of the Spirit has been kept in the bond of peace. The old paths have been firmly adhered to, and the Gospel of the Lord Jesus Christ has been found to be sufficient. No extraneous aids have been resorted to, and the Word of God unmixed with human novelties has proved effective to secure the accomplishment of God's purposes of blessing for both saint and sinner."

With the story of Dublin, our narrative of the rise and progress of the Brethren Movement, principally during the last century and the opening of the present, draws to a close. Our journey, leading along the avenue of years, may have been long and tedious to the patient reader, and yet, one is hopeful that in our sojourn together through days of sunshine and shadow, the flowers gathered by the wayside may yield a sweet and lasting fragrance at the remembrance of all the way the Lord has led His people.

PART III

EARLY DAYS IN THE FOREIGN FIELD

EARLY DAYS IN THE FOREIGN FIELD

THE early pages of this book recorded the setting out of a small party of pioneer missionaries upon what proved to be an enterprise destined to yield far-reaching results. This chapter, which is the last, again takes up the story and tells of a century's trials and triumphs in the foreign field.

In the plague-stricken city of Baghdad, an ambassador of Christ stood by the death-couch of his young wife. Within two years of leaving their home in Exeter, and less than eighteen months in this cesspool of disease and iniquity, her course was run. This tragic event, which cast two motherless boys into the lap of the unveiled future, marked the laying of the first stone in a missionary structure which in the hundred years that have since passed on, has grown to dimensions stretching almost from pole to pole. The toilsome years amid the arid sands of Persia—truly virgin soil where spade had not yet penetrated—though productive of meagre fruit, were testing years which brought through the fire of affliction, Anthony Norris Groves, who, under the guidance of God, may rightly be regarded as the founder of our far-flung missionary enterprise.

The tortuous journey from Baghdad to India, where his efforts in the Gospel met with happier results, impressed Groves with that country's need and its vast possibilities. He returned to England in the hope of creating an interest in the carrying of the Gospel to other lands. In this he was successful, and from Barnstaple there went forth to India in 1836, our first missionaries: William Bowden and George Beer, with their wives.

From that seemingly small beginning, mission stations sprang up in many parts of that vast country, giving impetus to the great work of evangelisation, which quickly spread from the East to the five continents. It was fitting that the occasion of a hundred years' missionary service should be marked by a time of united thanksgiving. Thus, on the first three days of April, 1936, a great concourse of upwards of four thousand Christians assembled in Narsapur, West Godavari District. Most of our missionaries were present, and about twenty delegates arrived from various parts of India. Elaborate preparations had been made for the housing and providing for so large a number, and the meetings were held in a large *pandal* erected for the occasion. At first it was feared that torrential rain—an unusual occurrence at that time of the year—would mar the proceedings, but God wonderfully answered prayer in suddenly driving away the storm clouds.

An interesting feature of the Convention was the reading of an historical survey of the work during the past century, from the arrival of Bowden and Beer up to the recent times. The mention of these notable names recalls the fact that descendants of those pioneers have, during that long period, found a place in the ranks of missionaries in India, and among those present at the centenary celebrations was C. J. Tilsley, a great-grandson of Mr. and Mrs. W. Bowden, representing the fourth generation of missionaries. "With those who welcomed the friends in the large meeting on 1st April," writes Mr. A. Naismith, "was Vasa Kottayya, a nonagenarian Christian of Narsapur, the son of one of the early converts from the weaver caste, and the only survivor of the second generation of the converts who came out in the lifetime of the pioneer missionaries. Mrs. Beer, now in her eighty-second year, the only surviving missionary of the second generation, was also present."

One cannot leave India without mention of the indefatigable labours of the veteran Handley Bird, whose impressive appeal at the London Missionary Meetings, on the occasion of his last visit to this country, is still remembered.

With the departure of the first missionaries from our assemblies on that memorable day in the spring of 1836, the machinery was set in motion. Across the country the Macedonian call was wafted on the winds of hope. That call was taken up. To Spain there went forth Robert C. Chapman, scattering portions of the Scriptures

EARLY DAYS IN THE FOREIGN FIELD

when that priest-oppressed country was closed to the Bible. Those who have read *The Bible in Spain* will appreciate some of his experiences and triumphs. Later, Hoyle, Blamire, Fenn, Payne and others, landed on that inhospitable shore. Years of hardship and persecution had its reward in the establishment of assemblies in many of the Spanish provinces.

What ultimate result the recent civil war will have upon what has already been accomplished by those who have borne the brunt of long years, cannot yet be known. One of the tragedies of unhappy Spain has been the desperate position into which the civilian population was suddenly plunged by the horrors of civil war. This chaotic state, for the time being, closed every door to the Gospel; native brethren were compelled to take up arms, while missionaries had to flee to the coast where ships were waiting to take them to safety. A pathetic figure amid the ruins of a life's work was the veteran brother Henry Payne, who, after braving the contrary winds of religious difficulties and persecution amongst the Spaniards for sixty-five years, was obliged to quit Barcelona, that hot-bed of revolution, and take refuge in a homeward-bound British vessel. Peering through the mists of uncertainty, it is difficult at this distance to predict what the outcome will be now that the war-clouds have passed. "One thing seems clear to me," said Mr. Payne, not long before his Home-call in 1938, "and that is that Spain has lost all confidence in the Church of Rome. Many still believe there is a God; but they have been kept in ignorance of the Bible, and the tendency is towards infidelity, and this points to what we now see: utter strife and confusion leading on to the acceptance of Antichrist."

In Italy, light was to come from within. The conversion of an Italian nobleman in a somewhat unusual way took place. This brought Count Guicciardini, the new convert, under the close observation of the Romish Ecclesiastical Authorities and exposed him to a tyrannical persecution. Rather than submit to the power of Rome, the Count chose to go into exile, and sought a haven of refuge in England. Here he met young Rossetti, a countryman of his own: a political refugee and an unbeliever, of whose conversion he became the instrument. How the two exiles increased in the knowledge of the Scriptures and prepared themselves for the evangelisation of their native land, to which they returned in the face of bitter opposition, is one of the marvels of missionary enterprise. The first Italian assembly was formed in the year 1846, when the Lord's Supper had to be observed in secret. It was not until 1871, when religious tolerance was announced in Italy, that services could be held openly, and six hundred Italian Christians came together in one building to remember the Lord in the breaking of bread. Men and women from the home country, among whom the names of Cole, Anderson and Honywill are remembered, have kept the light burning amid the darkness and superstition of that land of Romanism.

Other continental countries were reached and a testimony commenced, not infrequently under widely different circumstances. Men were raised up who had indeed been called of God. Thus in Belgium, some eighty years ago, an unknown Christian, A. M. Gaudibert, from the South of France, who came to reside in the industrial centre of Charleroi, was the means of establishing an assembly there, from which fourteen other assemblies have since been formed. Space forbids the mention of pioneer work in the broad mission field extending from the shores of Portugal to the Eastern frontier of Russia, a country so closely associated with the devoted labours of Dr. Baedeker.

While Groves was pioneering in the East, a young clergyman sent out from England as Rector of a parish church in British Guiana, became exercised as to the simple New Testament method of worship. He gave up a lucrative living and a manse, that he might devote his life and energies on lines which an independent study of the Scriptures had shown him to be the true way. Thus Leonard Strong, unaware of the historic Movement in Britain, was not only meeting, in like manner as we are to-day, with native Christians whom he had led into the light, but was laying the foundation of a

EARLY DAYS IN THE FOREIGN FIELD

missionary work which spread through the West Indies, where assemblies continue to the present day.

The distant Orient was still under the cloud of superstition and darkness with few to carry the light, when, about the year 1861, a Presbyterian minister residing in Penang, came under the influence of the Holy Spirit as to the truth of worship. This spiritual experience was deepened by the arrival of Alexander Grant in the city. He, too, had had his mind enlightened and his vision enlarged. The meeting of these two men, Chapman and Grant, and the severing of ecclesiastical ties which hitherto had restricted their outlook and activities, resulted in the founding of our present missionary work in the Straits Settlement, and afterwards in the Federated Malay States.

Since its doors were opened to the Gospel, China, with its four hundred millions, has claimed the lives of many heroes of the Faith. But God has honoured their labours in establishing mission stations in many parts of that vast empire, where, despite avalanche after avalanche of war and rebellion, which have devastated that unhappy country, there still remain those faithful to the cause of Christ, amid untold persecution. So many names are associated with China and the Gospel that one can mention but a few: Dr. Parrot, Dr. Case, Robert Stephen, H. C. Kingham, with their wives, and Miss Gates.

During the terrors of the "Boxer Rising" in 1900, when over a hundred missionaries belonging to various missions were ruthlessly killed, and about twenty thousand native Christians were brutally put to death because they refused to deny Christ, Mr. and Mrs. Kingham and their little daughter were the victims of an infuriated Chinese mob, while Miss Gates had an amazing escape from death.

Evangelisation in the priest-ridden continent of South America, since our first missionary arrived with the Gospel in the second half of last century, has met with encouraging results. God has indeed honoured the efforts of His labourers in that almost measureless vineyard, and to-day thousands of believers of many colours and nationalities meet together in happy fellowship. The work of such pioneers as Ewen, Payne, Torre, Jenkins and Clifford, in face of religious bitterness and persecution, shall ever remain a monument to the power of the Gospel over the darkness of Romanism.

With the Home-call in 1936, of James Clifford, at the close of forty years' service for the Lord in South America, there passed on yet another stalwart of the faith.

"Don Jaime, as every one knew him," writes a fellow-worker, "was known and beloved from the Bolivian border in the North, right to Montevideo, one hundred miles beyond Buenos Aires up the River Plate; over a thousand miles! He had a knowledge of the Scriptures that enabled him always to minister and refresh and build up the saints, with such ministry as was invaluable. When Tucuman was full of malaria and the work needed a helper, Don Jaime and his devoted wife willingly volunteered, and always after he was known as Don Jaime de Tucuman; and many souls were led to the Saviour."

And what of Africa, that vast continent of heathen darkness? David Livingstone revealed to the world the density of that darkness, and had turned aside the long grass of centuries which covered the untrodden paths leading to unreached tribes—paths that were soon to be traversed by another Scotsman. It was in the summer of 1881, at the immature age of twenty-three, that Frederick Stanley Arnot set out alone upon his long journey—a journey which was to end thirty-three years later, when he had traversed thirty thousand miles under the African sun. After seven years' pioneer work, during which time he journeyed from Durban on the east coast to Benguela on the west seaboard, often stricken down by sickness and encountering almost insurmountable difficulties, the intrepid missionary returned home bringing with him the story of Africa's desperate need. The response was spontaneous. In less than ten years, over sixty missionaries from assemblies in Britain went out to the Dark Continent. Stations were established across the great country, upon what is now known as the "Beloved Strip," and thousands who never before heard the sweetest Name on earth, were won for the Saviour. But those early days claimed many noble lives, and while the great structure was going up, the long, long trail from the coast line to the interior, was marked by a chain of graves. The loss sustained was grievous but the light continued its course, and to-day the triumphs of the Gospel are a living witness where once the savagery of heathendom held sway.

The Jubilee of 1931, when seventy missionaries assembled from many parts of the "Beloved Strip" to commemorate the setting out for Africa of F. S. Arnot, revealed what the coming of the Gospel had accomplished during the passage of those fifty years—years which had witnessed the horrors of the slave caravan, and the brutal atrocities of native practices (the demonic issue of fetish worship), being supplanted by the Living Word. Looking back upon that dark picture as it was presented to those pioneer missionaries, braving the dangers of the fever-laden swamps, in those days when medical science in its fight against tropical disease was yet in its embryonic state, one can but faintly comprehend the tremendous difficulties which had to be overcome before a single soul could be reached. To-day across that great belt of African soil, may be seen mission stations from which over one hundred and seventy missionaries radiate. There are now several thousands in Church fellowship. The work, which has attained to a very efficient standard, is fourfold: evangelical, medical, educational, and industrial. Through the schools, literally thousands have been won for Christ.

Regarding medical work in the foreign field, one cannot speak too highly of the devoted services of the doctors, who, while healing the body, have a rare opportunity of giving heed to the soul of the patient. As an instance of the amount of medical work carried on at one station, it is stated that during one year there were twenty-seven thousand four hundred attendances at the dispensary, three hundred and seventy-seven patients were seen in camp, and more than two thousand and seventy injections given, while four hundred and twenty-five operations—more than half of them on eyes—were performed.

But the fruits of to-day were only attained by the arduous toil and patient sowing of those hardy pioneers, who had few of the advantages enjoyed by the present-day missionary. Looking back: what a story!—"Years spent doggedly pushing ever forward with set purpose and unflagging zeal, pressing through thorny forests, crossing flooded rivers alive with crocodiles, trekking through waterless deserts, winning the confidence of hostile tribes, overcoming the innumerable obstacles, with pitifully slender material resources, but rich in faith and trust in the Lord, arriving at last at the capital of the chief of the Garanganze country!" Such was written of Arnot the pioneer, and such since then is applicable to many of our unknown missionaries who, unseen and unsung in some remote corner of the great vineyard, are content to labour on.

Nor would we forget the labours of those faithful ambassadors toiling in the obscure habitations of the earth and on the distant islands of the sea. They form part of the great army of nearly a thousand missionaries who have left home and friends for the Gospel.

God has indeed blessed and prospered the work in the foreign field since that almost forgotten day over a hundred years ago, when the little missionary party sailed down the Thames for the East, little realising that a page was being written in the history of a world-wide missionary enterprise, which has been used of God in carrying the Gospel to almost every clime and nation.

> "God speed the day when those of every nation,
> 'Glory to God' triumphantly shall sing;
> Ransomed, redeemed, rejoicing in salvation,
> Shout 'Hallelujah!' for the Lord is King!"

INDEX OF NAMES

Alford, A. G., 51
Aroolappen, —, 78
Ashby, —, 109
Arnot, F. S., 111, 118, 147, 196, 318, 319, 320
Adams, Sidney, 113
Adams, A., 113
Ainsworth, George W., 152
Anderson, James, 211, 212
Anderson, John, 213
Anderson, Hope Vere, 215
Adam, Joseph, 217
Adams, Harry, 221
Anton, James, 233, 243, 255
Anton, James, Snr., 243
Anderson, J., 287
Anderson, Sir Robert, 301
Anderson, J. A., 316

Bellett, J. G., 3, 4, 5, 6, 7, 8, 10, 11, 13, 22, 153, 201, 299, 300
Bowden, Wm., 9, 78, 313, 314
Beer, George, 9, 78, 313, 314
Batten, J. E., 20
Blake, H. T., 44
Barter, W. J., 44
Brown, Mrs. Matthew, 44
Brealey, George, 47, 188
Blow, Samuel, 48, 70
Baedeker, Dr. F. W., 57, 58, 111, 316
Bannister, F., 61, 62
Bunyan, John, 61
Binns, Chas., 72
Bennet, W. H., 73, 75, 156
Bragg, John, 73
Berger, W. T., 80, 84
Barnardo, Dr., 84, 309
Bilson, W. T., 92, 93
Bailey, Sergt., 92

Blackwood, Sir Arthur, 98
Bland, F. C., 104, 301, 303, 304, 309
Bilke, Robert, 108
Blamire, Thomas, 111, 315
Bilson, C. F., 112
Brodie, Wm., 129, 130, 131, 132
Brodie, Frederick, 129, 130
Benest, Mrs., 130
Baddeley, F. H., 131
Brown, Wm., 134
Brunton, John, 138, 139, 164
Booth, William, 145
Bewley, Henry, 149, 308
Bennett, Edwin H., 162, 171
Bennett, William, 162
Bright, —, 162
Buck, Jas., 163
Burt, W. J., 164
Brookes, Thos., 164
Burgess, Jas. Henry, 165, 166
Brocklehurst, Thos., 180
Birkett, G. N., 187
Brown, Tom, 206
Buchanan, Mrs. Ed., 217
Brown, Matthew, 236
Barclay, Miss Maggie, 236
Barclay, John, 236
Barnett, Robt., 238
Bonar, Dr. Andrew, 241
Beveridge, R. F., 243
Burns, Sandy, 245
Bayne, Alexander, 252
Barton, Dr., 253
Brown, Mrs., 258
Brown, Alexander, 259
Boswell, Albert, 261
Black, Dr. John, 269, 270
Brewster, J. H., 271
Boal, John, 288, 289
Boyd, Mrs., 292

BRETHREN

Bell, Archd., 297, 304
Bellett, George, 300
Brennan, John, 303
Buckley, Miss F., 305
Beer, Mrs., 314
Bird, Handley, 314

Craik, Henry, 3, 25, 26, 27, 28, 29, 30, 31, 53, 59
Chapman, R. C., 3, 47, 50, 52, 53, 54, 55, 56, 73, 80, 84, 124, 141, 164, 165, 182, 191, 315
Cronin, Dr. E., 5, 9, 12, 13, 14, 59
Cotton, Colonel, 9
Cole, W. H., 19
Cowper, William, 27
Coultas, —, 33
Chrystal, D. D., 34
Campbell, Sir A., 47, 59
Crawford, Mrs., 55
Cavan, Earl, 57, 58, 111
Cookson, General, 58
Congleton, Lord (*see* Parnell)
Charters, A. H. and Mrs., 93
Churchill, John T., 98, 101, 119, 120
Churchill, Mrs., 99
Crawford, Dan, 111, 196, 233
Cooper, Mrs., 112
Cummings, C. P., 131
Connor, John, 132
Cummings, A. J., 141, 142
Clifford, Jas., 152, 236, 318
Code, John Marsden, 153
Cooper, R. Boyd, 157
Cross, Thos., 164
Crewdson, —, 187
Carter, Wm., 191
Carr, Jonathan D., 193, 194
Carr, Henry, 194
Carr, Thomas William, 194
Carr, James, 194, 195
Chapman, Samuel, 206
Chapman, Robert, 207, 209
Cooper, Gavin, 211
Campbell, Colin, 213, 261

Close, Henry, 215
Campbell, George, 220
Caldwell, Wm., 220, 240
Caldwell, John R., 220, 239, 240, 253, 257
Cochrane, Thomas, 220, 240, 257
Campbell, Robt., 229
Campbell, Mrs., 233
Campbell, Murdo, 269
Cairns, Miss, 280
Campbell, James, 282, 288, 289, 290, 294, 295, 296
Crichton, Hugh, 296
Carrick, Earl of, 297, 301
Crosbie, William T., 304
Cole, L. B., 316
Case, Dr., 317
Chapman, — (Penang), 317

Darby, J. N., 3, 5, 10, 11, 13, 16, 17, 18, 20, 21, 22, 23, 24, 37, 39, 60, 77, 114, 143, 153, 202, 209, 279, 299
Deck, J. G., 3, 59
Denny, Sir E., 4, 154
Drury, Misses, 13
Dyer, W., 20, 187
Davies, E. T., 34
Dyer, Henry, 47, 70, 73, 74, 75, 76, 84, 141, 155, 164, 182, 187
Dorman, W. H., 78
Doddridge, Dr., 87
Dunning, W. H., 101
Denham, George, 145, 147
Dawson, J. C. M., 147, 151, 195
Dore, Joseph, 160
Dalling, Capt. and Mary, 165
Davies, George, 171
Dodds, Samuel, 218, 219
Dickie, John, 223, 230, 231
Duncan, Robert, 245, 250
Dalrymple, Wm., 252
Dunbar, Euphemia, 253
Dykes, Wm., 253
Downie, Henry, 255
Davidson, Henry, 256

INDEX OF NAMES

Dryden, Tom, 256
Darling, Dr., 297

Evans, Harrington, 52
Ewing, John Orr, 58
Elliott, John, 67
Eales, S. C., 67
Elliott, Russell, 147
Evans, Peter, 164
Eddis, Dr., 173
Edgar, Frank, 269
Evans, —, 279
Ewen, J. H. L., 318

Foley, —, 78
Freeman, T. K., 81
Fegan, J. W. C., 93, 104, 113, 114
Francis, S. Trevor, 104
Farie, Robert, 112
Fisher, Alfred W., 118, 119, 120
Foster, Col., 135
Fry, Oliver, 136, 137, 138
Fry, William, 149, 308
Fry, John, 162, 164
Ferguson, —, 164
Fox, George, 192
Forlong, Gordon, 238, 239, 275
Faulds, John, 245
Ferguson, John, 248
Fyfe, Robert, 250, 251
Fraser, Archie, 251
Fyfe, John, 251
Farquharson, Wm., 258
French, Joseph, 281
Finlay, Isaac, 286, 287
Fenn, Albert, 315

Groves, A. N., 3, 5, 6, 7, 8, 9, 10, 25, 30, 31, 47, 54, 59, 78, 80, 188, 313, 316
Griffiths, Mrs., 35
Gipps, Henry, 35
Griffiths, Dr., 35, 38, 39

Groves, Henry, 37, 60, 139, 155, 156, 164, 182, 184, 187, 188, 189, 261
George, William, 40
Griffiths, John, 40
Gribble, Robert, 55, 69
Guicciardini, Count, 61, 78, 315
Gosse, Philip, 65
Guinness, Dr. H. Grattan, 84, 309
Ginnings, A., 85
Grove, William ("Happy Bill"), 92, 100
Garstin, Arthur, 102
Gordon, General, 105
Grace, Mrs. Emma, 130, 132
Grove, —, 138
Gelder, R. N., 144
Graham, Richard, 146
Glover, Fred., 156, 164
Gale, —, 163
Grayson, E. J., 165
Green, Wm., 171
Groves, George, 182
Groves, Frank, 188
Gall, Robt., 196
Graham, John, 196
Greenshields, Michael, 204
Geddes, —, 204
Gilchrist, James, 207
Gilchrist, Jeanie, 208
Grant, Wm. J., 228, 249
Gibson, David, 228, 229
Gunn, Robert, 243
Garrey, Matthew, 250
Garriock, J. A., 259
Gerrie, Ernest, 262
Grant, James, 269
Graham, John C., 287
Gaudibert, A. M., 316
Grant, Alexander, 317
Gates, Miss, 317

Hutchinson, Francis, 13, 14
Hall, Captain P. F., 18, 22, 36, 37, 39, 43, 45, 49, 59, 154
Harris, J. L., 20, 24, 59
Harris, H. J., 33

Humfrys, —, 35
Hamilton, A., 40
Hake, Wm., 47, 54
Heath, Henry, 54, 80, 123, 124
Hull, T., 55
Hambleton, John, 62, 148, 164, 181, 182
Howard, John Eliot, 78, 79, 80
Hubble, W. J., 87
Hyde, G. J., 94, 120
Hucklesby, George, 101, 132
Hurditch, Russell, 101, 239
Holiday, A. J., 104, 145, 152, 185
Hunter, W. H., 111, 185
Hewitt, W. M., 125
Hewer, Sidney, 131
Henry, Shuldham, 132, 141, 309
Hoste, Lieut., 134
Harris, John, 139
Honywell, W. J., 140
Hill, Miss, 142
Henderson, Stewart, 142
Hughes, Edward, 151
Hurditch, Edward, 159
Hooper, William, 160
Hacker, Thos., 160
Hallett, Fredk. E., 164
Howe, Wm., 164
Hamilton, —, 164
Hamilton, Wm. L., 168, 170, 171
Hill, R. H., 171
Houghton, John, 173
Hopkins, Rice T., 174, 224
Hargreaves, W. B., 181
Howitt, Wm., 195
Hyslop, Joseph F., 204
Holt, —, 204
Hodgkinson, Arthur E., 205
Henry, Wm., 205
Hamilton, Daniel, 208
Henderson, —, 212
Hamilton, Mary, 213
Henderson, Ebenezer, 213
Hamilton, Wm., 214
Hynd, Peter, 221, 222, 223
Hynd, Thomas, 223
Hynd, Henry, 223

Hoste, Wm., 226, 227
Hoste, Gen. D. E., 226
Holmes, James, 228
Holmes, Alexander, 228
Houston, John, 230
Hogg, John, 232
Harris, Alexander, 243
Hill, David, 245
Hamilton, Andrew, 254
Haig, Misses, 272
Hamilton, A. (Belfast), 282
Henry, R. M., 283, 285
Hormon, —, 288
Halyburton, John, 292
Henderson, Jas., 293
Hoyle, J. C., 315
Honywill, —, 316

Inglis, Charles, 73, 101, 132, 297
Iles, Edmund and William, 99
Inglis, William, 243

Jarratt, —, 18
Jones, John, 92
Jordan, Joseph W., 113, 119, 120
Johnston, Howard, 127
Johnson, S. C., 166
Jones, David, 168, 169
Judd, C. H., 243
Joss, Fiddler, 297
Jenkins, Alfred, 318

Kitto, Dr., 8
Kelly, William, 48
Kenyon, "Daddy," 95
Kyd, A. Milne, 119, 120
Kirkham, Gawin, 145
Knox, John, 201
Kirk, John, 201, 202
Kennedy, Dr. Robt., 236
Kyle, William, 242
Kelly, James, 256

INDEX OF NAMES 325

Kerr, Robert, 256
Kenaran, —, 280
Kingham, H. C. and Mrs., 317
Kottayya, Vasa, 314

Lunell, J. E., 32
Lewis, W. R., 36, 157
Lear, Thomas, 72
Lincoln, William, 87, 88, 89, 90, 91
Lohr, Conrad, 93
Lane, W. R., 101, 146
Laing, J. W., 114
Lockhart, W. P., 148
Lloyd, H. G., 171
Lewis, Wm., 171, 172
Lorimer, Arthur, 176
Livingstone, Dr., 189, 318
Laing, John, 196
Loudon, John, 204
Loudon, James, 204
Lindsay, Wm., 214, 220
Lauder, Hugh, 224
Leith, Fred. A., 250, 251
Leggat, Robert, 256
Logg, Francis and Matthew, 272, 273, 298
Luke, Rodger, 281
Lepper, Charles, 282
Lowden, G., 287
Lough, Thos., 291
Lansdowne, Lord, 303

Müller, George, 3, 23, 25, 26, 27, 28, 29, 30, 31, 33, 48, 49, 53, 59, 81, 141, 164, 190, 223, 309
Mahon, J., 4
Magee, Bishop, 11
Maunsell, Thomas, 16, 39
Mackintosh, C. H., 16, 142, 143, 279, 281, 303
Miller, Andrew, 19
Maclaren, Dr., 29
Molesworth, Colonel, 34, 142, 265
McCall, T., 40, 41
Metcalfe, James, 42

Minett, —, 44
Marsom, H. E., 51, 71
Minchen, Col., 58
Morton, Charles, 62
Mogridge, F. C., 68
Maclean, Dr. John Lindsay, 73, 155, 157, 160, 161, 189, 261
Marks, G. H., 82, 84
Morley, John, 82, 86
McVicker, J. G., 83, 119, 220, 283, 285
Morris, Thos. H., 84
Marks, Mrs. H. F., 85
McCall, —, 94
Mudditt, B. R., 95
Morgan, R. C., 102
Mandeville, Lt. H. A., 104, 301
Moorhouse, Harry, 132, 145, 147, 148, 149, 150, 164, 173, 182, 239, 309
Macnutt, Dr., 132
Mitchell, Capt., 135
Moody, Dwight L., 136, 149, 173, 195, 240, 282, 289
Mackenzie, General, 141
Mills, Dennis, 142
Marshall, Alexander, 145, 146, 164, 178, 179, 207, 224, 239, 242, 256, 301
Maclean, Gen. Sir George, 155
Morse, Arthur, 161
McLay, A., 164
Moss, William A., 196
McAlpine, John, 204
Miller, Robert, 206
Montgomery, William, 210, 254
Millar, Charles, 210, 211
Massie, Arthur, 213
Muir, Jas., 216
Morton, Robt., 216, 217
McCrory, Robert, 217
McPhie, Mrs., 217
Meneely, Jeremiah, 219, 281, 285
Munro, Donald, 225, 266
Moule, Dr. Handley, 227
Milne, George, 241
McNab, Duncan, 242

McLaren, Thos., 242, 245
McInnes, R. G., 243
McKilliam, Dr., 243
Meneely, W. J., 246, 255
McAlonan, James, 248
McKenzie, Allan, 249
Morton, James, 250
McDermid, John, 250
McLachlan, John, 253, 254, 255
McAulay, Thomas, 254
Miller, Mrs., 257
Martin, —, 258
Mitchell, Robert, 260, 261
Mowat, R. G., 261, 262
Mowat, Henry, 262
Mackenzie, Alexander, 269, 270
Mackenzie, William, 270
Masson, George R., 271
Meiklejohn, Mr. and Mrs., 272
McLean, William, 275, 276, 285, 291, 292, 293
Matthews, Dr. W. J., 280, 291, 294, 295, 296, 297
McKee, Patrick, 280
Moore, Francis, 281
McDowell, Boyd, 281
McLaughlin, W. H., 281, 282, 287
Marshall, John, 281
McClay, R., 287
McCleery, Mrs., 289
McEwen, John Knox, 291
Matthews, Wm., 294, 295, 296
Megan, James, 296
McCracken, R., 297
Matthews, Abram, 297
Mahony, Richard, 301, 302, 303, 304
Mansfield, Joseph, 303
Milne, John, 303
Milne, Robt., 304
Mansfield, A., 304

Newman, F. W., 9, 17, 18
Newton, B. W., 18, 20, 23, 24
Neatby, W. Blair, 18
Newberry, Thomas, 58, 141

Newman, J. H., 73
Neatby, Dr., 108
Nicholls, Dr., 166
Nelson, Isaac, 184
North, Brownlow, 239, 277
Ness, William, 272
Napier, James, 276
Needham, George C., 303
Naismith, A., 314

Offord, George, 93
Orde-Brown, Capt., 103, 104, 105
Orde-Brown, Mrs., 103
Ord, Harrison, 132, 154, 239
Onslow, —, 135
Owles, Dr., 142, 173
Oliver, —, 294
Oswald, Gordon, 301

Parnell, J. V. (Congleton), 3, 5, 9, 14, 15, 37, 59, 60, 61, 78, 84, 110, 261
Powerscourt, Lady, 22
Paget, Miss, 47, 55
Peden, Alexander, 63
Pierson, Dr., 81
Pearse, George, 84
Poulton, Henry and Tom, 101
Penstone, John Jewell, 108
Pike, John, 108
Pike, Charles, 108
Panting, —, 140
Petter, Edward, 144
Peck, Edward, 152
Picket, Richard, 160
Pullin, Chas., 164
Perry, Douglas, 170
Pickering, John, 176
Pickering, James, 176
Podmore, Fred., 180
Paisley, Dr., 190
Pattinson, John, 190
Paton, Dr. John G., 194
Page, Edwin, 196

INDEX OF NAMES

Paterson, Wm., 204
Pattinson, —, 212
Paterson, Robt., 212, 213
Paterson, Mary, 213
Pearson, Miss, 221
Park, Alex., 223
Phillips, A. W., 227
Peebles, John, 236
Pickering, Hy., 242, 243, 252
Paton, John, 254
Pennefather, —, 275
Plunkett, —, 280, 281
Patton, James, 286, 287
Payne, Henry, 315
Parrot, Dr., 317
Payne, William, 318

Queensberry, Lady, 111
Quine, Edward C., 175
Quarrier, William, 259

Rhind, Captain W. G., 42, 43, 44, 45, 59
Royce, W., 44
Radstock, Lord, 57, 92, 104, 111, 129, 135, 148
Rice, General, 58
Russell, Douglas, 58, 173
Rossetti, Teodoro, 61, 315
Rutter, John, 72
Radwell, G., 108
Radstock, Lady, 111
Ranyards, Miss, 136
Radcliffe, Reginald, 148, 277
Russell, Chas., 159
Rea, David, 164, 256, 291, 293, 297, 298, 299
Robinson, Thos., 181
Rhodes, —, 187
Reid, Wm., 192, 193
Rankin, John, 217
Reid, Duncan M., 217
Ritchie, John, 221, 224, 225, 226, 244, 255, 267
Ritchie, John, Jun., 221
Ross, Donald, 225, 261, 263, 266, 267, 277, 278
Renfrew, William, 246
Robertson, Wm., 273
Ritchie, John (Aberdeen), 278

Stokes, W., 15
Soltau, H. W., 20, 47, 48, 49, 50
Short, E. R., 28, 33
Seward, W., 37, 39
Stafford, Col., 47
Strong, Leonard, 65, 66, 67, 316
Surridge, William, 69, 70
Surridge, F. W., 71
Stewart, Alexander, 78
Smith, J. Denham, 82, 83, 85, 86, 132, 135, 159, 275, 308, 309
Skelton, Mrs., 92
Smith, Gipsy, 92
Stevens, Edward, 107, 108
Stone, Huntingdon, 114
Stunt, Francis, 119
Stunt, W., 120
Salmon, —, 126
Steinle, John, 131
Sankey, Ira D., 150, 173, 195, 240, 282, 289
Smith, Frank, 151
Sparks, Robt. E., 156, 157, 287
Sparks, Mrs., 156
Sims, George, 161
Stephens, D. J., 170
Sylvester, —, 184
Showell, Jas., 187, 188
Stone, James, 212
Stewart, John, 223
Steen, J. Charlton, 226
Sharkey, Philip, 231
Steel, David, 243
Stokes, C. E. and Mrs., 253
Steel, John, 253
Sinclair, John, 253
Stewart, Alexander (Glasgow), 256, 257, 258, 259
Straiton, James, 262

Scott, John, 263
Smith, John, 266
Soutter, James, 271, 272
Soutter, Dr. W. R., 271
Smith, W. G., 271
Stephen, Robert, 276
Shaw, Martin, 281
Smith, James, 282, 288, 289, 290
Spence, Samuel, 282
Stewart, R. and J., 288
Scott, Alexander, 292
Stewart, James, 299
Stephen, Robert (China), 317

Tims, —, 13
Tregelles, Dr., 20, 78, 301
Tireman, Major, 32
Towers, Captain, 80, 123
Taylor, Hudson, 84, 111, 141, 194
Teskey, James, 93
Toplady, A. M., 122
Tidmarsh, —, 126
Tupman, Frank, 139
Tapson, E. D. J., 164, 167, 168, 169, 171
Thomson, Wm., 219
Thomas, Dr., 249
Tainsh, E., 255
Taylor, William, 256
Turner, Dan, 256
Turner, James, 274
Thompson, H. B., 287
Trench, George, 301, 304
Trench, Townsend, 303, 304
Tilsley, C. J., 314
Torre, W. C. K., 318

Underwood, —, 111
Usher, Edward, 149

Victor, —, 32
Vicary, J. A., 33, 34, 135
Venn, John, 35, 36, 37
Vivian, John, 63
Venn, Ephraim, 73, 101
Vine, John T., 73, 74, 103, 239
Varley, Henry, 102, 159
Vine, W. E., 157
Vance, Robert, 281

Wilson, Edward, 12, 13
Wigram, G. V., 18, 22, 23, 77, 78
Wigram, Sir George, 23
Welchman, —, 33
Wright, James, 33, 80, 81, 134, 164
West, Captain, 34
Wreford, Samuel, 47
Wreford, Dr. Heyman, 47, 48
Wylie, Judge, 58
Wallis, Ransome, 92
Want, Albert, 93
Wallis, Mrs. Ransome, 94
Wells, E. H., 101
Weaver, Richard, 101, 148, 184, 309
Wright, Ned, 102, 159
Wigston, James, 111
Wesley, John, 122, 193
Wood, George, 144
Walker, William, 145
Willington, W., 145, 146
Wallis, Horatio, 146
Widdison, A., 147
Webb, Frank, 154, 156
Williams, Edward, 159
Willie, George, 164
Williams, Evan, 168
West, —, 169, 170
Winn, John, 176
Wharton, Jas., 181
Wilson, Wm., 186, 187, 189
Wales, Thomas, 187
Wakefield, Edward, 187, 190
Wilson, Theodore, 189
Wardrop, John, 204, 212
Weir, James, 204
Watson, James, 228
Wilson, Alex., 229
Wardrop, Dr. James, 242, 243, 244
Wilson, James, 246, 247

INDEX OF NAMES

Wilson, Janet, 253
Wight, David and Mrs., 258, 259
Whitelaw, A., 271
Walbran, John, 287
Watt Brothers, 287
Watt, George, 296

Yapp, William, 35, 36, 38, 59, 111
Yapp, Mrs., 111
Young, H. G., 142
Young, James, 232
Young, George, 240, 241, 253
Young, Robert, 261

INDEX OF PLACES

Algeria, 34, 40, 142
Africa, 34, 40, 93, 94, 118, 132, 135, 147, 157, 161, 208, 223, 227, 233, 236, 243, 253, 255, 302, 318, 319
Argentina, 34, 152, 236
Aberystwyth, 35
Australia, 129
America, North, 149, 169, 189, 216, 217, 271, 278, 288, 294, 303
Adamsdown, 162, 164
Abergavenny, 168, 171
Abertillery, 169
Ambleside, 190
Avon, River, 210
Angola, 217
Ayr, 218, 233, 234
Ayrshire, 218, 220, 221, 223, 224, 228, 232, 233, 234, 250, 261
Aberdeenshire, 224, 274, 278, 303
Auchinleck, 229, 232, 233
Annbank, 234
America, South, 236, 317, 318
Aberlour, 266, 267, 268, 269
Aberdeen, 271, 273, 277, 278, 288, 304
Antrim, 281, 284
Ahoghill, 286
Ards Peninsula, 287
Armagh, County, 291, 292, 297, 298
Ahorey, 292
Agulas, 295
Ardfert, 301, 303, 304
Aboyne, 303

Bristol, 3, 9, 23, 25, 26, 27, 28, 29, 30, 32, 35, 48, 53, 59, 80, 81, 134, 189, 307
Baghdad, 7, 8, 9, 18, 31, 188, 313

Baltic Sea, 8
Barnstaple, 9, 47, 50, 52, 53, 54, 55, 80, 124, 165, 191, 313
Bethesda Chapel, Bristol, 27, 28, 30, 32, 33, 34, 35
Bedminster, 33
Bishopston, 34
Barbados, 34
Belfast, 40, 147, 281, 282, 283, 285, 287, 288, 289, 290, 292
Ballingham, 46
Bideford, 50
Bristol Channel, 57
Bedford, 61
Bedfordshire, 61, 62
British Guiana, 65, 66, 316
Babbacombe, 67
Bridford Mills, 69, 71
Blandford, 73, 74, 75
Beresford Chapel, 87, 88, 89, 90
Bury St. Edmunds, 126
Belgian Congo, 132
Baldock, 138, 139
Bath, 153, 154, 155, 156, 158, 160, 288
Box, 156
Birkenhead, 174
Barrow-in-Furness, 181, 182, 183
Bradford, 185
Bowness-on-Windermere, 187, 189, 190
Ballochmyle, 233
Bridge of Weir, 259
Bonnyrigg, 264
Berwickshire, 265
Banffshire, 266
Boham, 269
Brechin, 271
Ballater, 272
Boddam, 274
Banbridge, 280, 281

332 BRETHREN

Ballymena, 285, 286
Ballywalter, 287
Ballyhay, 287
Bangor, 287
Ballyholme, 287
Butterlump, 287
Ballymaconaghy, 288, 289
Ballywoollen, 289, 290
Bessbrook, 298
Bandon, 300, 301
Burma, 305
Barcelona, 315
Belgium, 316
Benguela, 318
Bolivia, 318
Buenos Aires, 318

Calary, 11
Clifton, 32, 226
China, 34, 84, 132, 135, 142, 157, 195, 253, 271, 317
Canada, 40, 119, 205, 217, 232, 233, 294
Cambridge, 43, 61, 227
Cheltenham, 43, 141, 142, 143
Chittlehamholt, 55, 56
Camden Town, 77, 117
Clapton, 82, 83, 86, 92, 94, 119
Camberwell, 90
Codymain, 122
Combs, 125
Cornwall, 143
Charlestown, 144
Chicago, 149, 150, 278
Cutsyke, 151, 152
Castleford, 151
Corsham Side, 156
Czechoslovakia, 157
Cardiff, 162, 163, 165, 167, 169, 171
Cogan, 162, 164
Canton, Wales, 164
Cathays, 164
Castletown, Wales, 166
Cefn Golau, 170
Cheshire, 174
Carlisle, 192, 193, 194, 195
Cumberland, 194

Calder, River, 203
Chapeltown, 208
Coalburn, 214
Carfin, 216, 217
Clyde, River, 230, 239, 246
Catrine, 232, 233
Chirnside, 265
Clonkeen, 281
Coleraine, 282, 284, 296
Cullybackey, 283, 285
Cardy, 287
Comber, 287
Crossgar, 289, 290
Cookstown, 295, 296
Cork, 300
Charleroi, 316

Dublin, 3, 4, 6, 7, 10, 11, 12, 13, 16, 17, 18, 60, 65, 72, 85, 105, 149, 153, 195, 210, 279, 280, 286, 297, 300, 307, 308, 309, 310
Devon, 25, 48, 50, 52, 54, 55, 59, 60, 62, 63, 69, 77, 124, 139, 171, 186
Dawlish, 60
Demerara, 65, 187
Dorset, 72, 73, 75, 76
Deptford, 113
Douglas, Isle of Man, 175
Denmark, 217
Dalry, 218, 219, 220, 228, 233
Dover Castle, 226
Darvel, 233
Dumbarton, 257
Davidson's Mains, 262
Dufftown, 268, 269
Dee, River, 272
Dingwall, 273
Down, County, 280, 287, 288, 289, 294
Derry, 284, 296
Donegal, 289, 296
Dromore, 289, 301, 302, 304
Dunadry, 292
Derriquin Castle, 301, 303, 304
Durban, 318

INDEX OF PLACES

Ennis, Co. Clare, 4
Exeter, 6, 10, 30, 31, 47, 48, 49, 50, 51, 69, 157, 188, 313
Exmouth, 50
Epping Forest, 94
East Finchley, 113
English Channel, 129, 227
Eastbourne, 129, 132, 133
Edinburgh, 155, 260, 261, 262, 263
Ebbw Vale, 171

Fownhope, 44
Fakenham, 123
Featherstone, 151, 152
Forgewood, 217
France, 227, 316
Ferryden, 266
Footdee, 278

Godaveri Delta, 9, 57, 314
Grove Common, 44, 45, 46
Georgetown, British Guiana, 65, 67
Geneva, 86
Greenwich, 113, 114
Glasgow, 145, 220, 230, 238, 239, 240, 241, 242, 243, 244, 245, 246, 247, 248, 249, 250, 251, 253, 255, 256, 257, 258
Garanganze, 147, 320
Grangetown, 164
Grosmont, 171
Germany, 195
Glenbuck, 214
Glengyron, 229
Galston, 233
Garngad, 246, 247, 249
Govanhill, 251
Groggan, 281
Guilley, 295
Galway, 302
Greystones, 304, 305, 307

Hampshire, 6
Hereford, 35, 36, 37, 38, 39, 40, 42, 43, 46, 61, 157, 171
Hoarwithy, 46
Heavitree, 51
Hackney, 78, 80, 81, 82, 84, 124
Harlesden, 107
Hertfordshire, 127, 138
Hunslet, 146, 147
Halifax, 149
Herefordshire, 171
Hamilton, 201
Hurlford, 233
Holywood, 287

India, 9, 34, 44, 59, 132, 135, 157, 188, 217, 227, 236, 313, 314
Ilfracombe, 55
Islington, 87
Isle of Wight, 134
Isle of Man, 175
Irvine, 218, 223, 228, 229, 230, 231, 233
Inverurie, 225, 267
Italy, 227, 315, 316
Inverness, 269

Japan, 34

Kroppenstaedt, 29
Kingston-on-Thames, 85, 136, 137
Kentish Town, 98
Kendal, 184, 186, 187, 188, 189, 190
Keswick, 187
Kirkcowan, 205
Kirkmuirhill, 214
Kilmarnock, 218, 221, 223, 224, 226, 228, 231, 233
Kilwinning, 233
Kilbirnie, 234, 235, 236, 250
Kilmacolm, 258, 259
Kells, 281, 286
Keady, 292
Killeen, 293
Karvagh, 293

Kilmore, 297
Kerry, 301, 302, 303, 304
Kenmore, 302, 303, 304
Kingstown, 308

London, 6, 7, 18, 23, 30, 43, 52, 75, 77, 78, 80, 82, 84, 85, 86, 87, 88, 90, 93, 102, 104, 105, 107, 110, 111, 113, 114, 117, 118, 119, 124, 157, 181, 226, 231, 234, 252, 286, 297, 304, 307, 314
Limerick, 16, 39, 279
Ledbury, 43
Leominster, 76, 141, 155, 157
Leyton, 92, 93, 94, 95
Lewisham, 103, 118
Leighton Buzzard, 109
Leeds, 145, 146, 148, 151
Lancashire, 148, 149, 176, 181
Liverpool, 150, 173, 174
Langland Bay, 166
Llanelly, 168, 169
Lancaster, 184
Low Side, 190
Lanarkshire, 201, 204, 206, 207, 210, 213, 214, 215, 218
Larkhall, 206, 207, 208, 209, 210
Lesmahagow, 211, 212, 213, 214
Leadhills, 214
Leith, 262, 263
Loanhead, 264
Lisburn, 280, 288
Letterkenny, 296
Limavady, 296
Lurgan, 297, 304

Madras, 9
Manchester, 29, 148, 150, 176, 180, 185
Montreal, 41
Malay States, 85, 113, 317
Malta, 155
Morocco, 157
Mackintosh, 164

Monmouthshire, 165, 167, 169
Mumbles, 165
Merseyside, 173, 174
Moscow, 188
Millheugh, 208, 210
Muirkirk, 214
Motherwell, 215, 217
Meldrum, 224
Maryfield, 232
Mauchline, 234
Manchuria, 271
Montrose, 271
Moneymore, 295
Montevideo, 318

Newton, Hampshire, 6
Northam, 50
Newton Abbot, 60
Newbridge, 105
Newport, Mon., 165, 167, 171
Newmains, 202
Nethan, River, 213
New Stevenston, 217
Newarthill, 217
Newmilns, 233
New Zealand, 270, 294
Nairn, 272
Newtonards, 286
Narsapur, 314

Oxford, 18, 22, 24, 66
Old Bailey, 120
Old Rayne, 225, 267
Old Cumnock, 233
Omagh, 294

Plymouth, 3, 6, 9, 18, 19, 20, 21, 22, 23, 24, 25, 28, 31, 35, 37, 42, 43, 49, 50, 72, 77, 153, 173, 186, 279, 300, 307
Plymstock, 24
Prestonpans, 30
Portugal, 34, 316

INDEX OF PLACES

Paris, 86
Preston, 87
Plumstead, 105
Pontefract, 151
Penarth, 162, 164, 169
Persia, 188, 313
Ponfeigh, 214
Prestwick, 220, 233
Plann, 233
Pollokshaws, 253
Paisley, 258
Portobello, 262
Penicuik, 264
Peterhead, 274, 275, 276, 285
Portavogie, 287
Portadown, 292, 297
Penang, 317
Plate, River, 318

Roumania, 34
Ross-on-Wye, 42, 43, 44, 66
Rougham, 123
Rangoon, 132
Ryde, 134
Rhymney, 171
Rock Ferry, 174
Ramsay, 175
Russia, 188, 316
Ravenscraig, 217
Regina, 232
Round Toll, 255, 256
Renfrewshire, 258
Rosewell, 263, 264
Randalstown, 281
Ramelton, 296

Somerset, 4
St. Petersburg, 8, 188
Shaldon, 25, 31
St. Andrews, 30, 31, 272
Spain, 34, 85, 157, 171, 314, 315
Switzerland, 34, 132, 306
Shaftesbury, 72, 73
Sherborne, 75

Suffolk, 80, 122, 123, 125
Southwark, London, 87, 88
Singapore, 93, 195
Southend, 93
Southampton, 114
Stowmarket, 123, 125, 126
St. Albans, 127
Shanklin, 134, 135
Sandown, 134
Surbiton, 136
Starcross, 139, 140
St. Austell, 143, 144
Shetlands, 146
Swindon, 159, 160, 161
Scranton, U.S.A., 169, 170
Sierra Leone, 189
San Domingo, 217
Stevenston, 223
Saskatchewan, 232
Springburn, 246
Shawlands, 253
Shrewsbury, 263
Spey, River, 268
San Francisco, 278
Scrabo, 287
Stranraer, 287
Straits Settlements, 317

Tiflis, 8
Teignmouth, 25, 30, 31, 48, 59, 60, 61, 62
Teign, River, 31
Taw, River, 56
Torquay, 60, 63, 64, 65, 67, 68
Tottenham, 78, 79, 80
Tostock, 122
Tawstock, 124
Trinidad, 129
Tredegar, 167, 168, 169, 170, 171
Tweed, River, 201
Troon, 220, 221, 222, 223
Thurso, 266
Torry, 278
Tyrone, County, 294
Tucuman, 318
Thames, River, 320

Uckfield, 129
Ulster, 280, 283, 291, 299, 307

Wicklow, 11, 13, 22, 142
West Indies, 42, 66, 135, 142, 155, 157, 217, 236, 317
Wye, River, 46
Whipton, 51
Weston-super-Mare, 57, 58
Woolpit, 80, 123, 124
Whetstone, 82
Walworth, 88
Walthamstow, 92, 93, 94, 95
Wimbledon, 98, 101
Woolwich, 103, 104, 105
Welbeck, 110, 111

Westminster, 120
Westport, 143, 282
Westcliffe-on-Sea, 144
Wiltshire, 159
West Cross, 165
Warrington, 180
Walney, 183
Westmorland, 186, 188
Windermere, 190
Wishaw, 201, 202, 204
Wigtownshire, 205
Woodside, 278

Yeovil, 75, 76, 156
Yorkshire, 84, 152